GREEK SCEPTICISM
Anti-Realist Trends in Ancient Thought

Virtually as old as philosophy itself, scepticism is the antithesis of movements such as Platonism, Aristotelianism, and Cartesianism. They celebrate rationality and our ability to discern the true nature of the world. Scepticism emphasizes the limits of reason and doubts our ability to establish objective truth. In *Greek Scepticism*, Leo Groarke argues that the ancient sceptics pose the central problems of both ancient and modern epistemology and that ancient scepticism provides a plausible alternative to the views that characterize contemporary epistemology. In the course of his argument he shows that scepticism offers a positive philosophy that not only moderates the sceptical critique of knowledge but is an ancient precursor to modern and contemporary anti-realism. Failure to appreciate the anti-realist nature of sceptical philosophy has led to the modern misconception that it is inconsistent or solely negative.

Groarke focuses on those aspects of scepticism and Greek epistemology that are most relevant to modern accounts of knowledge. In addition to his account of scepticism, he proposes a new reading of thinkers who influenced the sceptical tradition, among them Democritus, Protagoras, and the Cyrenaics. His account of Greek epistemology finishes with a discussion of its relationship to the work of contemporary philosophers. In the process he provides a sympathetic and accurate account of the heart of the ancient sceptical tradition and its relevance for modern thought.

Leo Groarke is a member of the Department of Philosophy, Wilfrid Laurier University.

McGill-Queen's Studies in the History of Ideas

1 Problems of Cartesianism
Edited by Thomas M. Lennon, John M. Nicholas, and
John W. Davis

2 The Development of the Idea of History in Antiquity
Gerald A. Press

3 Claude Buffier and Thomas Reid:
Two Common-Sense Philosophers
Louise Marcil-Lacoste

4 Schiller, Hegel, and Marx:
State, Society, and the Aesthetic Ideal of Ancient Greece
Philip J. Kain

5 John Case and Aristotelianism in Renaissance England
Charles B. Schmitt

6 Beyond Liberty and Property:
The Process of Self-Recognition in Eighteenth-Century
Political Thought
J. A. W. Gunn

7 John Toland: His Methods, Manners, and Mind
Stephen H. Daniel

8 Coleridge and the Inspired Word
Anthony John Harding

9 The Jena System, 1804–5: Logic and Metaphysics
G. W. F. Hegel
Translation edited by John W. Burbidge and George di Giovanni
Introduction and notes by H. S. Harris

10 Consent, Coercion, and Limit:
The Medieval Origins of Parliamentary Democracy
Arthur P. Monahan

11 Scottish Common Sense in Germany, 1768–1800:
A Contribution to the History of Critical Philosophy
Manfred Kuehn

12 Paine and Cobbett:
The Transatlantic Connection
David A. Wilson

13 Descartes and the Enlightenment
Peter A. Schouls

14 Greek Scepticism
Anti-Realist Trends in Ancient Thought
Leo Groarke

GREEK SCEPTICISM
Anti-Realist Trends in Ancient Thought

Leo Groarke

McGill-Queen's University Press
Montreal & Kingston • London • Buffalo

To Tom Lennon
Whose sceptical but open-minded attitude played a
crucial role in the germination of my ideas and whose
continued support has made this work possible

© McGill-Queen's University Press 1990
ISBN 0-7735-0756-6
Legal deposit second quarter 1990
Bibliothèque nationale du Québec

Printed in Canada on acid-free paper

This book has been published with the help of a grant from the
Canadian Federation for the Humanities, using funds provided by the
Social Sciences and Humanities Research Council of Canada.

Canadian Cataloguing in Publication Data
Groarke, Leo
Greek scepticism
(McGill-Queen's studies in the history of ideas; 14)
Includes bibliographical references.
ISBN 0-7735-0756-6

1. Philosophy, Ancient. 2. Philosophy, Modern—
20th century. 3. Knowledge, Theory of
I. Title. II. Series.

B525.G76 1990   180   C90-090004-0

Contents

Abbreviations ix
Acknowledgments xi
Preface xiii

I Toward a New Interpretation of the Sceptics 3
The Negative Side of Scepticism / Standard Criticisms of the
Sceptics / The Positive Side of Scepticism: Mitigated Scepticism / Moral
and Religious Scepticism / Scepticism as Anti-Realism / Scepticism
and Idealism / Contemporary Anti-Realism / Historiography and
the Sceptics

II Greek Epistemology before the Rise of Scepticism 31
Xenophanes / Heracleitus / Epicharmus / Parmenides / Zeno /
Empedocles / Anaxagoras / Summary

III The Rise of Scepticism 49
The Sophists / Democritus: Atomism, Idealism, and Equanimity /
Protagoras: Utility and Anti-Realist Truth / Metrodorus and
Anaxarchus: Idealism and Equanimity / Socrates: Mitigated
Scepticism / The Megarians / Monimus and Cynic Indifference /
The Cyrenaics: External Objects and Other Minds / Plato / The
Rise of Scepticism

IV Early Pyrrhonism 81

The Arguments for Early Pyrrhonism / Pyrrhonism as a Practical
Philosophy / Equanimity and Indifference / Appearances / Pyrrhonism
and Idealism / The Consistency of Early Pyrrhonism / Toward
Later Pyrrhonism

V Scepticism in the Academy 98

The Arguments for Academic Scepticism / Academic Arguments,
Probability, and Equal Opposition / Academic Equanimity / Arcesilaus
and Natural Belief / The Consistency of Arcesilaus' Outlook /
Arcesilaus and Sextus / Carneades and Plausibility / Cicero on the
Plausible / The Consistency of Carneades' Scepticism / Carneades,
Arcesilaus, and Pyrrho / Philo, Metrodorus, and Cicero

VI Later Pyrrhonism 124

The Arguments for Later Pyrrhonism / The Problem of the Criterion /
Practical Affairs / The Consistency of Later Pyrrhonism / Pyrrhonean
Anti-Realism / The Standard Interpretations

VII Ancient Scepticism and Modern Epistemology 143

Mental States / Contemporary Anti-Realism / The Sceptical Perspective

Appendix: Flourishing Dates of Ancient Thinkers 155
Bibliography 157
Index Locorum 165
General Index 173

Abbreviations

Ac	Cicero, *Academica*
Ad Col	Plutarch, "Adversus Colotem," *Moralia*
AM	Sextus Empiricus, *Adversus mathematicos*
Apol	Plato, *Apology*
Aris.	Aristocles
Bur	Descartes, *Conversations with Burnman*
Bibl	Photius, *Bibliotheca*
Con Ac	Augustine, *Against the Academicians*
Cons ad Apoll	Plutarch, "A Letter of Condolence to Appollonius," *Moralia*
Crat	Plato, *Cratylus*
De A	Aristotle, *De anima*
De An	Tertullian, *De anima*
De Fin	Cicero, *De finibus*
De Gen	Aristotle, *De generatione et corruptione*
Deip	Athenaeus, *The Deipnosophists*
De Rep	Cicero, *De republica*
De Sens	Theophrastus, *De sensu*
Dis	Epictetus, *Discourses*
DK	Diels and Kranz
D.L.	Diogenes Laertius
DND	Cicero, *De natura deorum*
Ench	Epictetus, *Enchiridion*
Enq	Hume, *Enquiry Concerning Human Understanding*
Eus.	Eusebius, *Preparatio evangelica*
Gel.	Gellius, *Attic Nights*
Haer	Hippolytus, *Refutatio omnium haeresium*

Lac.	Lactantius, *The Divine Institutions*
Lex	Suidas, *Lexicon*
Med	Marcus Aurelius, *Meditations*
Mem	Xenophon, *Memorabilia*
Met	Aristotle, *Metaphysics*
Non Epic	Plutarch, "Not Even a Pleasant Life Is Possible on Epicurean Principles," *Moralia*
Num.	Numenius
OC	Wittgenstein, *On Certainty*
Par	Plato, *Parmenides*
Ph	Plato, *Phaedo*
PH	Sextus Empiricus, *Outlines of Pyrrhonism*
Phaed	Plato, *Phaedrus*
Philo	Philo of Alexandria, *On Drunkenness*
PHK	Berkeley, *Principles of Human Knowledge*
Phys	Simplicius, *Aristotelis physica commentaria*
PI	Wittgenstein, *Philosophical Investigations*
Plut.	Plutarch
Prot	Plato, *Protagoras*
Rep	Plato, *Republic*
RFM	Wittgenstein, *Remarks on the Foundations of Mathematics*
Soph	Plato, *Sophist*
Stob.	Stobaeus
Th	Plato, *Theaetetus*
Tim	Plato, *Timaeus*
Tr	Hume, *A Treatise of Human Nature*
Tranq	Plutarch, "On Tranquillity of Mind," *Moralia*
Tus Dis	Cicero, *Tusculan Disputations*

Acknowledgments

I am indebted to Renato Cristi and John Chamberlin, who were always willing to discuss Greek and Latin, and to Rocky Jacobsen, Joe Novak, and Ken Dorter, who gave me useful comments on earlier versions of the book. The research office at Wilfrid Laurier provided a book preparation grant, and a course remission grant that helped me complete some chapters of the manuscript. I would also like to register my indebtedness to Michael Frede, Philip Hallie, G. B. Kerferd, Richard Popkin, Charles B. Schmitt, and other scholars who have recognized the significance of the sceptical tradition. The work of other scholars, most notably Myles Burnyeat, has forced me to defend my views more carefully than would otherwise be the case. Finally, I want to thank McGill-Queen's University Press, especially Philip Cercone, Joan McGilvray, and Connie Buchanan, for their work on the manuscript, and the anonymous readers whose comments have helped me revise it.

The following publishers have kindly granted permission to reprint material from the sources mentioned: Oxford University Press, from Plato, *Theaetetus*, translated with notes by John McDowell (Oxford: Clarendon Press, Oxford University Press, 1973); and Harvard University Press, from volume 2 of *Sextus Empiricus*, translated by R. G. Bury (Cambridge: Harvard University Press, Loeb Classical Library, 1967).

Preface

The present book attempts to summarize and introduce a whole tradition in philosophy, one that spans a great many thinkers over more than six hundred years. Given the breadth of the book's concerns, I have not been able to address all aspects of the sceptics' views, though I do discuss the most important features of their philosophy, the most prominent secondary literature, and many fine points of interpretation.

In deciding what should and should not be discussed, I have tried to focus on those aspects of scepticism relevant to modern philosophical concerns. The whole point of this book might be summarized as the claim that Greek scepticism is uniquely relevant to such concerns and represents an ancient analogue of those aspects of early modern and contemporary epistemology usually thought to have no precedent. If this is convincingly defended, the book may (especially in light of its discussion of the sceptics' predecessors) be understood more broadly as a history of Greek precursors of modern epistemology.

My interest in the sceptics' relationship to modern epistemology has meant that I approach them in a way that is, in some regards, distinct from that of much contemporary scholarship. The latter is primarily historical and deals with the intricacies of translation and philology, lacunae in the extant texts, and specific details debated in the secondary literature. As subsequent discussion should make clear, I think that such inquiry is important, and that a discussion of the sceptics must be wedded to an understanding of the technical terms they employ, a detailed account of important passages, and reliable texts and translations. This being said, I believe scholars place too much emphasis on such concerns and have thus obscured the philosophical significance of both sceptical views and Greek philosophy in general, encouraging a preoccupation with technical detail that rarely moves beyond it.

The standard emphasis on detail is founded on the reductionist assumption that an understanding of the parts of Greek philosophy is a necessary prerequisite to an understanding of the whole. Within limits this must be accepted, though it can go too far and need not precipitate a broader understanding. On the contrary, the usual approach often leads to an interminable conflict over detail that loses sight of broader issues. Any important word or passage can be variously interpreted, and the questions this raises are multiplied by our lack of extant information on many ancient thinkers, by the remoteness of the context in which their thought develops, and by a long tradition of scholarly research that has produced a sea of secondary literature both complex and contradictory. There is probably no substantive claim about Greek philosophy that is not disputed somewhere in the secondary literature. Too much emphasis on detail thus mires us in detail, producing an endless refinement of arguments and indefinitely postponing a more general understanding of Greek concerns. (In courts of law, attention to detail is often used to postpone a verdict.)

Anyone who wishes to discuss Greek philosophy in a way that recognizes its relevance to contemporary philosophical debates must walk a fine line between sufficient and excessive attention to scholarly detail. Important details must be addressed, but should not obscure philosophical issues at the heart of the discussion. This is what I have tried to do in my account of the sceptics, judging their philosophy in terms of its ability to answer fundamental questions about reality, knowledge, and the good life that still play an important role in philosophical discussion. In some cases, this means that controversial details have been consigned to the footnotes, though I have tried to address in one way or another all the major issues raised in the secondary literature. In the process, I have dealt with most opposing points of view. However, no one should expect the book to deal in a definitive way with every other commentator or every possible point of contention. Nor should it be assumed that I have nothing to say about points which have not been addressed.

The appoach to Greek philosophy I have adopted is, I think, an important one if we are to reestablish the relevance of ancient thought to mainstream philosophical debate. The standard approach obscures this relevance by driving a wedge between historical and philosophical concerns, leaving the study of Greek philosophy to specialists who are historians first, and philosophers only second. Those who do take mainstream philosophical issues as their primary focus—those best able to judge the contemporary relevance of any philosophical position—are left to play a marginal role in current debates about the history of philosophy. And so discussions of the Greeks are often predicated on a view of philosophy that lags behind the times. This failure to keep step with philosophical discussion is exacerbated by the weight of received opinion, which favours established outlooks and authorities, and is compounded by the usual attention to detail, which makes it difficult to progress beyond them (though received opinion is equally open to objection if one subjects it to the same microscopic scrutiny). In answer to such tendencies, it must be said that mainstream philosophical concerns can shed important light on the views of Greek philosophers, for their aim is a plausible reponse to perennial philosophical questions. In keeping with this, I shall argue that commentators have failed to understand the sceptics because they have misunderstood the *logic* of their philosophy. We must in contrast view it in terms of the distinctions that play a central role in contemporary epistemology. A grasp of modern philosophical issues and a good head for philosophical argument are the first prerequisites for understanding the sceptics.

The importance of reestablishing the relevance of the sceptics and other Greek philosophers to mainstream philosophical debate is difficult to exaggerate, given that increasingly narrow interests and specialized technical concerns have promoted the view that Greek philosophy is a dispensable frill in modern education. (The question why publicly funded institutions should devote considerable resources to its study needs to be taken more seriously than it is.) An appeal to something more than historical curiosity (or dubious clichés such as the claim that the world has never seen anything like the glory of Periclean Athens) is needed if the study of ancient thought is to be a vital part of intellectual debate. I believe it has this potential, but that the standard approach runs the danger of turning it into an esoteric discipline pursued by an elite few who are further and further removed from central philosophical concerns. In the case of scepticism, such a development would be unfortunate, for it has a relevance that extends beyond philosophical inquiry. Indeed, it might be said that the crisis now facing Western civilization is very much an extension of the arrogant and uncritical acceptance of reason the sceptics continually attack. Like the original sceptics, I offer my conclusions as an antidote to the attitude this implies.

GREEK SCEPTICISM

I

Toward a New Interpretation of the Sceptics

In the "Polemical Introduction" to his 1968 collection of selections from Sextus Empiricus, Philip P. Hallie complains that philosophers have deprived the word *scepticism* of its true meaning, making it "a rather empty but highly charged swear word." There have been some significant developments in our understanding of the sceptics since he made that charge but the present book still substantiates his suggestion that they "have been fallaciously criticized or simply ignored," more than any significant group of thinkers in the history of Western thought.[1] In this chapter, we begin by introducing the sceptics, the main features of the interpretation that will be proposed, and the way in which it differs from the accounts suggested or assumed by other commentators.

It hardly need be said that the most salient feature of the sceptics' views is their rejection of the commitment to reason which is celebrated in most accounts of the history of Western thought. Thinkers who espouse this commitment extol the human ability to discern the true nature of the world and proclaim the highest good to be the pursuit of rational inquiry. Plato exemplifies the spirit of such convictions when he writes that the sense of sight has given rise to number, time, and inquiry into the nature of the universe, thus bringing forth philosophy "than which no greater good ever was or will be given by the gods to mortal men" (*Tim* 47c Jowett).[2]

1. Hallie, "Polemical Introduction," p. 3.
2. The first quote from a classical work or author indicates the translation used. If I have used a different translation in any subsequent quote, this is noted in the text. Major, but not minor, amendments are mentioned in the text or in the notes.

In contrast, the sceptics expound the limits of reason and its inability to establish fundamental truth. The sceptical tradition thus represents the historical antithesis of movements like Platonism, Aristotelianism, and Cartesianism, and it is their popularity that has allowed it to be ignored, misunderstood, and underemphasized in philosophical debate. In recent commentary historians have begun to question this treatment of the sceptics, but their reevaluation is limited in its scope and it is difficult to take the sceptics seriously in an atmosphere that pays homage to the peculiar notion that Western philosophy is a footnote to Plato. The received view of Greek philosophy remains the one that Bernard Williams defends in describing the legacy of Greek philosophy, suggesting that, of all the Greeks, it is Plato and Aristotle who must count as "supreme in philosophical genius and breadth of achievement."[3] He accords the sceptics second-class status, complaining that their views "are not altogether easy to reconstruct from the accounts, rambling and sometimes inconsistent, offered by second- or third-rate thinkers such as Sextus or Cicero."[4] As we shall subsequently see, these charges cannot withstand careful scrutiny. For the moment, suffice it to say that the sceptical corpus is, at worst, no more obscure than Plato's *Parmenides* or Aristotle's *Metaphysics*, and that it is, at best, a lucid and compelling ancient analogue of some of the most important themes we find in philosophers such as Berkeley, Hume, and Kant.

The negative view of scepticism that characterizes contemporary philosophy is particularly marked in discussions of scepticism as a problem in philosophy. Defeating scepticism has become one of philosophy's main concerns; but philosophers have made little or no attempt to understand true scepticism and have rarely looked past Hume or Descartes in discussions of the issues it raises.[5] Their version of scepticism is a caricature that portrays it as a wild attack on all belief. In the process, they ignore a classical tradition that for more than six hundred years developed and discussed the very problems they address—a tradition that presented scepticism as the resolution rather than the cause of philosophical perplexity.

The present book attempts to provide a more sympathetic and accurate account of Greek scepticism and its relevance to modern and

3. Williams, "Philosophy," p. 202.

4. Ibid., p. 238.

5. There are a few exceptions (e.g., Reichenbach and Chisholm), but their discussions are problematic and fall far short of what is needed.

contemporary thought. It begins with an account of the development of scepticism in pre-Socratic times and ends with a discussion of scepticism's relationship to modern and contemporary epistemology. In answer to the usual assumptions that characterize philosophical discussions of the sceptics, it makes the following claims:

1. That the sceptics pose the central problems of ancient and modern epistemology
2. That scepticism is not solely negative and offers a consistent positive philosophy (indeed, a number of philosophies) that mitigates the sceptical critique of knowledge
3. That the sceptics' responses to sceptical arguments (and the responses of many of their predecessors) are an ancient precursor to modern and contemporary anti-realism
4. That ancient scepticism provides a plausible alternative to the views of contemporary epistemologists

In the process of arguing for these conclusions, we shall see that sceptical philosophy has been drastically misunderstood and underestimated; that it has been dismissed with straw-man arguments that misrepresent sceptics' views; and that the standard objections to scepticism are easily overcome.

I proceed chronologically after this introductory chapter, so these themes are recurring theses that will be defended in the context of the views of different sceptics at various points in my discussion. The consistency of the major schools of scepticism (early Pyrrhonism, academic scepticism, and later Pyrrhonism) is, for example, defended on pages 94–96, 111–12, 119–20, and 136–39.

THE NEGATIVE SIDE OF SCEPTICISM

In presenting scepticism, it is useful to distinguish a "positive" and a "negative" side. The negative side of sceptical philosophy is a critique of the human ability to establish truth. A variety of arguments lead to the general conclusion that truth is unattainable, or that it is unattainable in specific contexts. Though such arguments have been influential in the history of philosophy, the details of the negative side of scepticism are ignored in contemporary debate. The enormous catalogue of arguments in Sextus' critique of space, time, place, and innumerable other notions is, for example, rarely mentioned, and accounts of the arguments for scepticism usually focus on the claims of other thinkers. Even Hallie's defence maintains that "Socrates doubted more subtly and with more originality and power than they [the sceptics] did, and various philosophers who came after them, like Bayle in the seventeenth century and Hume, in the eighteenth, used doubt to invade more important dogmas . . ."[6]

This tendency to ignore the septics' arguments is reinforced by most accounts of modern thought, which suggest that the philosophies of Descartes, Berkeley, Hume, Kant, and other modern thinkers are an attempt to answer a new, more powerful sceptical challenge. According to M. F. Burnyeat, Richard Popkin, Wallace Matson, and apparently Descartes himself (*Bur* 4), the break with earlier arguments is seen most clearly in the latter's suggestion that our beliefs may be mistaken because we are the victims of supernatural deception—a suggestion that is said to raise a new, unheard-of ground for doubt. According to Burnyeat, Alfred Ewing, Matson, C. D. Rollins, and Williams, philosophers after Descartes are forced, for the first time, to grapple with the possibility that the world of our perceptions may not correspond to an objective, independent world of external objects (the problem of the external world). According to such accounts, Hume's critique of cause, and later questions about logic, religion, and morality, all add to modern scepticism, but it is Descartes' distinction between the internal and the external world that provides its core, making possible quasisceptical positions like solipsism and idealism. In keeping with this, Richard Rorty argues that it is a mistake to assume "that everybody has always known how to divide the world into the mental and the physical,"[7] and that the modern distinction is invented by Descartes. The picture of modern philosophy that emerges is well summed up by Norman Kemp Smith, who begins his *Studies in the Cartesian Philosophy* with the claim that Descartes' separation of mind and body forced "a reconsideration of the problem of knowledge," with the result that philosophy makes "a fresh start: a new set of problems has arisen and it is as the first to face these problems that he has been called 'the father of modern philosophy.'"[8]

Though I shall take issue with such views, it must be admitted that many of the sceptics' arguments, based as they are on ancient

6. Hallie, "Polemical Introduction," pp. 3–4.
7. Rorty, *Philosophy and the Mirror of Nature*, p. 17.
8. Smith, *Studies in the Cartesian Philosophy*, p. 1.

controversies and disputes, have lost their significance in the modern context. This being said, we shall see that other more central arguments raise the key issues in modern and contemporary epistemology. In particular, the sceptics discuss the reliability of sense impressions; the validity of inductive inference; the existence of the external world; the possibility of idealist truth; relativism (a problem that is, as we shall see in chapters 2 and 3, already pressing in earlier epistemology); the role that human nature and social convention play in determining belief; the possibility of a foundation for belief; and the certainty of the principles of logic, religion, and morality. (See, for example, the Pyrrhonean arguments discussed on pages 125–31.) We shall, in particular, note that the distinction between the mind and the external world is an integral part of ancient scepticism, and that the route sceptics take to their conclusions (via the problem of opposition, the different tropes, and discussions of specific issues) encompasses all the major kinds of doubt in ancient and modern epistemology.

There are some ways in which the sceptics' discussion of such issues is distinct from modern debate, but it would be a mistake to defend an emphasis on Descartes, Hume, and other modern thinkers by arguing that they offer superior formulations of scepticism's arguments. That ancient arguments are more, not less, worthy of attention is evident in discussions of specific problems. The academic analogue of Descartes' argument for scepticism clearly recognizes, for example, the question-begging nature of any attempt to refute scepticism by an appeal to clearness and distinctness (the marks of the Stoics' "cognitive" impressions, the *phantasiai kataleptikai*) as a guide to truth (see p. 103). In its discussion of inductive inference, Pyrrhonism more clearly recognizes the problem of induction, not exaggerating, as Hume does, the role of causal reasoning in such inference (see p. 129).

More generally, the sceptics have a better understanding of the fundamental issues that give rise to different kinds of scepticism. This aspect of their arguments manifests itself in the problem of the criterion, which suggests that there is no (noncircular) way to justify basic criteria for belief (see p. 131). Various versions of this problem are increasingly emphasized as sceptical philosophy evolves, becoming the focus of the most sophisticated form of ancient scepticism, later Pyrrhonism. Its lengthy and detailed discussions of the criterion demonstrate an appreciation of the theoretical foundations of scepticism that far surpasses philosophers such as Hume and Descartes. Indeed, if the account proposed here is correct, the original sceptics achieve an understanding of the sceptical critique of knowledge that equals (or surpasses) most contemporary epistemology.

STANDARD CRITICISMS OF THE SCEPTICS

Ancient scepticism is not, however, merely negative, and the assumption that it is has been the source of the most serious misunderstandings of the sceptics. The positive side of their views can best be understood against a background of the standard criticisms used to dismiss their views. The most striking feature of these criticisms is a failure to come to grips with the details of the sceptics' outlook.

For our purposes, it is important to note the carelessness that characterizes modern and contemporary criticism, though it should be noted that a similar failure to take the sceptics seriously informs the history of philosophy. Popkin cites many pertinent examples in his history of scepticism from Erasmus to Spinoza. The rejection of scepticism propounded by sixteenth- and seventeenth-century thinkers such as Pierre Le Loyer, Jean Daille, Paul Ferry, Jean Bagot, and Cardinal Sadoleto is, for example, little more than a denunciation of its tenets. As Popkin writes, "Cardinal Sadoleto's answer to academic scepticism is little more than a panegyric on the merits of ancient philosophy and human reason rather than an answer to the challenge. His overwhelming faith in the capacities of rational thought does not seem to be based upon any genuine analysis or answer to the arguments of the academics. Instead, he has tried to shift the locus of the attack, letting the academics' battery fall on the scholastics, while blissfully retaining unshaken confidence in man's rational powers, if properly employed."[9]

One might complain that Sadoleto's critique is out of date and of little interest, but a similar approach is shared by many modern thinkers. Bergmann, for example, offhandedly dismisses scepticism because it is "one of the silliest philosophies,"[10] Samuel Johnson "refutes" scepticism by the kicking of a rock, and Moore "proves" the existence of the external world by holding up his hand. Such bald assertions cannot, however, refute the sceptic—they ignore both the positive side of scepticism and the details of its arguments. The latter suggest that the kicking of a rock or the presentation of a hand may be

9. Popkin, *The History of Scepticism from Erasmus to Spinoza*, p. 27.
10. Bergmann, *Meaning and Existence*, p. 58.

illusory, and one cannot prove otherwise by *declaring* this to be obviously mistaken.

The lack of care that characterizes treatments of scepticism is seen in contemporary texts used to teach philosophy. In *Philosophy: Paradox and Discovery*, Minton and Shipka introduce and dismiss the sceptics in one paragraph, which begins: "A word first . . . about the philosophical minority: the radical sceptics. Since the very beginning of philosophical reflection, even before Socrates, there have been thinkers who denied the possibility of acquiring genuine knowledge, of distinguishing true statements from false ones. Legend has it that one of these early radical sceptics, Cratylus, was so adamant that our quest for knowledge is doomed, that he actually refused to speak . . ."[11] Cratylus is not, however, a sceptic, but a Heraclitean who reputedly gives up speaking because it is impossible to speak the truth about a world in flux. Minton and Shipka class him as a sceptic because he concludes that we cannot establish truth and because, as a result, he gives up ordinary ways of acting. The assumption is that scepticism undermines belief and must therefore destroy normal life. The Pyrrhonean endorsement of *aphasia* is the closest any sceptics come to the suggestion that we should not speak, however, and it is a refusal to speak on specific philosophical issues that explicitly leaves room for day to day affairs (see p. 92).

In defense of the caricature in Minton and Shipka, it is sometimes said that the sceptic so construed is of theoretical interest and therefore worth discussing. We would probably not accept such a cavalier attitude to historical accuracy in the case of other thinkers, though the crucial point is that the position attributed to the sceptics is *not* of theoretical interest, for it is obviously untenable. As Minton and Shipka themselves remark:

Anyone who shares this position faces logical difficulties if he chooses to defend it. If he says, in effect, "We can know nothing for sure," we might ask whether he is sure of that statement; if he answers "yes," he has contradicted his claim by asserting at least a single truth; if he answers "no," he has retracted his claim, and opened the door to an opposite one, namely that one can know *something* for sure. Further, if he offered arguments in support of his claim, he is presuming that both the conclusions and the premises are sound—truthful if you will—and again he is trapped. Finally, a radical sceptic's living usually puts the lie to his talking. If you examine his behaviour, you will find that he acts on statements of belief which he accepts as truthful implicitly. He wears clothes to

11. Minton and Shipka, *Philosophy: Paradox and Discovery*. p. 174.

protect him from the elements, and pays his bills on time, and eats regularly, all of which show that he implicitly affirms some truths about himself and his surroundings.

Another simplistic response to the problem of truth . . .[12]

This criticism would undermine scepticism if Minton and Shipka described it accurately, but the inconsistencies they note evaporate when they are exposed to real scepticism. It is nonetheless the caricature popularized by such authors that has become the focus of discussion of the sceptics, trivializing critiques of their views and ignoring the viable outlook they defend.

Though it is mistaken, the assumption that scepticism is purely negative, and the claim that its rejection of all belief is inconsistent with its own tenets, is a standard criticism. For example, Russell comments that Greek "Scepticism as philosophy is not merely doubt, but what may be called dogmatic doubt," and that "it is this element of dogmatism which makes the system vulnerable."[13] Russell does note that the sceptics deny asserting "the impossibility of knowledge dogmatically," but he fails to investigate the matter, simply remarking, "their denials are not very convincing."[14] The claim that sceptical conclusions are inconsistent is also found in Plato's criticism of Protagoras, and in criticisms of the major schools of scepticism propounded by the Stoics, Lucretius, Augustine, Maccoll, Stough, and Burnyeat. According to Johnson, sceptical philosophy has no way around the charge of inconsistency, and this is the "standard" objection to it.

The charge that scepticism is incompatible with life is an even more familiar theme. The Epicurean Colotes attacks the sceptics in this way in a work entitles *On the fact that the doctrines of the other philosophers make it impossible to live*. Lucretius echoes Colotes' sentiments when he writes that:

The senses cannot be refuted . . . /[do not] loose from your hands what is manifest,/and break the primary trust, and tear apart the foundations upon/ which the whole of life is solidly built./For not only would reason be destroyed,/ but life itself would collapse, unless we believe our senses,/avoiding precipices and pitfalls, and other things/equally to be shunned, seeking the opposites. (*De rerum natura* 4.483–512 Martinband)

12. Ibid.
13. Russell, *A History of Western Philosophy*, p. 6.
14. Yet Russell dubs scepticism "a lazy man's" philosophy.

The claim that we must avoid these precipices and pitfalls alludes to apocryphal anecdotes according to which Pyrrho refused to do so. More generally, Galen questions "whether the Pyrrhonist expects us to stay in bed when the sun is up for lack of certaintly about whether it is day or night, or to sit on board ship when everyone else is embarking, wondering whether what appears to be land really is land."[15]

Emotionally charged criticism along these lines typifies modern discussion. As Hallie writes of the French philosopher Alain, "he described the sceptic (and he was thinking of the founder of scepticism, Pyrrho) as being somebody who 'holds himself immobile and indifferent so that the sleep of death may take him alive; . . . for there is one true sceptic, and he insists that nothing is true; and he insists on it dogmatically.' In an essay written in 1922 he had said that scepticism is 'systematic negation' and 'oriental indifference,' and that it sees life as a 'vain illusion.'"[16] One finds similar claims in more recent commentary. According to Kekes, scepticism leads to a life that is "nasty, brutish and short."[17] According to Johnson, "the sceptic's peace of mind is a goal purchased at the expense of living a life comparable to that of a sleep walker or of someone sunk in a coma, a level that is surpassed by the more intelligent animals. Not only would a life like that signal the death of the intellect . . . it would make it impossible for us to engage in any activities we consider . . . human."[18] Rescher writes that scepticism is, "as far as the cognitive venture goes, a doomsday bomb that levels everything in sight."[19] C. I. Lewis writes that scepticism is "worse than unsatisfactory, I consider it nonsense to hold or imply that just any empirical judgment is as good as any other—because none is warranted. A theory which implies or allows that consequence is not an exploration of anything, but merely an intellectual disaster."[20]

Similar remarks are made by Slote, Maccoll and others. In marked contrast, Hallie holds that "philosophically induced life negation has nothing to do with scepticism as it really is."[21] The sceptics and their supporters throughout the history of philosophy concur, pointing out that scepticism is consistent and compatible with life, and rejecting claims to the contrary. To take but one example, Plutarch ridicules

15. Burnyeat, "Can the sceptic Live His Scepticism?" fn. 4.
16. Hallie, "Polemical Introduction," p. 6.
17. Kekes, "The Case for Scepticism," p. 38.
18. Johnson, *Scepticism and Cognitivism*, p. 119.
19. Rescher, *Scepticism: A Critical Reappraisal*, p. 206.
20. Lewis, "The Given Element in Empirical Knowledge," p. 175.
21. Hallie, "Polemical Introduction," p. 6.

Colotes, calling him a "pettifogger" and claiming that the details of Arcesilaus' views get from him "the response a performance on the lyre gets from an ass" (*Ad Col* 1122B).

THE POSITIVE SIDE OF SCEPTICISM: MITIGATED SCEPTICISM

Understood within a broader context, the negative side of scepticism (and the sceptics' emphasis on the negative) is a response to other schools (Platonism, Stoicism, Epicureanism, etc.) that are too confident of their ability to establish truth. In answer to their overconfidence, the sceptics preach a more humble attitude, but not a complete rejection of all claims. On the contrary, they adopt a variety of outlooks that explicitly include a positive basis for belief. Philosophers who assume or argue otherwise reject a position that is not actually adopted by the sceptics or, it appears, by anyone else in the history of philosophy. If such a position were compelling, their discussions might be instructive, but it is patently inconsistent and has only served to divert philosophers from the positions sceptics really advocate.

Like the negative side of scepticism, the sceptics' positive philosophy can be understood in modern terms and is uniquely relevant to contemporary discussion. There is, however, a great deal more that must be said about the positive side of scepticism. It is useful to begin with Hume's distinction between "mitigated" and "unmitigated" scepticism. Suppose that sceptical arguments lead one to the conclusion that what is true cannot be established. One might follow Molière's Marphurius in *Le Marriage Forcé* or Lucian's Pyrrhonean in the *Sale of the Philosophies* and *give up* on reason and the senses, suspending judgment on the truth of all belief. One might adopt unmitigated scepticism. As Minton and Shipka and many others point out, this position is extremely problematic. It is hard to see how it can be compatible with a belief in scepticism, for example, or with living, eating, walking, talking, or any other action, for actions are founded on belief (the belief that certain objects exist, that we are capable of certain thoughts and actions, that our senses are reliable, and so on). Unmitigated scepticism thus gives birth to the hapless character maligned by Lucian and Molière—a character now invoked as the epitome of the sceptic.

In contrast, mitigated sceptics respond to sceptical conclusions in a different way. For though they conclude that a belief in the external world, the principles of reason, and so forth cannot be justified, they still accept them. As Popkin says, " 'sceptic' and 'believer' are not opposing classifications. The sceptic is raising doubts about the rational and evidential merits of the justification given for beliefs; he doubts that necessary and sufficient reasons have been or could be discovered to show that any particular belief must be true . . . But the sceptic may . . . still accept various beliefs."[22] This acceptance of belief that is ultimately unjustified is the mark of so-called mitigated scepticism. The kind of life that it entails is portrayed not by Lucian or Molière but by Calderon in *La Vida es Sueño*, where Segismundo concludes that it is impossible to determine whether he is dreaming or awake, and decides that he will act as though awake. The mitigated sceptic also deals with everyday circumstances by accepting the use of reason and the senses, at the same time granting that they may be mistaken. Why does the sceptic accept belief that is ultimately unjustified? Because it seems impossible to do otherwise, and psychological constraints (pain and pleasure, logical intuition, and emotion and sensation) and the goal of happiness seem to leave no other choice.[23]

Hume himself is usually suggested as the classic example of a mitigated sceptic. For though he concludes that there is no way to justify the senses, causal inference, and reasoning in general, he still claims that ordinary life and human nature do not allow us to reject them. On the contrary, the sceptic is "absolutely and necessarily determined to live, and talk, and act like other people in the common affairs of life" (*Tr* 296). To take but one example, "the sceptic . . . must assent to the principle concerning the existence of the body, tho' he cannot pretend by any arguments of philosophy to maintain its veracity. Nature has not left this to his choice, and has doubtless esteem'd it an affair of too great importance to be trusted to our uncertain reasonings and speculations . . . 'Tis vain to ask, Whether there be body or not? That is a point which we must take for granted in

22. Popkin, *The History of Scepticism from Erasmus to Spinoza*, p. xix.

23. The psychological constraints underlying sceptical beliefs will be very much in evidence if we try to doubt the existence of a heavy metal object as it descends toward our toes, or the existence of food when we suffer hunger pangs. The psychological traits accompanying unmitigated scepticism on the other hand, require bizarre and abnormal dispositions. Frankl reports one case in which a psychosis was brought to crisis when a patient read Kant's *Critique of Pure Reason* and was overwhelmed by "the thought that the objects of the world might not be real" (*The Unheard Cry for Meaning*, pp. 133–40; I am indebted to David Noar for this example). It is in keeping with the mitigated sceptic's emphasis on the psychology of belief that Frankl cures his patient's doubts, not by rational argument, but by therapy that changes his psychological propensities.

all our reasonings" (*Tr* 218). According to Hume's analysis, it is "animal faith" and the inclinations that accompany it that must provide our ground for acting and believing.

Unlike Hume, the ancient sceptics are usually said to be unmitigated sceptics. Hume himself is guilty of this assumption in his discussion of the Pyrrhoneans, whom he characterizes as "that fantastic sect." His view of their philosophy is reflected in his account of cause. On the one hand, he accepts that a Pyrrhonean will triumph if he holds "that we have no argument to convince us, that objects, which have, in our experience, been frequently conjoined, will likewise, in other instances, be conjoined in the same manner; and that nothing leads us to this inference but custom or a certain instinct of nature, which it is indeed difficult to resist, but which, like other instincts, may be fallacious and deceitful" (*Enq* 127). On the other hand, Hume holds that a Pyrrhonean cannot expect

that his philosophy will have any constant influence on the mind, or if it had, that its influence would be beneficial to society. On the contrary, he must acknowledge, if he will acknowledge anything, that all human life must perish, were his principles universally and steadily to prevail. All discourse, all action would immediately cease; and men remain in total lethargy, till the necessities of nature, unsatisfied, put an end to their miserable existence . . . When he awakes from his dream, he will be the first to join in the laugh against himself and to confess that all his objections are mere amusement, and can have no other tendency than to show the whimsical condition of mankind, who must act and reason and believe, though they are not able, by their most diligent enquiry, to satisfy themselves concerning the foundations of these operations, or to remove objections, which may be raised against them. (*Enq* 128)

One can find exceptions, but modern philosophical discussion takes a similar view of all of ancient scepticism. Scepticism is, according to it, unmitigated. When Smith points out that Hume accepts "natural" beliefs, he concludes he is a naturalist *rather* than a sceptic. We shall see, however, that there are no unmitigated sceptics and that all the schools of ancient scepticism mitigate their views in one way or another. For example, the Pyrrhoneans offer not merely Hume's critique of cause but also the core of his response, suggesting that the everyday belief in cause be accepted because this seems necessary to day-to-day living. As both the academics and the Pyrrhoneans recognize, the sceptic "is not sprung from a rock or an oak primeval" and must participate in practical affairs (*Ac* 2.101, *AM* 11.161; the allusion is to Homer).

MORAL AND RELIGIOUS SCEPTICISM

Though a detailed discussion of the positive side of scepticism must wait till later, we might illustrate its mitigated nature by turning to religion. Modern commentators sometimes suggest that the sceptics' critique of religious arguments is the only redeeming feature of their outlook, but this critique is easily misunderstood. The sceptics do attack arguments usually offered in support of religious dogma, but this does not mean that they are "religious sceptics" in the sense that they reject religious claims. On the contrary, they reject atheism and endorse religion, claiming that the latter must be accepted without a philosophical foundation (on the basis of faith rather than reason). The sceptics are in this sense the precursors of Kierkegaard and Pascal rather than Hume and Holbach.

The sceptics' commitment to religion is reflected in Sextus' discussion of arguments against the notion that God is an efficient cause in book 3 of the *Outlines of Pyrrhonism*. Thus he begins by "first premising that, . . . following the ordinary view, we [the sceptics] affirm undogmatically that Gods exist and reverence Gods and ascribe to them foreknowledge" (*PH* 3.2 Bury). In "Against the Ethicists," he similarly tells us that "the sceptic, as compared with philosophers of other views, will be found in a more defensible position, since in conformity with his ancestral laws and customs, he declares that the Gods exist, and performs everything which contributes to their worship and veneration, but, so far as regards philosophic investigation, declines to commit himself rashly" (*AM* 9.49 Bury). One finds a similar attitude in Cicero's *De Natura Deorum*, when Cotta, the academic sceptic, outlines his position in answer to the Stoic Balbus:

I am considerably influenced by your authority Balbus, and by the plea . . . that I ought to uphold the beliefs about immortal gods which have come down to us from our ancestors, and the rites and ceremonies and duties of religion. For my part I always uphold them and always have done so, and no eloquence of anybody, learned or unlearned, shall ever dislodge me from belief in the worship of the immortal gods which I have inherited from our forefathers . . . There, Balbus, is the opinion of a Cotta and a pontiff; now oblige me by letting me know yours. You are a philosopher, and I ought to receive from you a proof of your religion, whereas I must believe the word of our ancestors even without proof. (*DND* 3.5–6 Rackham)

The same sentiments are echoed when Cotta responds to Epicurean arguments for religion with the remark that

I, who am a high priest, and who hold it to be a duty most solemnly to maintain the rights and doctrines of established religion, should be glad to be convinced of this fundamental tenet of the divine existence, not as an article of faith merely, but as an ascertained fact. For many disturbing reflections occur to my mind, which sometimes make me think that there are no gods at all. But mark how generously I deal with you. I will not attack those tenets which are shared by your school with all other philosophers—for example, the one in question, since almost all men, and I myself no less than any other, believe that the gods exist, and this accordingly I do not challenge. At the same time I doubt the adequacy of the argument which you adduce to prove it. (*DND* 1.61–62)

Here the issue is not the correctness of religion, but the correctness of philosophical arguments allegedly supporting it. It is philosophy, not religion, that is called in question, and it is philosophy (in the sense of a rational basis for belief) that is ultimately rejected. [24]

Something similar must be said about the sceptics' relationship to so-called moral scepticism. Often the term is used to refer to thinkers like the *physis* sophists, Hobbes, Mandeville, and Nietzsche. They reject conventional (typically, altruistic) moral claims in favour of an explicit commitment to self interest ("self love"). This is not the view of the ancient sceptics, who would argue that it, like any other conception of

---

24. Penelhum's critique of the sceptical approach to religion in *God and Scepticism* seems to me fundamentally misguided. In this regard it is worth noting that later thinkers link scepticism with religion by using the ancient sceptics' reasoning to argue that scientific reasoning cannot be justified and is not, therefore, preferable to religion. As Schmitt writes in his discussion of Gianfrancesco Pico:

The use which Pico made of sceptical arguments might appear somewhat startling to those who tend to identify scepticism with the anti-religious. The sceptic can certainly be one who entertains religious doubts or disbelief, but as Pico's writings indicate so well, scepticism can also be used in the service of religion. In fact, a careful examination of the reintroduction of scepticism into the West during the sixteenth century discloses that it was used more often in behalf of Christianity than in opposition to it. Gentian Hervet's Preface to his translation of Sextus Empiricus (clearly) indicates that he was of one mind with Pico on this point . . . It is now beginning to be realized although the process has been painfully slow, that we cannot make a simple equation between scepticism and irreligion . . . We have been given a variety of epithets to characterize . . . early modern philosophy. One speaks of "Christian humanism," "Christian philosophy," "the Christian Renaissance." Could we not with as much justification speak of Gianfrancesco and other as "Christian sceptics"? (*Gianfrancesco Pico*, pp. 7–9)

The outlook here expressed is a natural extension of the views of ancient sceptics.

morality, is vulnerable to attack. Given that no morality can be defended in a way that defeats scepticism, they propose an acceptance of traditional moral views and, in this sense, of mitigated scepticism. In many ways, their moral outlook is similar to emotivism, denying as it does our ability to establish objective moral principles but endorsing ordinary moral sentiments nonetheless. As Sextus puts it when he proposes the Pyrrhonean "practical criterion" as a guide to life, "the tradition of customs and laws" determines the sceptics' opinions on pious and good conduct (*PH* 1.23–24). There is much to be said about the details of this view; for the moment let us simply note that it is not the rejection of morality implied by unmitigated scepticism.

SCEPTICISM AS ANTI-REALISM

Unlike mainstream philosophers, scholars who study the history of philosophy are more receptive to the notion that ancient scepticism is a mitigated scepticism. Some commentators (in early modern philosophy, Bayle, and in more recent discussion, Brochard, Hallie, Stough, Barnes, and most significantly, Frede) recognize the positive side of scepticism, though other commentators (most notably, Burnyeat, Zeller, Maccoll, Johnson, Couissin, and Striker)[25] take issue with their views. In some cases, those who portray ancient scepticism as unmitigated do not pay enough attention to specific texts—for instance, Cicero's discussion of Clitomachus' account of Carneades' views (see below pp. 117–19)—though a more important problem lies behind their views.

The case for the unmitigated nature of ancient scepticism is founded on the sceptics' claim that they suspend judgment (practice *epoche*) on the truth of any claim. As Burnyeat and other commentators point out, this seems to drive a wedge between them and a philosopher such as Hume, whose commitment to mitigated scepticism means that he does *not* suspend judgment on the truth of all claims, but accepts some claims as true (while admitting that they cannot be rationally established). Cicero, Philo, and Metrodorus espouse a similar view within the context of academic scepticism, but the most important ancient sceptics explicitly reject all claims to truth and it seems to follow that they endorse unmitigated scepticism.

25. It is important to distinguish Striker's view of Pyrrhonism (which she sees as mitigated) and academic scepticism (which she sees as unmitigated). Her view of the latter has been particularly influential and I shall concentrate on it in the present book.

To account for this apparent incongruity, Frede and other commentators who recognize the sceptics' acceptance of belief have argued that sceptical *epoche* is (despite appearances) not intended universally, and applies only to scientific or philosophical belief. According to Barnes, the Pyrrhoneans simply overstate their views, sometimes acting as "sober," and sometimes as "drunken," sceptics. In answer, Burnyeat and others have argued that such interpretations are *ad hoc*, and that a literal interpretation of Pyrrhonean claims suggests that any claim to truth should be rejected. Striker defends a similar view in her account of the major academic sceptics.

The claim that *epoche* is intended universally is difficult to dispute, but it is problematic, for it makes scepticism inconsistent and incompatible with life, undermining the sceptical commitment to practical affairs—a commitment that manifests itself in the explicit claim that we should accept appearances, the *eulogon*, the *pithanon*, and the practical criterion. The suggestion that sceptics simply fail to see such obvious problems is not convincing,[26] especially as their philosophy develops in a context sensitive to the charge of inconsistency. As Frede says, "the ancient sceptics, starting with Arcesilaus at the latest, were quite familiar with this objection [to their views]."[27] Indeed, concerns about consistency are emphasized in Greek philosophy long before Arcesilaus, in reductio ad absurdum arguments against philosophers such as Parmenides and Heracleitus. The apparent inconsistency of views that tend to scepticism is already recognized by Democritus, who attacks Protagoras on these grounds, and by Metrodorus of Chios, who explicitly qualifies his scepticism to avoid the charge of inconsistency (see pp. 61, 64). Especially as Democritus and Metrodorus play an important role in Pyrrho's own development, it is implausible to suppose that Pyrrho and later sceptics do not recognize the danger of

26. It is difficult to believe that any philosopher (much less thinkers as acute as Pyrrho, Carneades, or Arcesilaus) could accept such an obviously untenable position, much less ignore its inconsistency with their lives. As Norton suggests:

. . . it is easy to *caricature* the sceptic—the man who never rows because he cannot tell if the oar is straight or bent, or who develops bed sores because he cannot tell if he is awake or dreaming, or who would starve the plain man, telling him he does not know that he has food in his mouth— . . . although it does seem safe to say that sceptics have not only rowed, arisen, or eaten, but that they have displayed little interest in dissuading others from a forthright engagement in such activities. (*David Hume*, p. 240, cf. pp. 288–90)

27. Frede, "The Sceptic's Two Kinds of Knowledge," p. 180.

falling into inconsistency. The charge of inconsistency, Frede remarks, must somehow overlook "some crucial aspect" of sceptical views, for "the issue was raised again and again over the source of centuries," though "clearly, they [the sceptics] felt it did not really tell against their position."[28]

The key to understanding both the consistency and the mitigated nature of the ancient sceptics' outlook is an appreciation of crucial differences that separate modern and classical accounts of truth, belief, and knowledge. *Nothing* is more important to an understanding of the sceptics than an appreciation of the Greek commitment to a "realist" account of truth. It maintains that a claim is true if it corresponds to an objective world that exists independently of the mind. A claim is not, in view of this, true simply because it appears so given the structure of the human mind, of perception, of one's society, of one's historical circumstances, or of personal propensities; truth must encompass what is true from (as Hilary Putnam puts it) "a God's eye point of view." Truth must be objective and transcend subjective determinants of belief.

Greek philosophy's assumption that "truth" (*aletheia*) means realist truth, and its consequent assumption that what is and what exists is independent of the mind,[29] is obvious in thinkers such as Pythagoras, Heracleitus, Parmenides, Plato, Aristotle, and the Stoics, and has been recognized by many commentators on the sceptics. Frede alludes to Greek realism when he notes that the philosophers the sceptics attack "believe it is possible to go behind the surface phenomena to the essence of things, to the nature of things, to *true* reality . . . [and] that it is reason . . . that can lead us beyond the world of appearances to the world of *real* being; and thus for them it is a matter of reason, what is to count as *real* and as *true* . . . "[30] Burnyeat makes the same point when he remarks that truth in Greek philosophy always refers to "a real objective world outside the mind."[31] We shall see that this might be questioned in the case of Protagoras and his followers, (see pp. 58–61), but it need not detain us, for they are exceptions to the rule.

Given the Greek account of truth, Greek philosophy can be contrasted

28. Ibid.
29. By "what is and what exists" I mean what is denoted by the Greek verb *einai* ("to be"). As it encompasses both notions, I have used one or the other where appropriate.
30. Frede, "The Sceptic's Two Kinds of Knowledge," p. 187.
31. Burnyeat, "Idealism in Greek Philosophy," p. 48 (cf. 38, where he remarks that *alethes* "means truth as to real existence, something's being true of an independent reality").

with modern "anti-realism," which makes truth relative to subjective determinants of belief. It begins with idealism, with Berkeley's rejection of the external world. Rather than maintain that true claims are true of such a world, he interprets the assertion that something exists as meaning that we have certain kinds of perceptions. Kant similarly argues that knowledge must be understood in terms of our subjective outlook, and that the objects we know are appearances or "phenomena" rather than "things in themselves."[32] Contemporary philosophers such as Wittgenstein go further, arguing that notions of truth and knowledge are relative to language and, ultimately, to our form of life. In more recent discussion, Putnam argues that truth is relative to "internal" rather than "external" criteria for belief. In these and similar cases, modern philosophers reject or amend the realist notions assumed by Greek philosophy, replacing them with a more subjective account of truth.

The anti-realist bent of modern accounts of truth is particularly important to an understanding of the sceptics, for they assume a realist account of truth and it follows that they do *not* attack truth as many modern philosophers define it. In keeping with this, sceptical arguments are put forward as an attack on realist truth, countering the notion that we can transcend our subjective outlook by arguing that our beliefs are necessarily relative to human nature and perception, the culture that we live in, philosophical commitments, and so on. This reasoning culminates in the decision to suspend judgment on the truth of any claim, but here as elsewhere the concern is truth in the realist sense. The rejection of such truth leaves room for the acceptance of belief in an anti-realist sense, however, and in view of this, the negative side of scepticism is compatible with beliefs that are defined as relative to human nature, sense impressions, forms of understanding, psychological propensities, and custom and convention. The sceptics' *epoche* is thus universal, though it universally rejects all claims to *realist* truth and thus leaves room for anti-realist beliefs.

Unlike modern philosophers who defend anti-realism, sceptics define the word *truth* (*aletheia*) as realist truth, but they still endorse

32. Perhaps the most radical appeal to subjectivity is the account of moral claims proposed by Hume and the emotivists, but their proposal that ethical claims cannot be judged true or false puts their views at odds with the developments at issue here. (For an account of moral truth that is implicitly anti-realist, see Bambrough, *Moral Scepticism*. He himself portrays his account as a way to save objective truth, but in making that truth relative to linguistic—i.e.,social —conventions he is not an objectivist in the realist sense.)

anti-realist views when they suspend judgment on all realist truth in favour of subjective notions of assent that correspond to anti-realist truth. In this way, the sceptics anticipate modern anti-realism. In answer to the standard criticisms brought against them, it may be replied that the rejection of (realist) truth is quite compatible with the endorsement of specific kinds of (anti-realist) claims, and that these claims make possible an endorsement of both scepticism and day to day affairs. As the sceptics, in defending themselves, put it, their philosophy expels the claim that it is true along with all other (realist) claims ("as laxatives expel themselves with the body's wastes," *PH* 1.207), though this still allows them to accept appearances in an "undogmatic" way. In the context of practical affairs, this makes possible a mitigated scepticism that accepts anti-realist beliefs, though sceptics would admit that any of their beliefs may be mistaken from a realist point of view (and thus reject claims to realist truth).

The strength of this proposed interpretation of sceptical views can be seen if we contrast it with accounts proposed by other commentators. Scholars sympathetic to the sceptics recognize the positive side of their philosophy but fail to understand that their universal rejection of (realist) truth is compatible with the acceptance of anti-realist beliefs. Other scholars who deny that sceptical philosophy has a positive side recognize the universal nature of *epoche*, but mistakenly assume that the rejection of a Greek account of truth (one committed to realism) eliminates all belief. Scholars on both sides of the dispute repeatedly confuse the ancient and the modern claim that truth should be rejected, forgetting that the latter is much broader than the former, and that the former leaves room for qualified belief.

A detailed defense of this acount of scepticism must wait till chapter 6; for now, the equivocation that characterizes standard discussions can be illustrated with Stough's analysis of Pyrrhonism. Like many other authors, she recognizes that the Pyrrhonean adopts "'belief' only in a benign sense that has no implication as to [realist] *truth* and *real existence*,"[33] but she overlooks this in her analysis, arguing that the Pyrrhonean rejects *any* claim "that something is the case (is true)" and therefore "makes no claims about what is so," rejecting "factual claims" and all belief "about what is the case."[34] Stough is forced to conclude that Sextus does not recognize Pyrrhonism's fatal implications for

33. Stough, "Sextus Empiricus on Non-Assertion," p. 161.
34. Ibid., pp. 138–39.

ordinary life.[35] The real problem is her own confusion of realist and anti-realist claims. Her claim that the sceptic rejects all beliefs about what is, or what is true, is acceptable only if one interprets the words *true* and *is* in realist terms, but this invalidates her conclusion, that the sceptic must give up *all* belief about what is the case. It is possible to formulate anti-realist notions of "factual" claims "about what is the case" and "what is so"; in view of this, beliefs can be compatible with scepticism.

Assuming some such account of ancient scepticism, the usual view of modern anti-realism is mistaken in at least two ways: first, because it proposes anti-realism as an answer to the sceptics, failing to see that anti-realist notions are incorporated in scepticism; and, second, because it assumes that anti-realist notions originate in Berkeley, Kant, and contemporary philosophy. In answer to the latter claim, it must be admitted that modern anti-realism differs from ancient scepticism in specific ways, but it is simply not true that modern anti-realists introduce a radically new notion of belief defined in terms of subjective outlooks—a view propounded or assumed by philosophers such as Hegel, Ewing, Williams, and Burnyeat, and typified by Putnam's remark that it is "impossible to find a philosopher before Kant (and after the Presocratics) who was *not* a metaphysical realist."[36] Any such assumption ignores the sceptical endorsement of similar notions and persists only because we continue to ignore the sceptics. Nelson Goodman begins a recent book by suggesting that his work belongs "in that mainstream of modern philosophy that began when Kant exchanged the structure of the world for the structure of the mind . . . ,"[37] but it could as easily be said that his outlook continues a tradition that begins with ancient scepticism.

SCEPTICISM AND IDEALISM

Having pointed out the affinity between scepticism and modern anti-realism, we must note the differences, especially as they make scepticism a plausible alternative to modern views. Historically, the most important form of anti-realism is idealism. Idealism tries to answer scepticism, suggesting that we know our mental states (for we

35. Ibid., p. 163.
36. Putnam, *Reason, Truth and History*, p. 57.
37. Goodman, *Ways of Worldmaking*, p. x.

experience them) and therefore know that they, at least, objectively exist. Scepticism arises because we attempt to step beyond these states and establish that they correspond to external objects in an objective world. According to idealists, we can know that we perceive chairs, tables, and automobiles, but we cannot establish their independent existence. The idealist thus makes sense impressions the fundamental constituents of reality and interprets claims about the world by reference to them. Berkeley's claim that *esse est percipi* ("to be is to be perceived") turns a claim about the existence of an object into a claim that one has certain impressions and he concludes that we establish what exists. As Berkeley himself puts it:

All this scepticism follows from our supposing a difference between *things* and *ideas*, and that the former have a subsistence without the mind or unpreceived. It were easy to dilate on this subject and show how the arguments urged by the sceptics in all ages depend on the supposition of external objects.

So long as we attribute a real existence to unthinking things, distinct from their being perceived, it is not only impossible to know with evidence the nature of any unthinking being, but even that it exists . . . But all this doubtfulness . . . vanishes if we annex a meaning to our words . . . I can as well doubt of my own being as the being of those things which I actually perceive by sense; it being a manifest contradiction that any sensible object should be immediately perceived by sight or touch, and at the same time have no existence in nature, since the very *existence* of an unthinking being consists in *being perceived*. (*PHK* 87–88)

Kant moves in a similiar direction when he proposes phenomena as objects of inquiry, for the nature of phenomena is relative to the structure of the mind and need not exist beyond it.

If we are to understand idealism as it relates to ancient scepticism, we must begin by noting that it does not, despite its denial of the external world, reject all aspects of the realist point of view. In particular, Burnyeat is mistaken when he maintains that it introduces a new notion of truth that allows one to include "one's own [mental] experience as an object for description ."[38] Obviously, ancient philosophers allow mental states to be objects of description (as in such mundane claims as "He is in pain, " "I doubt the truth of such and such a view," "She dreams about her father," and "The perceptions of those with jaundice differ from our own"). Their account of truth maintains

38. Burnyeat, "Idealism in Greek Philosophy," p. 49, cf. 48.

that something exists if it is independent of the mind, not in the sense
that it is (physically) outside the mind, but in the sense that it actually
exists and is not merely *imagined* or *thought* to exist.[39] Idealists do not
reject this claim; they merely hold that mental states are the only things
we can establish as certainly existing. Idealism thus accepts specific
kinds of realist claims (that is, claims about sense impressions and other
mental states) as a paradigm of objective knowledge, and thus
constitutes an amendment rather than a rejection of realism—an
amendment that accepts claims about mental states, but no other
claims, as encompassing realist truth.

Comparing idealism to sceptical trends in Greek epistemology, we
find an analogue in the philosophy of Aristippus and his followers, the
Cyrenaics. Like modern idealists they attack realism by arguing that
belief is founded on impressions, and that it is impossible to transcend
perception. Given this conclusion, they interpret their beliefs as claims
about sense impressions rather than about external objects, arguing
that this allows them to know the truth of their beliefs. With the
exception of a lingusitic thesis noted in chapter 3, the Cyrenaics
differ from modern idealists only in recognizing that the arguments
for idealism also undercut our knowledge of other minds (for we
experience only our own impressions). This forces them to reject
claims about other minds as well as claims about external objects,
restricting their beliefs to claims about their own impressions (modern
idealism does not probe so deeply; it ignores the problem of other
minds).

The major schools of scepticism take the Cyrenaic critique of realist
knowledge further, employing many arguments that extend beyond
idealism's critique of the external world. The critique still plays a
central role in their philosophy, however, and they respond to it and
other arguments by endorsing claims interpreted in terms of sense
impressions and subjective states. The Pyrrhoneans' acceptance of
appearances (see pp. 92–94, 135) is particularly close to the idealist
notion of belief, though it must be emphasized that Pyrrhoneans and
other sceptics reject the assumption that we have an incorrigible
knowledge of our mental states, seeing this as yet another dogma of
philosophy. It follows that they interpret their own claims in terms of
impressions, but still accept them as possibly mistaken and only use

39. Burnyeat's mistake is his confusion of these two ways that something can be
independent of the mind.

them as a way to mitigate their scepticism (in contrast, the idealists see such claims as providing access to a restricted realm of realist truth). It is this that makes the sceptics mitigated sceptics rather than idealists. In the context of modern anti-realism, their positive philosophy is in this sense closer to the kinds of anti-realism propounded by contemporary philosophers who reject any realist truth.

A second way in which ancient scepticism differs from idealism is in its interpretation of ordinary language. For though the sceptics accept beliefs interpreted as beliefs about impressions, they do not (with the possible exception of the early Pyrrhoneans) forward them as a correct interpretation of ordinary claims. Rather, they accept the day-to-day assumption that ordinary claims refer to external objects and therefore see their own claims as a distinct departure from ordinary parlance.[40] In contrast, idealism proposes an interpretation of ordinary claims as claims about perception, and in this way saves them from sceptical attack. As Berkeley puts it, our doubts about these claims vanish if we annex "a meaning to our words." In the present book, we leave a discussion of what this implies for language for chapter 7, though it may from the start be said that sceptical views are more in keeping with the assumptions characterizing ordinary discourse, and that it begs the question to adopt the idealist account of language because one wants to defeat the sceptic.[41] The important point is that the thesis that ordinary claims should be interpreted in terms of impressions is a *linguistic* thesis, and a secondary matter when idealism and scepticism are compared as philosophies. From a philosophical point of view, it is the idealist claim that we can know our impressions that is the major difference between sceptics and idealists. Even this difference does not, however, undermine their substantial similarities, for both philosophies reject full-fledged realist claims in favour of claims about impressions. Idealists and sceptics are in this sense philosophical cousins (not strangers) motivated by similar concerns.

40 Pyrrho and Timon may be exceptions to the rule (see chapter 4), though even they accept the meaningfulness of realist claims and do not attack them on linguistic grounds.

41. That this is the basis of Berkeley's views shows just how cavalier he is in his assumption that scepticism must be incorrect. As we shall subsequently see, there is no need to refute the sceptics and their views can simply be accepted. (Philosophers often confuse the ability to interpret claims in an idealist way with a proof that this is how they were intended in the first place. Suffice it to say that such proof would require an independent analysis of language and probably an empirical study of actual linguistic practice.)

CONTEMPORARY ANTI-REALISM

In part because of problems with idealism, contemporary anti-realists pose a more radical answer to sceptical arguments. Rather than grant phenomena and sense impressions a special epistemic status (one guaranteeing our ability to know certain realist truths), they completely reject the realist account of truth, proposing various alternatives that make truth attainable. According to their accounts, it makes no sense to talk of truth from a transcendental point of view and we must be satisfied with an account of truth that is relative to our particular language. Truth is attainable according to such analyses, but it is not the truth of the realist-sceptical debate.

This response to scepticism in contemporary philosophy is popular with influential philosophers such as Wittgenstein, Putnam, Winch, Black, Bouwsma, Bambrough, and Davidson.[42] We have already seen that it is misleading to portray their views as a direct attack on ancient scepticism, though they often write as though they have defeated it and vindicated truth. The problem is that the truth they vindicate is not the truth that serves as the butt of sceptics' attack. Indeed, they defend a truth relative to human nature, historical circumstance, and cultural perspective, and this is quite in keeping with beliefs propounded by the sceptics. An appeal to social conventions is, in particular, an integral part of ancient scepticism.[43] Philosophers who fail to recognize this gloss over the distinction between anti-realist concepts and the traditional Greek notion of truth. This gloss cannot eliminate the fundamental change in perspective it implies, however—a change that takes us from transcendental truth and a god's-eye point of view to more humble horizons dictated by social conventions and other subjective determinants of belief. A defense of this change in perspective is the heart of ancient scepticism, and it follows that contemporary anti-realists agree with, rather than defeat, the sceptics when they reject realism and adopt more subjective notions of belief. The only difference is the contemporary claim that words such as *truth* and *knowledge* can be applied to the kinds of beliefs anti-realists and sceptics both accept.[44] This makes it look as though contemporary thinkers

42. Davidson would not classify himself as an anti-realist, but this is because he uses the term differently than I do.

43. Most obviously in their appeal to moral norms, but more broadly in their acceptance of ordinary beliefs and day to day affairs.

44. As we shall see in chapter 3, Protagoras actually goes further, propounding an ancient (though in some ways more radical) analogue to the anti-realist account of truth.

save truth from sceptical attack, but they in fact have only changed their definitions to extend truth to claims endorsed by sceptics. In contrast, the sceptics accept the realist definition of truth, not calling their claims true (*alethes*), but accepting them as basis for action nonetheless.

Putting aside the fundamental similarities, the question whether scepticism or contemporary anti-realism is more plausible turns on the linguistic question whether realist conceptions of belief are ingrained in ordinary language. This is a question the present book cannot address in detail, though it is discussed in chapter 7, where I suggest that the anti-realist view of language is implausible and *ad hoc*, and that it has (like the idealist interpretation of ordinary claims) been influential because it provides an apparently easy answer to the sceptic. In view of this, scepticism provides an alternative to anti-realism that should be taken seriously in contemporary discussion.

HISTORIOGRAPHY AND THE SCEPTICS

It is difficult to reconcile the account of scepticism I propose and standard treatments of it. In critical commentary, the latter manifest an antipathy backed by no serious attempt to come to grips with the details of sceptical views. There is more of an attempt to understand the sceptics within historical scholarship, but even here their views have been misunderstood, their significance has not been appreciated, and they are treated as being of secondary interest. I cannot pursue the causes of this neglect in detail here, though it should be said that they are tied to allegiances to specific individuals, ideals, and doctrines that exclude the sceptics. The effects of such allegiances are exacerbated by a tendency to portray the history of philosophy as a series of great men (Plato, Aristotle, Augustine, Aquinas, Descartes, Berkeley, Hume, Kant, and so forth) who stand above their contemporaries. Specific individuals are unduly venerated, while the accomplishments of other thinkers, in particular their adversaries, are belittled.

Within Greek philosophy itself, the extent to which individual allegiances can distort the interpretation of particular philosophers is seen in the history of Plato's Academy, which offers a series of diametrically opposed interpretations of his views. The interpretations all justify a philosophical position (anti-scepticism, scepticism, and eclecticism) adopted by one or another head of the Academy. An allegiance to Plato forces each to hold that he defends Plato's own position, and Plato becomes a figurehead rather than a real philosopher. The attitude to alternative philosophies that such allegiances encourage is seen in Epicurus' follower Colotes, whose claim that "the doctrines of the other philosophers make it impossible to live" is not directed solely at the sceptics, but also at Democritus, Aristotle, Parmenides, Socrates, and virtually everyone but his mentor. As Plutarch suggests, it is Colotes' allegiance to Epicurus and his goal of undermining other views, not a responsible attempt to compare and understand the different schools, which is the source of Colotes' conclusions.

Many of the gaps, errors, and inaccuracies that characterize the contemporary view of the history of philosophy can be explained by similar commitments to specific individuals.[45] Not merely scepticism but all of Hellenistic thought has been neglected by historians and epistemologists, who tend to portray it as an afterthought to Plato and to Aristotle. Despite recent interest, the usual attitude is still the one reflected in Maccoll's book on the sceptics, which begins by noting that ancient thinking culminates in Plato and Aristotle, and that scepticism and the philosophies contemporaneous with it evolved in a time when "speculation in its highest sense ceased to be."[46] As Sedley retorts when he answers Cornford's charge that Hellenistic philosophy is "of greatly inferior value,"

The truth is that the leading Hellenistic philosophers lived neither in Aristotle's nor in anyone else's shadow. Certainly Socrates, Plato, and Aristotle, together with a whole range of other thinkers, were integral to the intellectual background from which the new generation emerged, and not infrequently their work was, consciously or unconsciously, taken into account. But in the vital first half-century of Hellenistic philosophy it was contemporary debates, issues and theories that set the keynote. The result was one of the most exciting and prolific periods of ancient thought, in which some of the fundamental problems of philosophy were put on the map for the first time. [47]

45 As Kerferd shows in the case of sophism, and Popkin and Schmitt show in the case of later scepticism, the evolution of philosophy is influenced by many trends and thinkers we ignore. To take an example from medieval thought, modern scepticism is anticipated by al-Ghazali and Nicholas of Autrecourt, who get almost no attention in mainstream philosophical or even historical debate (see Groarke, "Descartes' First Meditation: Something Old, Something New, Something Borrowed," and "On Nicholas of Autrecourt and the Law of Non-contradiction"). In particular, Burnyeat's suggestion that there is something new in Descartes' doubts about the body is erroneous in both cases. Nicholas explicitly suggests that one cannot know whether any proposition is true, or whether one has "a beard, a head, hair and so forth" ("Letters to Bernard," 659).

46 Maccoll, *The Greek Sceptics*, p. 2.

47 Sedley, "The Protagonists," pp. 1–2.

Specialists are increasingly aware of Sedley's point, though students of philosophy are still introduced to ancient thought with texts like Brumbaugh's *The Philosophies of Greece*—a book that (despite its many merits) sees fit to devote two pages to Greek philosophy after Aristotle. We could improve our view of ancient philosophy by adding the names of prominent sceptics (Pyrrho, Arcesilaus, Carneades, Aenesidemus, Sextus) to the standard list of great philosophers. This would invite a more objective view of the history of philosophy, though still place too much emphasis on specific individuals. Some of the sceptics are, of course, particularly influential or insightful, but scepticism is best understood as the product of a community of individuals within a paricular intellectual milieu, and not as a perspective invented by individuals (say, Pyrrho or Arcesilaus). Indeed, the differences between sceptics and competing schools of thought are fewer than we think and Greek scepticism can be most profitably viewed as a natural (one might say, inevitable) response to problems that are the focus of discussion in all of Greek epistemology. The history and development of scepticism must, therefore, be seen as a response to a set of historical circumstances that includes prevailing modes of thought, cultural and intellectual ideals, various intellectual traditions, and the influence of the sceptics' (sceptical and non-sceptical) contemporaries. Contributions to scepticism come from multifarious philosophers inside and outside the formal schools themselves; a whole tradition of philosophy, not specific individuals, produces the sceptical perspective.

The sceptics' indebtedness to philosophers such as Democritus, Metrodorus of Chios, Protagoras, Socrates, Monimus, and the Cyrenaics is (as we shall see in chapters 2 and 3) particularly important, for we already find in their philosophy a critique of realism, an adoption of more subjective notions of belief, and a moral outlook that culminates in later scepticism. Such trends are significant, both because an understanding of them is the best preparation for an understanding of the sceptics, and because other commentators have ignored the extent to which they anticipate modern epistemology (standard histories of philosophy overemphasize the ontological concerns of early Greek philosophers). Scepticism is in this sense a continuation of an earlier move toward an anti-realist conception of belief rather than a rejection of the philosophical currents of the day.

To stress this aspect of scepticism, we begin our look at its history with an account of the sceptics' ties to early Greek philosophy—to Parmenides, Heracleitus, Epicharmus, and other pre-Socratics, for they present the problems that ultimately give rise to scepticism. Their philosophy already contains the seeds of anti-realism, and their affinity with the sceptics is often underestimated. Many of the details of their views will be familiar to the specialist. They must be presented, however, for the benefit of nonspecialist readers, and because they set the stage for subsequent discussion.

II

Greek Epistemology before
the Rise of Scepticism

Traditionally, the founders of Greek scepticism are said to be Pyrrho and Arcesilaus, both of whom founded later schools of scepticism. Their views, however, reflect prevailing themes and currents rather than original inquiry. In the present chapter, we trace the questions that motivate their philosophies, emphasizing the relevance of pre-Socratic thought to ancient and modern epistemology.

It should be noted that many commentators look for the origins of scepticism in earlier claims that truth is difficult or impossible to know. Sedley, for example, argues that sceptical claims come first, and that reasons are then collected to support them.[1] In contrast, we shall see that one can better understand the sceptics by focusing, not merely on sceptical conclusions, but on the *problems* that give rise to them—problems often emphasized by thinkers who eschew the sceptical point of view. Thus the most important schools of scepticism spring from two antisceptical philosophies, Democritean atomism and Platonism.

Ultimately, scepticism is founded on the problem of "opposition" or "antithesis." It can be put as the question, How can we decide between opposing points of view? Within metaphysics, the ancient fascination with opposing forces manifests itself in attempts to reconcile various opposing notions, states and substances—Parmenides' being and not being, Pythagorean and Aristotelean contraries, and the Heraclitean world of opposites. Within epistemology, the same interest manifests itself in the problem of antithesis, in attempts to reconcile opposing points of view.

From our present perspective, it is difficult to appreciate the

1. Sedley, "The Motivation of Greek Scepticism," p. 10.

perplexity that characterizes Greek concern about antitheses, though we can better understand it if we remind ourselves that for the Greeks, rational inquiry is still in its infancy and unable to choose between opposing points of view; science does not boast practical and theoretical successes to force consensus; opposing philosophical perspectives proliferate; a burgeoning interest in other cultures illuminates conflicting customs and traditions; mysticism and irrationalism are influential forces opposed to common sense; society cultivates and rewards the ability to argue any claim; and a variety of social forces (war, political rivalry, and a religion that pits god against god, man against man, and even god against man) makes it possible to adopt opposing ways of looking at almost any situation.

Greek epistemology is founded on the fundamental questions that arise whenever one attempts to choose between competing claims or outlooks. Different answers to these questions ultimately distinguish philosophers such as Heracleitus, Protagoras, Plato, and the sceptics from each other, though there is an underlying unity to their emphasis on opposition. Heracleitus and Protagoras respond to it by concluding that opposing views are true; Plato concludes that we must transcend the ordinary world because it is besieged by opposition; and the sceptics conclude that it is impossible to know which claims are true. Their mutual concern with similar oppositions explains many of the anomalies characterizing the development of later Greek philosophy (Aenesidemus' renunciation of his scepticism in favour of a Heracleitean outlook, the Academy's endorsement of scepticism, and so on).

Within the present context, the important point is that Greek concern with opposition casts doubt on the notion that absolute (realist) truth can be established and forces philosophers to take seriously the possibility that our view of the world is defined by our interests, perceptions, social context, human nature, and a variety of other subjective factors. This, coupled with the conclusion that reason cannot choose between opposing points of view, eventually results in the different schools of ancient scepticism. Thus one finds in pre-Socratic emphasis on opposition an anticipation of the sceptics and the beginnings of the ancient debate over the possibility of realist truth.

XENOPHANES

The earliest explorations of antithesis are found in arguments propounded by Xenophanes. Pairs of opposition play a role in still earlier philosophy (in Pherecydes, Acusilaus, and Anaximander, and in the Pythagorean table of contraries), but Xenophanes seems to be the first to invoke the contrast between opposing points of view. In his critique of anthropomorphic conceptions of God, he writes: "Mortals believe the gods to be created by birth, and to have their own raiment, voice and body. But if oxen (and horses) and lions had hands or could draw and create works of art like those made by men, horses would draw pictures of gods like horses, and oxen of gods like oxen, and they would make the bodies (of their gods) in accordance with the form that each species itself possesses. Aethiopians have gods with snub noses and black hair, Thracians have gods with grey eyes and red hair (frags. 14–16)."[2] Such opposing conceptions of the gods are, according to Xenophanes, equally (in)valid and there is no reason for preferring one to another. Our view of the gods is, this suggests, not a perception of objective (realist) truth, but something defined by human nature and social customs (forms of life). According to Xenophanes, we can overcome these subjective influences. But his account of God need not concern us here. The important point is his use of opposition to illustrate the relative nature of most religious claims. The sceptics take his position further when they use the same oppositions to back the conclusion that it is impossible to choose between opposing views of God (*DND* 1.76–77, cf. 81–83).

One finds another example of antithesis in Xenophanes' suggestion that we "would say that figs were far sweeter if God had not created yellow honey" (frag. 38). Again, the moral is that belief is relative to subjective circumstances, and not indicative of transcendental truth. The Pyrrhoneans argue similarly when they suggest we judge an object's value by its "constancy or rarity of occurrence" in our lives,[3] and cannot, therefore, establish the true value of any object "in itself" (*PH* 1.141–44 and D.L. 9.87–88).

Given such antitheses, Xenophanes concludes that no one can know clear truth, and that conjecture (*dokos*) is wrought over all things (frag. 34). According to Sextus, he compares the search for truth to a search for gold in a dark room because one cannot know when one has found it (*AM* 7.52). He nonetheless suggests that mortals can learn to understand things better (frag. 18), proposing his own metaphysics as

2. References to fragments follow the order in Diels and Kranz (section B) or as indicated. If not stated otherwise, translations are from Freeman.

3. Gold is rare and valuable, water plentiful and of little value (though it is more important).

conjecture similar to reality (frags. 23–26). As both the academics and the Pyrrhoneans acknowledge, this commitment to a more subjective outlook anticipates later scepticism (see *PH* 1.224–25 and *Ac* 2.74, and note that Pyrrho's student, Timon, adopts Xenophanes as a protagonist in his *silloi*). However, it is not Xenophanes' conclusions but his way of establishing them (via antithesis) that is his most important contribution to the trends culminating in ancient scepticism.[4]

HERACLEITUS

Despite his antipathy to Xenophanes, Heracleitus is the next important pre-Socratic who shows an interest in antithesis. His claim that the world is full of change and opposition commits him not only to opposing states (war/peace, winter/summer, hunger/satiety), but also to opposing points of view that are enumerated in many of his aphorisms. "A road up and down is one and the same," he writes (frag. 60 Robinson), and can be seen either way. Within the circle beginning and end coincide (frag. 103), and when we write the path is both straight and crooked (frag. 59). "The fairest universe is but a dust-heap piled up at random" (frag. 124 Freeman). "We both step and do not step" into the same river (frag. 49a), for the water always changes.[5]

So many of Heracleitus' remarks refer to antithesis that it is impossible to consider them in detail here and we must restrict ourselves to remarks that anticipate the sceptics.[6] The claim that "[the sun's] breadth is that of a human foot" (frag. 3) is a case in point. Freeman interprets it literally, finding it "astonishing" that Heracleitus "seems to ignore the fact that . . . [distance] decreases apparent size."[7] This is not Heracleitus' point, however. On the contrary, he simply wishes to contrast the size of the sun judged from a perceptual and a rational point of view. Fragments 46, 54, 56, 107 and 123[8] have

4. Contrast Barnes, *The Presocratic Philosophers*, ch. 7 (cf. *PH* 1.224–25, 2.18–19 in this regard).

5. Cf. Wilbur and Allen, *The Worlds of the Greek Philosophers*, p. 67. The version of the dilemma found in fragment 12 can be similarly interpreted (cf. Robinson, *An Introduction to Early Greek Philosophy*, p. 91), as can Plato's claim (frag. A.6, *Crat* 402a) that Heracleitus says a man cannot step into the same river twice. Plato does not adopt this reading, but his account is vague, not in keeping with fragments 12 and 49a, and questioned by many commentators—among them, Robinson (ibid.); Kirk (*Heracleitus*, p. 366); and Kirk, Raven, and Schofield (*The Presocratic Philosophers*, pp 195–97).

6. But see fragments 58, 79, 96, and 99.

7. Freeman, *Companion to the Presocratic Philosophers*, p. 112.

8. The relevant portion of fragment 123 is rejected by Kirk.

convinced some that this comparison expresses doubts about the sense of sight, but this is contradicted by Heracleitus' remarks elsewhere.[9] More likely he holds that judgments of the sun's size are relative to reason and perception (from the point of view of perception, it is true that the sun is the breadth of a human foot). Whatever one decides, the distinction between reason and perception here implied becomes a fundamental theme in scepticism, for it establishes the subjective nature of perception.[10] The contrast between the real and apparent size of the sun is used by Cicero (and much later, by Ghazali) when he attacks the senses (*Ac* 2.82 and *De Fin* 1.20). Similar contrasts between the apparent size of objects viewed from different distances are a common theme throughout sceptical discussion and are formalized in the fifth of the Pyrrhoneans' ten modes (*PH* 1.118–23, D.L. 9.85–86, and Philo 181–83).

Heracleitus' affinity with scepticism is also seen in his comparison of subjective states—sleeping and waking (frags. 21, 26, 75, 88, 89), drunkenness and sobriety (frag. 117)—that offer different perceptions of reality. Especially within the context of a culture that accepts dreams, visions, and frenzies as a potential source of highest truth, abnormal states cannot be easily rejected, and the contrast between them and ordinary perception becomes a standard way of eliciting antithesis. In the process, philosophers demonstrate that human beliefs are relative to one's perceptual states.

More general determinants of belief are invoked when Heracleitus contrasts the views of different species, building on themes already found in Xenophanes. As he puts it, human beings prefer fresh water to mud and gold to chaff, but pigs prefer mud to clear water (frag. 136) and donkeys prefer chaff to gold (frag. 9). "Sea water is very pure and very foul—for fish drinkable and life-sustaining, for people undrinkable and lethal" (frag. 61). Though Heracleitus still holds that the human view of things is superior (frags. 82, 83), the examples he cites become the basis of the opposite conclusion in many later sceptical arguments (*PH* 1.40–79, D.L. 9.79–80, and Philo 171–75).

9. Fragment 55: "Whatsoever things are objects of sight, hearing, and experience—these things I hold in high esteem." Contrary to Guthrie's suggestion (*A History of Greek Philosophy*, 1: 432), sight need not be discarded to appreciate the Heracleitean one. Sight confirms it (by, for example, showing that the way up and the way down are one and the same).

10. See, for example, Carneades' arguments against the criterion (*AM* 7. 159–64), Sextus' claim that sense impressions separate us from reality (*PH* 2.72–75), and the discussion in subsequent chapters.

Heracleitus departs from sceptical ways when he formulates his philosophical response to opposition. For though he adopts a cautious attitude toward knowledge, his warnings that "nature likes to hide" (frag. 123 Freeman) and that "the eyes and ears are bad witnesses for men who have barbarian souls" (frag. 107 Freeman) imply that truth is difficult, not unattainable.[11] It can still be discovered in a philosophical stance that leaves room for opposing outlooks. In contrast, the sceptics respond to antithesis by suspending judgment on the truth of any claim. As different as these two conclusions are, they are founded on a mutual commitment to the equality of opposing points of view.

In later Greek philosophy, Heracleitus' affinity with scepticism manifests itself in Aenesidemus, whom Brochard calls "with Pyhrro, the most illustrious representative of the sceptics in antiquity."[12] Though he is a key figure in ancient scepticism (the reviver of Pyrrhonism and the first to formalize its arguments), he subsequently defects and becomes a Heracleitean (see *De An* 9.5, 14.5 and *AM* 7.349, 9.336–67, 10.216). According to Sextus, he and his followers see scepticism as "a road (*hodos*) leading to Heraclitean philosophy, since to hold that the same thing is the subject of opposite things which appear to be the case is a preliminary to holding that it is the subject of opposite realities" (*PH* 1.210). As Sextus replies, the two philosophies are not at all compatible, though this does not mean that we should question Aenesidemus' defection.[13] On the contrary, that move is a natural one given the centrality of antithesis in scepticism and its importance in Heraclitean views. As Brochard describes the likely transition, "meditating on the opposition and the equivalence of contraries in human thought, was he [Aenesidemus] not likely to ask from where this opposition and this equivalence comes? The human mind, especially the mind of such a man, is not content for long, it wants an explanation. After it has doubted all, it wants to know why it doubts. The Heraclitean system offers it an answer it adopts. The contraries are equal in the mind, because they are equal in reality."[14] Aenesidemus' defection from scepticism (or perhaps, as Bury sug-

11. Fragment 78 ("Human nature does not have right understanding, divine nature does") may seem to indicate a more radical scepticism, but Heracleitus believes that we can grasp the divine (cf. frag. 86).

12. Brochard, *Les Sceptiques Grecs*, p. 241. Translations of Brochard are my own.

13. As does Zeller, *Stoic, Epicureans and Sceptics*, p. 278, and *Socrates and the Socratic Schools*, p. 302.

14. Brochard, *Les Sceptiques Grecs*, p. 285.

gests, the defection of his followers) is thus an understandable continuation of his philosophical development.

One finds another early anticipation of the sceptics in Alcmaeon, who claims that the gods have certainty, but that humans must employ evidence for conjecture.[15] The development of antithesis is not, however, prominent in the fragments of his philosophy,[16] and Barnes makes too much of his sceptical inclinations. A more important and more neglected precursor of the sceptics is Epicharmus, who contrasts the differences in species and ridicules pride, suggesting that our beliefs are relative to human nature and thus not credible as absolute truth.[17] "It is not at all remarkable that we should speak thus of these things and should afford pleasure to ourselves and think ourselves well endowed by nature. For dog too seems very handsome to dog, and ox to ox, and donkey very handsome to donkey, and even pig to pig" (frag. 5). "What then is the nature of men? Blown up bladders!" (frag. 10). Such remarks capture well the spirit of later scepticism, which is championed as an attack on dogmatists who think too highly of their ability to establish transcendental truth. As Timon puts it, alluding to Epicharmus, "Men are but bags with vain opinions filled" (Aris. in Eus. 763c).[18]

Epicharmus also casts doubt on ordinary views and elicits antithesis in his epigram, "I am a corpse. A corpse is dung, and dung is earth. If Earth is a god, then I am not a corpse but a god" (frag. 64). Carneades, the most important academic sceptic, constructs a whole series of conclusions along these lines, arguing against standard conceptions of God by showing that they entail the conclusion that every stream, river, day, month, thought, mountain, stone, and cliff must be a god (*AM* 9.182–90). The content of Epicharmus' argument is not, however, as

15. Fragment 1, but see 1a, where he says that men have understanding.
16. Though he does have an account of physical opposites and fragment 2 might be construed as antithesis.
17. According to Freeman, Epicharmus here *parodies* Xenophanes, but this does not sit well with the tone of fragments 5 and 10, nor with his other uses of antithesis. The question is complicated given fragment 15, but it is a different matter and even it could (despite Aristotle) be interpreted differently.
18. One can find similar sentiments in Renaissance painting, where the ephemeral nature of life is often depicted in the form of children blowing up the bladder of a butchered pig.

important as the form it takes; for it is a clear precursor of the sceptical suggestion that one can deduce an antithesis from any claim by taking it through successive inferences.

This method of eliciting antithesis is also seen in Epicharmus' parodies on Heraclitean views (frag. 2), founded on the notion that everything is changing. According to Plutarch, these parodies are the basis of many of the sophists' arguments against the flux—arguments that take it to imply that the guest who comes to dinner is not the guest invited, and that the one who owes money is not the one who borrowed it. According to a famous story, Epicharmus wrote a play in which a Heraclitean is beaten by a lender because he refuses to repay a loan, claiming he has changed and is no longer the man who borrowed it. When he is charged with assault, the lender turns the tables, arguing that he is not the guilty party, for everything is in flux and he is not the man who committed the assault. Such scenarios (besides providing comedy, for which Epicharmus is justly famous) set up an antithesis between common sense, which suggests that we remain the same person, and Heraclitean doctrine, which tells us that we change. It is easy to see why such oppositions are subsequently used in reductio ad absurdum arguments, for the simplest way to eliminate this contradiction is by rejecting Heraclitean views. This is not a satisfactory answer to the problem from the point of view of scepticism, however, for sceptical philosophy subsequently argues that every view (including alternatives to Heraclitean doctrine) can be equally opposed.

PARMENIDES

According to Burnyeat, scepticism begins with Parmenides.[19] Given the trends we have already noted, this is a misconception, though we shall see that it contains a grain of truth. It is even possible that Parmenides is a student of Xenophanes, for this is claimed by some ancient commentators and Parmenides employs antithetical modes of argument to establish similar conclusions (that reality is one, uniform, and motionless).[20]

19. Burnyeat, "Protagoras and Self-Refutation in Later Greek Philosophy," p. 60.
20. See *Met* A5, 986b18, *Phys* 22–24, D.L. 9.21–23, and *Soph* 242d. At the very least, Parmenides' ties cannot be rejected on the grounds that there are important differences in their outlooks—as they are by Tarán (ibid., 3) and Kirk, Raven, and Schofield (*The Presocratic Philosophers*, 165, but see pp. 240–41, where they write that "certainly there are echoes, not merely verbal, of Xenophanes' theology and epistemology in Parme-

At first glance, Parmenides seems irrelevant to the development of antithesis that culminates in scepticism, for contrasts between different outlooks are not particularly prominent in his philosophy. He does suggest that the mind is relative to the constitution of the body; the latter, he writes, is a consequence of the "union of the much wandering limbs" (frag. 16 Gallop).[21] But his most important contribution to scepticism is found elsewhere, in his conviction that reason is too weak to deal with opposition.

In some ways, Parmenides' main argument is reminiscent of the epigram of Epicharmus we have already mentioned, for both begin with initial statements that take us through a series of inferences ultimately leading to an opposing point of view. In Parmenides' case, the initial statement is the assumption that we can investigate, think, and talk about what is not; it leads to the paradoxical conclusion that what is not, is. Parmenides aligns himself with the negative side of scepticism when he goes on to the reject backward-turning path (the *palintropos keleuthos*) of ordinary reasoning, which assumes what is and what is not (hence being and not being). It is along this path of inquiry that

mortals knowing nothing
Wander, two-headed; for helplessness in their
Breasts guides their distracted mind; and they are carried
Deaf and blind alike, dazed, uncritical tribes,
By whom being and not-being have been thought both the same
[for both are]
And not the same [for not being is not]; and the path of all
is backward-turning (frag. 6.4–9).

Here Parmenides argues that our commitment to what is and what is not pulls us in two directions, making us "two-headed." Humans are, therefore, "dazed, uncritical tribes" who wander about in ignorance of

---

nides. And Parmenides' decision to write his philosophy in hexameter verse may well have been prompted partly by the example of Xenophanes, who spent the latter part of his long career in Sicily and South Italy"). One might just as well conclude that Zeno was not Parmenides' pupil, or that Wittgenstein did not study under Russell.

21. According to Aristotle and Theophrastus, he goes on to say that it is "the substance of the limbs" that thinks, though some contemporary commentators disagree (see, e.g., Gallop). It seems to me implausible to suppose that Aristotle and Theophrastus are so far off the mark, especially as alternative interpretations make it difficult to understand the connection between the first and the last two lines within the fragment.

the ultimate nature of reality,[22] and ordinary claims turn back on themselves, entailing (as the sceptics suggest) opposing points of view.

Parmenides' affinity with scepticism is limited by his commitment to a metaphysics encompassing being and the One (a metaphysics the sceptics emphatically reject), though it is unlikely that he believes his claims in this respect to be immune to opposition. On the contrary, his arguments undermine all claims, including those about being and the One, for they depend on distinctions he denies (distinctions between what is and what is not, between coming to be and perishing, between different colours and locations, between past, present, and future).[23] Taken to its logical conclusion, his commitment to a reality that is changeless, indivisible, and uniform undermines the very notion that he speaks or thinks (much less utters truths), denying as it does speakers and thinkers as discrete individuals.[24] Parmenides himself recognizes this when he rejects the distinctions made by mortals (frags. 8.21–30, 38–41, 44–49 and *passim*).[25]

The universal nature of Paramenides' commitment to antithesis is also seen in Plato's *Parmenides*, which depicts the earlier philosopher illustrating a method of dialectic that leads repeatedly to opposing points of view (cf. *Par* 136a–c). Taking as an example his own conclusion that the One exists, Paramenides contrasts at times not just two but three or four conclusions, ending with the claim that "whether the One is or is not, the One and the others in relation to themselves and to each other all in every way are and are not and appear and do not appear" (166c Fowler). Many commentators find it puzzling that Parmenides would deduce contradictions from his own philosophy, but this is because they interpret them as a refutation of his views.

22. Tarán (*Parmenides*, pp. 69–72) and Bernays (see Tarán) have portrayed the passage as an attack on Heracleitus. The criticisms it contains pertain, however, to mankind in general (which clearly rejects Parmenides' outlook), and a more specific target is not in keeping with general talk of "mortals" and "dazed, uncritical tribes." For what seem to be decisive defenses of the interpretation I have adopted, see Gallop ("Introduction," p. 11), Mourelatos (*The Route of Parmenides*, p. 78), Stokes (*One and Many in Presocratic Philosophy*, pp. 193–94), and Kirk, Raven, and Schofield (*The Presocratic Philosophers*, pp. 247–48).

23. The latter is a matter of dispute, but see Groarke, "Parmenides' Timeless Universe," and "Parmenides' Timeless Universe, Again."

24. Cf. Gallop, "Introduction," p. 28.

25. I cannot defend it here, but I believe the correct conclusion is that Parmenides sees his commitment to being and the one as a commitment that transcends language, and thus all claims. Such a view resolves any contradictions in his thought (cf. fn. 26 below) and makes his philosophy more in line with the suggestion (by West, Bambrough, and Verdenius) that he adopts a mystical perspective.

Parmenides probably sees them as yet another indication of the weak and fickle nature of ordinary reasoning.[26] Indeed, his philosophy is vindicated by such deductions, for a true grasp of being and the One must transcend human reason (it is no accident that he puts his philosophy into the mouth of a goddess). By demonstrating reason's weakness, conclusions that "contradict one another about the same things in relation to the same things, and in the same respect" can, as the Eleatic stranger says in the *Sophist*, prepare the ground for knowledge (230b Cornford).[27]

Given his ultimate rejection of reason and ordinary views, Parmenides anticipates the positive side of scepticism when he proposes a qualified endorsement of opinion (*doxa*). Declaring it unreliable and "deceitful" (frag. 1, 8), he nonetheless offers a detailed cosmology as the best that can be hoped for. Like Xenophanes' metaphysics, this qualified acceptance of conjecture in lieu of objective truth anticipates mitigated scepticism, though the sceptics propose the latter as a basis for practical affairs rather than metaphysical speculation.

ZENO

Antithesis is also important in the arguments of Parmenides' philosophical heir, Zeno of Elea. His attack on plurality argues that it entails things both "finite and infinite" (frag. 11), "large and small" (frag. 9), "like and unlike" (frag. 12).[28] Variants of the specific arguments he uses to attack the many are employed by sceptics (see, for example, D.L. 9.72 and *PH* 3.65–80), though his influence is much broader. It is the notion that *any* claim can be argued and refuted that is his legacy to later thinkers.[29]

26. There is a great deal of tension in the usual interpretation of Parmenides that reveres his commitment to reasoning (*logoi*) in fragment 7.5. According to Cornford, he is "the prophet of a logic which will tolerate no semblance of contradiction" (*Plato and Parmenides*, p. 92). Against this, West (*Early Greek Philosophy and the Orient*, pp. 221–22) is right to complain, for such a title hardly sits with views that are obviously contradictory.

27. This interpretation of Parmenides' views eliminates many of the difficulties raised by Plato's *Parmenides*. The emphasis on the One rather than being might (*à la* Tarán) still be criticized, though criticism along these lines seems misguided: Parmenides' views suggest the two cannot be separated. The strength of the impression Parmenides makes on Plato (see *Par, Theat* especially 183e–4 and *Soph*) suggests familiarity with his views.

28. I have used the numbering and translation in Lee.

29. Those commentators who argue that Zeno does not confine his dialectic to a critique of plurality (see Freeman, *Companion*, p. 157; Cornford, *Plato and Parmenides*, pp. 67–68; Von Fritz, *Real Encyclopadie*; and most importantly, Solmsen, "The Tradition about Zeno") seem to me substantially correct, though it is the prevailing view of Zeno in later Greek philosophy, not his actual philosophy, that is most important in the present context.

It is often said that Zeno's commitment to the Parmenidean One is incompatible with a commitment to universal opposition, but we have already seen that Parmenides himself apparently endorses both positions. According to Eudemus, Zeno claimed he could speak about existing things if someone could explain to him the One (frag. 5, cf. DK A21). As Simplicius suggests, this seems to mean that the One needs an explanation, and that Zeno does away with the many *and* the One.[30] Whatever one decides in this regard, Zeno's attack on units is based on a principle (that anything that has extension is divisible), which implies that the One has no magnitude (and does not exist) or is divisible and does not exist (because it encompasses plurality). It is hard to understand how Zeno could fail to see this, especially as he uses the principle in many other arguments.[31] The specific steps he takes to establish that the many must have both zero and infinite magnitude (frags. 1, 2) are, in particular, easily applicable to the One. As Kirk, Raven, and Schofield remark, "It is hard to resist the conclusion that . . . [this] does indeed undermine Parmenides' *Truth*, and that Zeno was perfectly well aware of this. Perhaps he enjoyed the thought that common sense and Parmenidean metaphysics can be embarrassed by precisely the same dialectical manoeuveres."[32] The important point is

30. Though Alexander takes it to mean that he attacked the many by attacking the units (ones) it is composed of. It is, however, unlikely that Zeno would have failed to see that the One could be rejected on precisely the same grounds, and the distinction between units and the One (see, e.g., Lee, *Zeno of Elea*, p. 26) seems foreign to ancient ways of thinking (see Solmsen, "The Tradition about Zeno," pp. 138–39).

31. Consider, for example, the paradoxes of motion. Here the use of the principle is obvious in the case of the dichotomy and the Achilles, though it can also be found in the arrow and the stadium. These paradoxes are usually interpreted as an attack on spatial and temporal indivisibles, but this does not show that Zeno denies that extension implies indivisibility, for the points in question have zero magnitude (cf. Furley, *Two Studies in the Greek Atomists*, pp. 71–75, and Kirk, Raven, and Schofield, *The Presocratic Philosophers*, p. 265). For example, the points of the arrow's flight must have zero spatial extension, for these are the only points in which the arrow occupies "a space equal to itself," and zero temporal extension, for time is analogous to space and the flight of the arrow is continuous. Such an interpretation seems to be confirmed by Zeno's arguments for the claim that points have no magnitude.

Something similar might be said of the stadium, though it is difficult to accept the standard suggestion that it is an attack on indivisibles. Rather, there seems no good reason to reject Aristotle's account. To suggest, as Lee does, that it makes Zeno's arguments "puerile" is to fail to appreciate the context in which the argument is offered (in which modern notions of relativity are still being formulated). On Lee's account, we would have to reject as puerile Plato's worries about relative judgments, which provide one of the fundamental reasons for accepting a world of forms.

32. Kirk, Raven, and Schofield, *The Presocratic Philosophers*, p. 269.

that Zeno never does deny the contradictory nature of the One, and that his arguments against the many show that it is *also* contradictory, opposing any metaphysics. Zeno's use of antithesis extends as well to his arguments about place, the paradoxes of motion, and the millet seed, and to one of the arguments reported by Philoponus. None of these arguments is presented as an attack upon the One.[33]

Later ancient thinkers therefore associate Zeno with antithesis in an unqualified way. Plato, for example, asks how "we can fail to see that the Palamedes of Elea [Zeno] has an art of speaking, such that he can make the same things appear to his audience like and unlike, or one and many, or again at rest and in motion" (*Phaed* 261d 6–8 Hackforth). In a similar vein, the Pyrrhonean Timon writes of "great Zeno's strength which, never known to fail; on each side urged, on each side could prevail" (D.L. 9.25). Plutarch mentions the latter comment in his *Life of Pericles*, where he says that Zeno perfected the ability to bring his opponents to a state of ignorance (*aporia*) through the use of opposing arguments (IV.3). The commitment to antithesis this implies probably accounts for Aristotle's claim that Zeno discovered dialectic (D.L. 8.57); for the suggestion that he is a sophist in the *Alcibiades* (1.119A–B);[34] and for Isocrates' remarks in the beginning of *Helen*, where Zeno is grouped with the sophists, Gorgias and Protagoras.[35] Galen goes further, classing Zeno as a sceptic along with Anaxarchus and Pyrrho (DK A.15), suggesting that he rejects all claims to truth.

EMPEDOCLES

An exact chronology of pre-Socratic thinkers after Zeno is difficult (perhaps impossible) to determine. It is enough for us to note that these thinkers contribute to the rise of scepticism. Empedocles is an

33. The arguments against motion can be *construed* as attacks on plurality, but this is not how they are presented, and it is impossible to interpret them in this way without begging the question of whether Zeno was committed to the one.

Lee's treatment of the fragment from Philoponus betrays his unwillingness to question the view that Zeno restricts his attack to plurality. One of the reasons he gives for rejecting it as genuine is that "*all* other arguments attributed to Zeno contain an infinite regress . . . " (my emphasis), though he himself footnotes two exceptions. Another is the character of the argument, which is, he says, more in keeping with later fifth-century arguments. We could more aptly conclude that Zeno is the forerunner of the sophists (cf. Kerferd, *The Sophistic Movement*).

34. For a criticism of this claim, see Vlastos, "Plato's Testimony."

35. He suggests that Zeno and the others deny the possibility of falsity or contradiction, referring to popular sophistic arguments to this effect. For a discussion of the matter, see Kerferd, *The Sophistic Movement*, pp. 91–92.

important case in point. Attempting to answer the Parmenidean attack on perishing and becoming, he explains them as a change in the configuration of basic ingredients of the world (ingredients that do not themselves become or perish). According to his account, these ingredients are the forces of attraction (love) and repulsion (hate), and the four "roots": fire, water, earth, and air.

Empedocles recognizes the subjective nature of perception when he suggests that "we apprehend earth by participation in earth and water by partaking in water, and air by participation in air, and similarly in the case of fire" (*AM* 7.121 Bury, cf. 115–16; *Phys* 160, 26; *Met* B4, 1000B6; and *De Sens* 9). For though Empedocles thinks that our perceptions correspond to an objective world, this makes thought dependent on our physical constitution (cf. frags. A86, 105, 106, 108, 109 and *Met* G5, 1009b, 10–25). The divine is therefore beyond our reach, for it transcends the physical (frag. 134, cf. *AM* 7.122).

Empedocles explains the operation of the senses by saying that they are passages that capture effluences from existing things. In the *Meno* Socrates asks: "Do you agree with Empedocles that existing things give off certain effluences? . . . And that they have passages into which and through which the effluences travel? . . . as Pindar puts it: colour is an effluence of shapes which is commensurate with sight and perceptible . . . [And this] will also put you in a position to say also what voice is, and smell, and many other such things" (76c–e Kirk et al.). According to this account, the impression "that comes through sense-perception is necessarily true" (*Met* G5, 1009b, 15–20), being an effluence that originates in existing things. This does not, however, mean that we can transcend subjective determinants of belief, for the shape and size of the sense passages restrict the effluences we receive. Only those effluences that fit the passages of sense can be received, and thus they afford only a partial vision of reality.

Empedocles' attitude to the limits and abilities of the senses is seen in his answer to traditional questions that arise because the different senses stand in opposition to each other. As Sextus puts the problem, "to the eye paintings seem to have recesses and projections, but not so to the touch. Honey, too, seems to some pleasant to the tongue but unpleasant to the eyes; so that it is impossible to say whether it is absolutely pleasant or unpleasant . . . " (*PH* 1.92). In attempting to resolve such differences, Empedocles adopts "the same theory about all the senses, maintaining that perception arises when something fits into the passages of any of the senses. This is why one sense cannot judge the objects of another, since the passages of some are too wide, of others too narrow for the object perceived, so that some things pass straight through without making contact while others cannot enter at all" (*De Sens* 7 Kirk et al.). From this point of view, the senses are not contradictory or in opposition, and only seem so because they reflect different (and partial) aspects of the world that are expressed by specific kinds of effluences. To understand the world in a comprehensive way we must accept all the senses, and all the different aspects of the world that they reveal. Empedocles writes, "Come, now, observe with all your powers how each thing is clear, neither holding sight in greater trust compared with hearing, nor noisy hearing above the passages of the tongue, nor withhold trust from any of the other limbs, by whatever way there is a channel to understanding, but grasp each thing in the way it is clear" (*AM* 7.125 Kirk et al.). Whether such a move satisfactorily resolves the kinds of oppositions that characterize the different senses is debatable, but here we need only note the implication that each sense gives us a limited picture of the world.

Empedocles himself does not use such considerations as a basis for rejecting realist truth, but it is easy to see that they make our view of the world relative to the size and shape of our sense passages. He himself emphasizes the limited nature of subjective experience:

> Short is the span of unlivable life beholden by mortals
> Swift is their doom, as whirl'd like smoke, they are
>   lifted and vanish,
> Each persuaded only of what himself has encounter'd,
> Carried about all ways; yet each keeps foolishly boasting
> How he has found the Whole. (*AM* 7.123)

ANAXAGORAS

Like Empedocles, Anaxagoras holds that the world is composed of basic ingredients of being. These "seeds" are, however, too small to be perceived, so Anaxagoras opposes the senses, claiming that their infirmity does not allow us to judge what is true, demonstrating this infirmity by noting our inability to perceive the gradual change in colour when we add black to white one drop at a time (*AM* 7.90).[36]

Despite the claims of Kirk, Raven, and Schofield,[37] Axaxagoras'

36. The appeal to gradual change is in some ways reminiscent of Zeno's argument of the millet seed. Both anticipate the use of the *sorites* argument by the sceptics.

37. Kirk, Raven, and Schofield, *The Presocratic Philosophers*, p. 384.

scepticism about the senses is also seen in other extant fragments, for they emphasize the relative nature of perception and the subjective nature of belief.[38] Thus: "Anaxagoras thinks that perception is by opposites, for like is not affected by like ... A thing that is as warm or as cold as we are does not either warm us or cool us by its approach, nor can we recognize sweetness or bitterness by their like; rather we know cold by warm, fresh by salt and sweet by bitter in proportion to our deficiency in each" (*De Sens* 27ff Kirk et al.). The significance of this passage can hardly be exaggerated, for it makes perceptual knowledge relative to subjective states, claiming that the perception of warmth, sweetness, or freshness is not a direct indication of the way things are in themselves, but equally an indication of our subjective states. "Sense appearances," Anaxagoras comments, "are the subjective vision of those external objects which lie beyond perception" (*AM* 7.140).[39]

Judging by Aristotle's claim that he told his disciples things "would be for them as they judged them to be" (*Met* G5, 1009b, 25–30), Anaxagoras interprets belief as referring to the ways our subjective states are affected by reality. So understood, we do seem to know the way things are given that we know our subjective states. Adopting this reading, Anaxagoras' epistemology is a remarkable anticipation of modern anti-realism, for it insulates ordinary belief from philosophical doubt by understanding it as referring to the ways we are affected by the world rather than the external world itself. Anaxagoras stops short of complete idealism only because he believes that reason can transcend the subjective limitations of the senses and establish some objective truth (*AM* 7.91–92). As we shall subsequently see, one finds similar moves in Democritean thought.

---

38. One might note in this regard Anaxagoras' sophism, "Snow is frozen water, and water is black; therefore snow is black" (*PH* 1.33), though one must wonder whether it could be seriously intended as an attack on the senses.

39. That the word *phainomena* here refers to sense impressions is made clear by the context and by the explicit reference to a specific sense (sight). On Diotimus' account of Democritus' views (which Sextus is discussing), see the discussion in the next chapter.

Bury translates the last phrase in the quote (*ton adelon*) as "nonevident objects," though we shall see that these objects correspond in the realm of sense perception to what we call external objects. For the moment, we may note that nonevident objects are defined as things perceived through other things (*PH* 2.98) and that this means, in the context of sense impression, those things existing beyond it. (On the nature of the nonevident, see our subsequent discussion.)

SUMMARY

It is against the background of pre-Socratic thought that we can better understand the views of the sceptics' immediate precursors. Even before these precursors turn their attention to the problem of opposition, it is an integral part of Greek epistemology that raises questions about the relative nature of belief and casts doubt on the human ability to establish realist truth. In presenting specific oppositions to illustrate the subjective nature of belief, critiquing reason's ability to choose between contrasting views, and developing ingenious arguments for a variety of unintuitive conclusions, philosophers such as Xenophanes, Heracleitus, Parmenides, and Anaxagoras help prepare the ground for the discussion that gives birth to scepticism.

This being said, it should be noted that the sceptics are influenced by a variety of trends in pre-Socratic thought we have not considered. Sextus exhibits their familiarity with the philosophers Thales, Pythagoras, Anaximenes, and Anaximander, for example, in his catalogue of the different schools of thought (Sextus' own work has been valued primarily for the light it sheds on other schools). The diversity of these and other philosophical opinions invites scepticism; they stand in opposition to each other and it is difficult to choose between them. The development of early Greek philosophy is in this sense a process of antithesis that the sceptics recognize when appealing to the opposing views of various "dogmatist" philosophers. Here as elsewhere, the sceptics are an integral part of their own intellectual milieu, invoking standard conflicts inherited from earlier philosophers.

From the point of view of modern epistemology, the oppositions found in the pre-Socratics are of secondary interest. It is arguable that we still have to come to terms with paradoxes such as Zeno's, but the significance of Greek discussion does not depend on claims to this effect. For though the specific oppositions that are discussed by pre-Socratic thinkers may no longer seem so pressing, they do suggest that belief is relative to our subjective outlook and raise the possibility that reason is not able to determine what is true from a god's-eye point of view. The significance of such questions is found in the fruit they bear in subsequent discussion of our ability to establish realist truth. Ironically, it is in part because this discussion is motivated by disagreements we no longer find compelling that the problem of opposing views becomes so prevasive and is the focus of such intense debate. Without such an apparently overwhelming problem, philosophers might not have delved so deeply into investigations of the foundations of belief.[40]

40. In contrast, Aristotle's treatment of the problem of scepticism is surprisingly unsophisticated and unsatisfactory, in part because his commonsense way around many of the traditional oppositions makes it less important that he resolve the sceptical problems they imply. Like modern philosophers, he overlooks the fact that these oppositions are founded on more basic problems which are not so easily eluded.

III

The Rise of Scepticism

Historically, scepticism is the culmination of three trends in the views of the sceptics' immediate forerunners. The first is a critique of realism. The second is the adoption of more subjective (anti-realist) notions of belief. The third is a commitment to the moral and psychological goal of equanimity. We have already discussed the first two trends in pre-Socratic thought. To see how they continue to evolve, to see how opposition becomes a vehicle for establishing equanimity, and to set the stage for scepticism, we need to turn to those philosophers who play important roles in the birth of scepticism.

THE SOPHISTS

While it is a mistake to write about the sophists as though they form a unified school of thought, it is important to note their collective contribution to the rise of scepticism. Leaving a detailed account of Protagoras' views for later, we may begin our account of the sceptics' immediate predecessors by noting that sophistic views and arguments create an atmosphere that invites antithesis and thus prepares the way for scepticism.

The kind of argument that characterizes the sophists is seen in the *Dissoi Logoi* (*Twofold Arguments*), an anonymous treatise found attached to the works of Sextus Empiricus. Rather than defend a definite point of view, it deals with a variety of topics by recounting standard arguments ("put forward in Greece by those who philosophize") for and against a series of opposing points of view, suggesting that they are equally convincing. Though some commentators have claimed the author to be a follower of Protagoras, the arguments usually associated

with his school do not receive special attention and there are signs of
other influences (section IX praises mnemonic theory, and section IV is
not in keeping with Protagoras' account of truth). For our purposes, it
is enough to note that the *Dissoi Logoi* is an elaborate presentation of
antithesis.

Those sections of the *Dissoi Logoi* that deal with value judgments are
especially instructive. Its first section begins with a defense of the thesis
that the good and the bad are one and the same, citing a long list of
oppositions that demonstrate the relativity of value judgments. "Death
is," for example, "bad for those who die but good for undertakers and
grave diggers," while "the battle between the Centaurs and the Lapiths
was good for the Lapiths, but bad for the Centaurs" (3, 10 Sprague).
Listing many such examples, the author turns to the opposite
hypothesis—that the good and the bad are not the same—defending it
by arguing that its denial leads to unacceptable antitheses. If you have
done your enemies wrong, it will follow that you have done them good,
while if it is bad to be sick, it will be good to be sick, and so on. Specific
oppositions are thus used to support both sides of the major opposition
—that good and bad are and are not the same. The repeated moves
from major to minor opposition are reminiscent of the *Parmenides*.

In a later section of the *Dissoi Logoi*, the author discusses value in
terms of the "seemly and disgraceful," defending the claim that they
are one and the same with a long list of oppositions. It is, for example,
seemly for women to wash themselves indoors, but disgraceful for
them to do so in the palaestra. For men, it is seemly to do both. Other
examples illustrate the relative nature of the seemly and disgraceful by
referring to "the things which cities and peoples regard as disgraceful."
The Macedonians consider premarital intercourse seemly for young
girls; the Greeks think it disgraceful. Tattoos are a comely ornament
for the Thracians; the Greeks use them as punishment.

The Scythians think it seemly that who(ever) kills a man should scalp him and
wear the scalp on his horse's bridle, and having gilded the skull or lined it with
silver, should drink from it and make a libation to the gods. Among the Greeks,
no one would be willing to enter the same house as a man who behaved like
that. The Massagetes cut up their parents and eat them, and they think that to
be buried in their children is the most beautiful grave imaginable, but in
Greece, if anyone did such a thing, he would be driven out of the country and
die an ignominious death for having committed such disgraceful and terrible
deeds. (13–14, cf. Bates)

Continuing this list at length, the author concludes that "if someone should order all men to make a single heap of everything each of them regards as disgraceful and then again, to take from the collection what each of them regards as seemly, not a thing would be left, but they would all divide up everything, because not all men are of the same opinion" (18). Opposing views thus cancel one another, undermining any possible consensus. Using the same kind of comparison, and some of the specific examples cited, the sceptics subsequently argue that there is no way to establish moral and religious principles (see D.L. 9.83; *PH* 1.145–63, 3.218–34; Philo 193–202; *De Rep* 3.4.8–32;[1] and *DND* 1.63, 81–88).

In other contexts, sophistic anticipation of the sceptics is evident in antitheses employed by Euthydemus, Antiphon, Critias, and others. Gorgias develops a rhetorical method that progresses through opposing views and argues, in apparent opposition to Parmenides, that nothing exists, that if it did exist we could not know so, and that if we did know its existence we could not communicate it (frag. 3, *AM* 7.65–87). It is difficult to tell whether his conclusions are intended seriously or for rhetorical display, but this is a secondary matter. Either way, they can be used in opposing any claim, and the sceptics frequently employ them in this way (see *PH* 2.50–60). In the *Outlines of Pyrrhonism*, Sextus thus preserves our most important fragment of Gorgias' reasoning.

More generally, the sophists' ingenuity in argument and their commitment to rhetorical dispute helps popularize the notion that one can argue for any claim. Sophistic *eristic* and sceptical modes of argument therefore have a great deal in common, though there are differences as well. In particular, the former aims for victory in argument, the latter for a state of indecision and a renunciation of desire.[2] Perhaps because of this, the sophists place more emphasis on equivocation and merely verbal contradiction, though they are also seen in scepticism and the sceptics are quite capable of rhetorical

1. Much of the description of Carneades' argument is lost, but there is enough left for us to know that Carneades used the kinds of antitheses in question (cf. Lac. 5.16.2–4, 6.6.2–4, 6.6.19, 23). It is in this regard worth noting that he also uses arguments similar to the sophists' arguments for injustice, claiming that it is more in keeping with self interest (see Lac. 5.16.12).

2. The sceptics would, of course, argue that it is in our own interest to eliminate desire, but this conception of self-interest is very far removed from the one characteristic of the sophists.

display. The most famous example is Carneades' trip to Rome, where he is said to have argued with great eloquence for justice and on the next day to have argued with equal force against it. His speeches read, according to Maccoll, "more like a page out of the life of Gorgias in the fifth century than of Carneades in the second" (41).[3] It might better be said that they demonstrate the continuity of these two centuries.

DEMOCRITUS: ATOMISM, IDEALISM, AND EQUANIMITY

We know Democritus as an atomist. His claim that atoms and the void are the ultimate constituents of reality might seem to make him an unlikely candidate for an influential role in the birth of scepticism, but there are three important ways in which he contributes to its development. As they correspond to three distinct aspects of his philosophy, we may distinguish them as we proceed.

Atomism

Despite its commitment to realist truth, there is a negative side to Democritus' atomism that anticipates the sceptics. Democritus doubts the veracity of the senses and ordinary claims, for they are contradicted by his claims about atoms we cannot see or feel. The senses are too weak to perceive them and knowledge through the senses is therefore illegitimate or "bastard." "Genuine" knowledge must be gained through reason and the intellect, which must take over "whenever the bastard can no longer see any smaller, or hear, or smell, or taste, or perceive by touch, but [things are] finer" (*AM* 7.138–39, Kirk et al., cf. frag. A.37).

Assuming such an outlook, our day to day dependence on the senses limits our knowledge of reality and creates a false picture of the world. As Democritus puts it, bastard knowledge of the senses exists only by human convention (*nomos*, frag. 9, 11, cf. 125 below), and we are separated from and know nothing of reality (frags. 6, 7, 8, 10). The sceptical attitude this implies is seen in the ancient claim that Democritus endorsed the formula *ou mallon* ("No more this than that")—a formula the sceptics use when they announce that opposing views are equally convincing. Judging by the accounts in Sextus (*PH* 1.213–14), Theophrastus (*De Sens* 69), and perhaps Colotes, Demo-

---

3. Maccoll, *The Greek Sceptics*, p. 41.

critus uses it to indicate that opposing sides in an ordinary disagree-
ment are equally *in*valid, for they both assume the existence of
ordinary objects.[4] Thus used, the formula indicates deference to atoms
and the void rather than a fully blown scepticism, though its rejection
of ordinary belief is an important step toward the latter. Democritus
himself suggests that it provides a basis for a more comprehensive
scepticism when he implies that intellectual knowledge is grounded in
the senses. How, he asks, can our "wretched mind" overthrow them?
(frag. 125).

Idealism

The sceptical aspects of Democritus' atomism have been widely
recognized. In contrast, his connection with idealism has been virtually
ignored. This is in part because commentators have overemphasized
his attempt to answer Parmenidean arguments that deny the possibility
of change (by denying that being can become not being, and vice
versa. Looked at from the Parmenidean point of view, Democritus'
philosophy is an obvious failure (it countenances the existence of a not
being that cannot be explained), and this suggests that he is motivated
by other kinds of problems.

According to Aristotle, Democritus develops his epistemology in
order to account for a variety of traditional oppositions. They include
the by now familiar contrast between humans and other species
("things appear quite the opposite to many of the animals," *Met*,
G5,1009b9, cf. frag. 154), as well as opposition between the views of

4. Despite this evidence, DeLacy argues ("*Ou Mallon* and the Antecedents of Ancient
Scepticism," p. 59) that comments by Aristotle (*Met* A4, 985b9) and Plutarch's "emphatic"
rejection of the proposed interpretation (*Ad Col* 1108F) show otherwise: Democritus' *ou
mallon* means only that being (constituted of atoms) is no more real than not being (the
void). However, Plutarch's emphasis is a sign of his pronounced disdain for Colotes
(evident throughout his commentary) rather than certitude on this particular point, and
his retort is an attack on an interpretation more radical than Sextus'. In keeping with this,
the atomists' use of the *ou mallon* principle is broader than he allows (see Aristotle,
Physics G4, 203b25S and frag. A.8 Leucippus) and Plutarch qualifies his rejection of the
sceptical interpretation, beginning his next paragraph with the phrase "But whatever we
may think of that . . . " His further argument, that Epicurus' views entail *ou mallon* (and
not his interpretation of the phrase *ou mallon*), is the crux of his defense of Democritus'
views (cf. 1110F).

As for Aristotle, he suggests elsewhere that Democritus uses the formula *ou mallon* as a
basis for sceptical conclusions (*Met* G5,1009b10–11). Perhaps this shows that Democritus
employed both interpretations, especially as they are both consistent with his outlook.

different individuals. The same thing appears sweet to some and bitter to others, while people who are diseased or insane have different perceptions of the world than those who are not. Indeed, if all but a few men were diseased or insane, the healthy would be judged unbalanced (ibid., and 1–10, cf. *PH* 1.213). Still other differences characterize the view we have of the world at different times—when we are sick and well, young and old, and so on.[5]

Atomism is attractive precisely because it provides an explanation of the opposing impressions of the world that this implies. The key point is that the body is composed of atoms, and that its interactions with the world and its perceptions of it are the result of atoms colliding and impinging on the body (see *Met* G5, 1009b7 and *AM* 7.136). It follows that perceptions change when the atoms of the body change, and that the same thing will appear contrary to one man and another through "the changes in the compound [of the body],[6] and will be altered by a small admixture and appear altogether different because of that single alteration" (*De Gen*, A1 315b6). Differences in the body's atoms thus explain the opposing views acceptable to different species, different individuals, and different states of mind.

The negative side of this account of opposing views is Democritus' conclusion that we cannot know what exists "in truth" (*etee*), for "we in actuality grasp nothing for certain, but what shifts in accordance with the condition of the body and of the things [the atoms] which enter and press upon it" (frag. 9, *AM* 7.136 Kirk et al.). It is, on this account, the subjective nature of perception that puts realist truth beyond our reach. Because belief is relative to the constitution of the body, we "in reality know nothing about anything; but for each of us there is a reshaping [of the atoms]—belief" (frag. 7, *AM* 7.137 Kirk et al.).

Democritus' epistemology is not wholly negative, however, for it suggests that we can know what is true relative to our own bodies, even though we cannot perceive what independently exists. Here we find the idealist strain in Democritus' thought: our immediate awareness of our sense impressions means that we can, despite the limits of perception, know the true nature of the world *relative to our subjective nature*. In his *Confirmations*, a book that promises to vindicate the senses, Democritus therefore claims that humans only grasp what shifts in

5. It might be experiments to this effect that account for the behaviour Diogenes Laertius reports at 9.38–40.

6. The "compound" is not the atoms that make up some object; they remain the same unless the object changes.

accordance with the body, still suggesting that this can be known. Commentators have been misled by Sextus' refusal to accept this vindication of the senses, failing to see that he is refusing to allow them access to realist truth. In contrast, Democritus is confirming them only in the sense that they can be used to establish an idealist analogue.

Democritus' commitment to our ability to know the nature of the world relative to our subjective nature also helps explain Aristotle's claim, in reference to Democritus, that the latter believed "truth is subjective," and that the perceptions suffered in a swoon are true (*De A* 404a 29, Hett). The latter are not, of course, true in the sense that they correspond to an independent world of external objects, but true in the sense that they tell us truly how the world appears from our point of view. We can know our perceptions, and know that they are the result when the world interacts with our bodies. In this way "truth lies in the appearances [*phainomena*]" (*De Gen* A1, 315b6 10–11). A rational commitment to atoms and the void still undermines the claim that the objects of the world are solid, bitter, cold, or hot, but not the claim that they appear so when our bodies interact with atoms and the void.

So understood, Democritus' philosophy offers appearances (*phaino-mena*) as a second-best alternative to the knowledge of the atoms that lies beyond the senses. As Diotimus reports, they constitute a second criterion of truth that allows us to judge, in a subjective way, the "nonevident" that exists beyond the senses (*AM*, 7.140). Appearances can thus be used to judge external objects, so long as we remember that they only show how they appear to us, and that "the sense appearances are the [subjective] vision of the external objects."[7]

Equanimity

Democritus' ideas about appearance make more understandable his commitment to practical affairs, which requires something more than metaphysical speculation about atoms and the void. The truth of appearances is not, however, a sufficient basis for ordinary action (it requires a decision on how we will respond to appearances). According to Diotimus, Democritus therefore employs the affections (*pathoi*) as a third criterion "of choice and aversion," which allows us to decide how

7. Note again that nonevident objects are things that "never appear of themselves, but may be apprehended, if at all, owing to other things" (*PH* 2.98). Compare the earlier discussion of Anaxagoras.

to act. "That which we feel is congenial to us is choiceworthy, but that which we feel is alien is to be regarded with aversion" (*AM* 7. 140).[8] This view is a natural extension of Democritus' commitment to sense appearances, and some such view is needed to complete his philosophy, making it a comprehensive basis for metaphysical speculation, ordinary beliefs, and practical affairs.

The Democritean suggestion that we do what seems appropriate is not, it must be emphasized, the suggestion that we should act impetuously. This would bring calamity. We should therefore judge acts with caution. Elaborating this suggestion, Democritus proposes a method of attaining happiness through moderation, which is best seen as a response to the problem of antithesis. Noting that opposing views are equal,[9] he proposes that we choose views and ways of acting that will make us happy and content:

Cheerfulness is created for men through moderation of enjoyment and harmoniousness of life. Things that are in excess or lacking are apt to change and cause great disturbance in the soul. Souls which are stirred by great divergences are neither stable nor cheerful. Therefore one must keep one's mind on what is attainable, and be content with what one has, paying little heed to things envied and admired, and not dwelling on them in one's mind. Rather must you consider the lives of those in distress, reflecting on their intense sufferings, in order that your own possessions and condition may seem great and enviable, and you may, by ceasing to desire more, cease to suffer in your soul . . . One must . . . [compare] one's own life with that of those in worse cases, and must consider oneself fortunate, reflecting on their sufferings, on being so much better off than they. If you keep to this way of thinking, you will live more serenely . . . (frag. 191, cf. frag. 3)

Here the suggestion is that equanimity can be achieved by dwelling on thoughts that oppose those thoughts that disturb it.[10]

This notion of focusing on those worse off is sometimes associated with apathy and a dour acceptance of any condition whatsoever. But

8. For modern analogues, one might look to Hume's account of the passions or Mill's account of what is desirable in *Utilitarianism*.

9. On the relativity of judgments of good and bad: "Those same things from which we get good can also be for us a source of hurt . . . [D]eep water is useful for many purposes, and yet again harmful; for there is a danger of being drowned" (frag. 172).

10. Modern commentators pay too little attention to the fact that the method *works*. The problem is our natural tendency to compare ourselves to those less deserving and those better off, comparisons that produce (as Democritus warns) bitterness and envy.

Democritus preaches moderation and enjoyment, declaring that one must submit "to the necessary conditions of life" (frag. 289 Freeman), that a life without festival "is a long road without an inn" (frag. 230 Freeman). As Diogenes Laertius describes it, his goal of "imperturbable wisdom" implies that "the end of action is happiness (*euthumia*), which is not identical with pleasure . . . but a state in which the soul continues calm and strong, undisturbed by fear or superstition or any other emotion" (D.L. 9.45). It follows that we should be cautious about what we undertake, but not that we should reject activity (it is only excessive desire and expectation that need be rejected). Democritus himself is said to have been referred to as *gelasinos* ("laughter") because he laughed at the folly of men and the extravagance of their desires.[11]

The historical significance of Democritean ideals exhibits itself in subsequent developments in Greek ethics, which fasten on mental equanimity as a moral goal and on antithesis as the means of achieving it. Once Democritus points out that one can oppose unhappiness by considering those worse off, others quickly recognize that there are many other ways to oppose unhappiness (by reminding ourselves that good may come from bad, that it is internal rather than external things that matter, and so on). For the moment, we need only note that Democritus' adoption of this technique is passed on to ancient scepticism, which takes issue with views that produce discontent and disturb our peace of mind.

PROTAGORAS: ANTI-REALISM AND UTILITY

According to a number of ancient commentators (Diogenes Laertius, Philostratus, Hesychius, and Apuleius), Protagoras is a student of Democritus. This suggestion is usually rejected as spurious because of

11. When the Abderites ask him to cure Democritus of his madness and laughter, Hippocrates is said to conclude that Democritus is sane and even wise. Other anecdotes are associated with a tradition that views Democritus as a devotee of the magic lore of Egypt and the East, apparently because of his extensive travels. Pliny believed him to be the exponent of magic as Hippocrates was the exponent of medicine, and reports that there are commentaries of Democritus recommending the use of human bones for a potion to cure disease. The bones of the head of a criminal are said to be more beneficial for some complaints, and those of a guest preferable for others. Syncellus says that Democritus wrote on gold, silver, and precious stones that were transmuted from other substances. A very different set of anecdotes relates Democritus' scientific endeavours, which reputedly save the Abderites from disaster.

the difficulty of reconciling the standard dates associated with their lives. It is probably impossible to decide the issue in a final way, though Owens proposes dates that make them contemporaries and Protagoras' study under Democritus makes philosophical sense; the two express similar concerns.

The Problem of Opposition

Protagoras' commitment to opposing views is seen in Diogenes Laertius' claim that he is "the first to say that there are two arguments [*logoi*] concerning everything, each opposed to the other" (D.L. 9.51, cf. A.20). Specific antitheses must have been enumerated in his two books of "opposing arguments" (the *Antilogiai*, D.L. 9.55), but these works have not survived. According to Plato and Sextus, Protagoras contrasts humans and other species (*Prot* 333e–4c), and the views we have when young and old, awake and asleep, and sick and well (*PH* 1.219, *AM* 7.60–64). Aristotle similarly holds that Protagoras and Democritus are motivated by the same antitheses. Other kinds of oppositions are implied by Protagoras' remark that he does not know whether the gods exist, because life is too short and the question too obscure (DK A.23, *AM* 9.56).

Anti-Realist Truth

Protagoras' response to opposition is more readily understood if we compare it to the views of other ancient anti-realists. We have already seen that Democritus concedes that we cannot perceive the true nature of the external world, arguing that we can still establish that it appears to us in certain ways. This is an important move away from ordinary realism, though he still grants our ability to know our mental states and the realist truths that this implies. Indeed, reason, he holds, can still establish that the ultimate constituents of reality are atoms and the void. In contrast, Protagoras' anti-realism goes much further, rejecting all realist truth and defining truth in terms of subjective appearance. In the process he rejects the sceptical side of atomism (the notion that we cannot "in reality" establish "truth") insofar as his definition makes reality and truth accessible. He might be compared to contemporary anti-realists who define truth in terms of forms of life, though he goes much further, understanding it as relative to specific individuals.[12]

12. Some (though not many) commentators have suggested that Protagoras makes truth relative to human nature—to man as a species rather than an individual. This view

Protagoras' views are reported in Plato's *Theaetetus*. Protagoras, Plato tells us, holds that "as each thing appears to me, so it is for me, and as it appears to you so it is to you" (386a, O'Brien). This implies that there are different truths for different individuals, but Protagoras accepts this consequence. To take a traditional example that may make his philosophy more plausible, there is no single answer to the question whether the wind is warm or hot or cold. On the contrary, individuals from different climates, of different ages, and in different states of health judge the same wind to be cold, mild, and warm, and we can only say that it is one or the other for certain individuals. In modern thought, we take for granted the notion that judgments of warmth, size, taste, and numerous other concepts are relative to specific individuals, though we usually assume that this distinguishes them from other kinds of judgments (for example, scientific claims) that are true in an absolute sense. In contrast, Protagoras holds that all truth is relative to specific individuals, and thus eliminates higher (realist) truth. It is in this way that he establishes his startling conclusion that all claims are true, even those that conflict with each other (*AM* 7.60, D.L. 9.51, DK A.13, 14, 15, 21a). Protagoras announces this with the formula *ou mallon* (*Ad Col* 1109A). The individual becomes, on his account, "the measure of all things," for "as things appear to me, so they actually are for me, and as they appear to you, so they actually are for you" *Crat* 386a (O'Brien, cf. ibid.).

This radical rejection of the realist conception of truth explains Sextus' suggestion that Protagoras does away with the criterion of truth. Protagoras is committed to universal truth, but such truth is subjective, and Sextus takes the criterion of truth to refer to realist truth, which cannot be subjective. As he explains:

Some . . . have counted Protagoras of Abdera among the company of philo-sophers who abolish the criterion, since he asserts that all impressions and opinions are true and that truth *is a relative thing* inasmuch as everything that has appeared to someone or been opined by someone is at once real in relation to him . . . Hence also the madman is a trustworthy criterion of the appearances which occur in madness, and the sleeper of those in sleep, and the infant of

is contradicted not only by the Greek (see Kerferd, and Guthrie, *A History of Greek Philosophy*, 3: 188–89) but also by the kinds of oppositions used to establish Protagorean relativism. They include the contrast between humans and other species but also focus on that between the impressions of individuals who are drunk or sober, young or old, sick or well, and so on. This emphasis on the individual is characteristic of the times (cf., e.g. the Cyrenaics).

those in infancy, and the ancient of those that occur in old age. Nor is it
appropriate to disallow one set of circumstances in favour of a different set [for
it begs the question to choose one set rather than another] . . . As some have
supposed, this man rejects the criterion, seeing that it purports to be a test of
things in themselves and to discriminate between the true and the false,
whereas he does not admit falsehood or the existence of anything in itself. (*AM*
7.60–64)

Protagoras' notion that what is true is relative to individuals is here
contrasted with things or states of affairs that are true absolutely and in
themselves. According to Sextus, it is not only Protagoras that rejects
realist truth; Euthydemus and Dionysodorus "are also said to have
shared these views; for they too regarded both the existent and the true
as relative things" (*AM* 7.64). In all three cases, we have clear examples
that contradict the usual suggestion (by Burnyeat and others) that all
the Greeks adopt a realist account of truth.

Sextus throws further light on Protagoras' views in the *Outlines of
Pyrrhonism* (*PH* 1.216–19), where he describes Protagorean doctrine in
order to distinguish it from scepticism. Having noted that both
Protagoras and the Pyrrhoneans introduce relativity and posit only
what appears to each individual, he goes on to differentiate their views.
Protagoras maintains that the world and our bodies are in flux, and
that the causes (*logoi*) of all appearances exist in the world and act upon
us depending on our subjective states. Those in a particular state grasp
those causes that appear, in one way or another, to those in such a state.
"Man" thus "becomes the criterion of things in themselves," not in the
sense that humans know these causes from a god's-eye (realist) point of
view, but in the sense that they know them from a human point of
view.[13] As Democritus has already suggested, perception is thus
relative to both the changing external world and our subjective states.
In contrast, the Pyrrhoneans do not dogmatize "about the fluidity of
matter and . . . the subsistence therein of the causes of all appearances,
these being non-evident matters about which we suspend judgment"
(*PH* 1.219, adapting Bury). From the Pyrrhonean point of view, the

13. It makes no sense to interpret this remark at *PH* 1.217 to mean that humans can
judge things in themselves in the realist way, for this is at odds with the passages already
noted and with Sextus' claim that Protagoras introduces relativity. Sextus' summary (*PH*
1.219) of the nonevident Protagorean doctrines the Pyrrhoneans take issue with does not
include the claim that we can establish what has absolute existence (something that would
be a paradigm of a nonevident truth the Pyrrhoneans reject).

problem with Protagoras is his assumption that a changing external world exists that contains the causes of perception, for the Pyrrhoneans eschew all reference to the external world, rejecting any claims about it, holding that it may not exist (see chapter 6).

Utility

According to many ancient commentators, the relativism proposed by Protagoras is untenable, inconsistent, and absurd. Aristotle gives the classic criticism of Protagoras' views: "He said that of all things the measure is man, meaning simply that what appears to each person also is positively the case. But once this is taken to be so, the same thing turns out both to be and not to be, and to be bad as well as good, not to mention the other opposites, since often what seems beautiful to this group of people will seem the opposite to that group, and what appears to each man is taken to be the measure" (*Met* K6, 1062b13 O'Brien). Elsewhere, Aristotle ridicules Protagoras by suggesting that he must maintain that the same thing is a ship, as wall, and a man (*Met* G4, 1007b18). In earlier philosophy, both Plato and Democritus criticize Protagoras in a similar way, arguing that he must accept the falsity and the truth of his own views, for they appear false to some (*AM* 7.389).

Such reasoning has been uncritically accepted by many modern commentators, though it is difficult to sustain. To begin with, it would not be obviously inconsistent for Protagoras to hold that Aristotle speaks the truth when he says that Protagoras is mistaken; this is true to Aristotle, which is nonetheless compatible with its being false to Protagoras or someone else (there is no contradiction in saying that vanilla ice cream tastes good to you and bad to me). Contradictions arise only if one begs the question and assumes that truth cannot be interpreted in the subjective way Protagoras proposes.

One might still argue that Protagoras leaves us with no way to pick between beliefs (every one is true), but this would ignore his appeal to practicality as basis for choosing between opinions. He can defend his own outlook in terms of it and still argue against his critics' views without having to maintain that they are false, for it suffices to point out that, while true, they have little utility. Socrates impersonates Protagoras in order to explain how this might make his relativism compatible with the claim that he is wise and his opinions are preferable to others:

I do say that the truth is as I've written: each of us is the measure of the things which are and the things which are not. Nevertheless, there's an immense difference between one man and another in just this respect: the things which are and appear to one man are different from those which are and appear to another. As for wisdom or a wise man, I'm nowhere near saying there's no such thing; on the contrary, I do apply the word "wise" to precisely this sort of person: anyone who can effect a change in one of us, to whom bad thing appear and are, and make good things both appear and be for him . . . to a sick man what he eats appears, and is, bitter, whereas to a health man it is, and appears the opposite. Now what must be done isn't to make either of them wiser . . . nor is it to accuse the sick one of being ignorant because he makes the judgements he does, and call the healthy one wise because he makes judgements of a different sort. What must be done is to effect a change in one direction; because one of the two conditions is better. In education, too, in the same way, a change must be effected from one of two conditions to the better one; but where a doctor makes the change with drugs, a sophist does it with things he says.

. . . when, because of a harmful condition in his mind, someone has in his judgements things which are akin to that condition, then by means of a beneficial condition one [the wise man] makes him have in his judgements things of that same sort—appearances which some people, because of ignorance, call true; but I call them better than the first sort, but not at all truer.

. . . where bodies are concerned, I say it's doctors who are the wise, and where plants are concerned, gardeners—because I claim that they, too, whenever any of their plants are sick, instil perceptions that are benefiical and healthy . . . instead of harmful ones. My claim is, too, that wise and good politicians make beneficial things, instead of harmful ones, seem to their states to be just. If any sort of thing seems just and admirable to any state, then it actually is just and admirable for it, as long as that state accepts it; but a wise man makes beneficial things be and seem just and admirable to them, instead of any harmful things which used to be so for them. And according to the same principle the sophist is wise, too . . . (*Th* 166d–67c, McDowell)

According to this account, all beliefs are true, but some are better or worse depending on their utility—on the good or bad effects they have upon our lives. As Socrates explains in his example, it is true that the same food is sweet to the healthy and sour to the sick, but it is preferable for food to taste sweet; the view of the healthy man is better in this sense. Someone who is wise can change the sick person so that his food is no longer sour, exchanging better views for worse. In other contexts, the wise can take an unsuccessful man and make him successful, or take a whole community and exchange harmony for turmoil.

Protagoras therefore holds that, as individuals, we should choose our own opinions by accepting what is advantageous to us. We should, for example, accept the norms and customs of society, for they are preferable to anarchy and a situation ruled by insecurity and injustice (*Prot* 320c–f, cf. Kerferd chap. 6).[14] In deciding who we should accept as wise we may rely on ordinary observation, looking to see who is successful in promoting health, teaching children, making individuals more successful, and dissipating turmoil. There may be no infallible recipe for making such decisions, and there will be opposing arguments that obscure the issue, but it is still possible to form an opinion about who is cured of sickness and whose situation changes for the better (human nature provides some basis for consensus). Practical results should be a basis for decision when we must choose between competing thinkers and opinions.[15] We already employ a similar method in many cases—when we decide, for example, for or against a medical procedure, not by listening to technical arguments we may not understand but by observing its usual outcome.

Given such an outlook, Protagoras can claim he is wise by noting that others see the improvement of his students when they study with him (*Prot* 318a). His willingness to accept other people's judgments (and his faith in the possibility of practical consensus) is seen in his confident stipulation that students need not pay his fee if they will swear his teachings are not worth it (328c–d). His practical concerns and the high regard in which he is held is attested by his appointment as the author of the constitution of Thurii, and by the report that he and Pericles spent a whole day discussing an athlete killed by a javelin, attempting to decide by the most correct argument (the *orthotatos logos*)[16] whether the cause was the javelin, the man who threw it, or those who organized the games.

A more detailed account of Protagoras' outlook is difficult to establish, though, it should by now be clear, it encompasses a positive philosophy that cannot be dismissed in the perfunctory way of

14. One finds another defence of *nomos* in the *Anonymous Iamblichi*, which suggests that men cannot live alone and must associate with others if they are to survive and flourish.

15. There is, therefore, no reason to accept Socrates' suggestion about Protagoras, that he must have thought the unwise have false beliefs about what is advantageous; this view contradicts Protagoras' main conclusions; Socrates himself says that Protagoras might lambast him for talking nonsense (ibid., 171). Protagoras can grant that all individuals have true views of the advantageous, though some have more practical success (for truth is relative to individual opinion, not practical success).

16. The *orthos* logos is "most straight" or, harking back to Parmenides, the least "backward turning."

Aristotle, Democritus, and Plato. The crux of his epistemology is an appeal to practical success as a way of avoiding opposites and determining those beliefs we should accept. This outlook is particularly sigificant in that it anticipates modern pragmatism. Unlike Protagoras, pragmatists argue that utility determines what is "true," though they still endorse a similar appeal to utility as a basis for belief. In both cases, transcendent truth and metaphysical speculation are rejected for more practical criteria for belief. The most important point here is that Protagoras' moves in this direction take us one step closer to the sceptics.

METRODORUS AND ANAXARCHUS: IDEALISM AND EQUANIMITY

The philosophies of Democritus and Protagoras provide a general background that illuminates the role less influential thinkers play in the rise of scepticism. Their views push Democritean and Protagorean themes toward a more explicit scepticism. Unfortunately, our lack of extant information makes an account of some important thinkers (for example, Nausiphanes)[17] too tendentious to be worth pursuing, though our knowledge of general philosophical trends and specific fragments enables us to sketch the views of the most important thinkers to contribute to the rise of scepticism.

Metrodorus of Chios

Sextus describes Metrodorus of Chios as one who does away with the criterion of truth, holding that "we know nothing, not even whether we know nothing" (*AM* 7.48, 87–88). As a follower of Democritus he must be familiar with the standard oppositions, which suggests that he propounds, in a rudimentary form, the negative side of scepticism. It has sometimes been said that this aspect of his philosophy is incompatible with his claim, "Everything exists which anyone perceives" (frag. 2), but any contradiction is eliminated if we understand it within the Democritean context. As we have already noted, the latter suggests that what is perceived can be known to exist (only) as an element of subjective experience, and this is compatible with the claim that we cannot know the nature of ultimate reality. So understood,

17. Who adopts equanimity as a moral goal (frag. 3) and holds that things appear equally to exist and not to exist (frag. 4).

Metrodorus' position is a natural extension of the idealist trends we have already noted in Democritus' views. His scepticism, however, goes much further, rejecting the notion that we can establish the ultimate existence of atoms and the void. And so his epistemology is that much closer to idealist trends in modern thought.[18]

Anaxarchus

Metrodorus' influence extends through his student, Diogenes of Smyrna, to Pyrrho's teacher, Anaxarchus. Though Galen classifies Anaxarchus as a sceptic (frag. DK A.15), the claim that he likened "existing things to a scene-painting," supposing them "to resemble the impressions experienced in sleep or madness" (A.16), suggests a position closer to idealism. Anaxarchus' anti-realism grants that we perceive certain objects, asking only whether they exist as absolute realities (the sceptics even doubt our ability to know what we perceive). In answer to the assumption that ordinary objects do exist, he compares them to a scene painting or the impressions received in sleep or madness; the latter need not reflect an external world. Full-fledged realist truth is thus exchanged for a more subjective anti-realism.

Within the moral realm, Anaxarchus also emphasizes the subjective nature of belief, propounding the Democritean method of attaining equanimity by opposing anything that disturbs us. According to Diogenes Laertius, he is called the "happy" one (*eudaimonikos*) in view of his contentment, and he retained his composure when he died a horrible death at the hands of the tyrant Nicocreon (D.L. 9.60, 59). That episode is probably apocryphal, but it seems that Anaxarchus was notably successful in trying to oppose unhappiness. In a famous incident, he cures the despondence of Alexander the Great after the latter has killed a friend in anger. The gentler methods of his associates having failed, Anaxarchus rebukes the king, shouting, "Here is Alexander, to whom the whole world is now looking; but he lies on the floor weeping like a slave, in fear of the law and the censure of men, unto whom he himself should be a law and a measure of justice, since he has conquered the right to rule and mastery, instead of submitting like a slave to the mastery of vain opinion. Knowest thou not

---

18. Metrodorus' idealism proves that Metrodorus is not (as Sedley holds) the first sceptic. On the contrary, the sceptics propose a more radical position that rejects even idealist truth.

. . . that Zeus has Justice and Law seated beside him, in order that everything done by the master of the world may be lawful and just?" (Plutarch, *Alexander* LII Perrin). Putting aside the question whether Anaxarchus acts appropriately or not, his comments are a good example of Democritean methods. Thus he confronts the king with an opposing way of looking at the murder he committed (one suggesting that what he did was right, not wrong) and restores his balance. Others who accepted Alexander's judgment were powerless to help him.

SOCRATES: MITIGATED SCEPTICISM

Democritean thinkers like Metrodorus and Anaxarchus play an especially important role in early Pyrrhonism. Academic scepticism stems from Plato and is more indebted to Protagoras and the sophists. According to the academics, even Plato is a sceptic, though it is Socrates who plays the most important role in this regard.

Socratic Dialectic

Socrates' sceptical tendencies are often underemphasized, sometimes to absurd extent.[19] Plato portrays him as in *search* of knowledge, but repeatedly demonstrating that we are mistaken in thinking we have found it. No ethical terms are, for example, ever satisfactorily defined. Instead, particular definitions are shown to be wanting. The standard strategy is *elenchos* argument, which begins with an answer to a question, deduces a contradiction, and ends with the opposition this implies. As Zeller writes, "of the various sides to every question, he [Socrates] brings out the opposition which every notion contains either within itself or in relation to some other . . . "[20] Traditional antitheses are sometimes used in such deliberations (see *Mem* 1.1.11–14, 3.8.4–10, 4.2.12–23), but they play a very minor role and Socrates, like later academics, typically relies on his ability to crossexamine and uncover inconsistencies in almost any view (see D.L. 2.28 and *Mem.* 2.8.4–10).[21]

A good example of Socratic dialectic is the *Euthyphro*. It begins with the suggestion that Euthyphro's decision to prosecute his father needs an exact and advanced account of piety (4b, 4e), and evolves into a

19. As in Zeller's *Socrates and the Socratic Schools.*
20. Ibid.,132.
21. It is interesting to compare these comments on Socrates with the comments on on Arcesilaus by Numenius (Eus. 730c) and Diogenes Laertius (4.37).

discussion of piety's nature. Socrates then demonstrates the contradictions that follow from Euthyphro's answer to the question of what is pious (7e–8b, 10). In answer to this, Euthyphro complains that his claims have been bewitched and are traveling in a circle, refusing to stay where they are put. (Socrates answers that they, like Daedalus' statues, run off on their own.) The discussion culminates when Euthyphro moves "full circle" to the point where he began, espousing views he has rejected (15b–c). By the end of the dialogue we are convinced that Euthyphro cannot defend his views, but we are left without an alternate, positive account of piety.

The scepticism behind such inquiry is seen in the *Apology*, where Socrates defends his dialectic and suggests that he has been brought to trial because he has embarrassed those who think they have knowledge. The Delphic oracle has deemed otherwise, declaring him to be the wisest man in Greece, apparently for having recognized his own lack of wisdom. "What is probable, gentlemen, is that in fact the god is wise and his oracular response meant that human wisdom is worth little or nothing, and that when he says this man, Socrates, he is using my name as an example, as if [to say,] . . . 'This man among you, mortals, is wisest who, like Socrates, understands that his wisdom is worthless'" (23a–b Grube).

Mitigated Scepticism

Despite his sceptical conclusions, Socrates might seem to reject scepticism when he claims that he "knows (*oida*) that it is wicked and shameful to do wrong, to disobey one's superior, be he god or man" (*Apol* 29b). The heart of scepticism is, however, the claim that *reason* cannot establish what is true, and this is compatible with conviction. Indeed, it is compatible with the use of the verb "to know," provided it expresses a certainty based on other grounds. Socrates is committed to such certainty because he grounds his convictions, not on reason, but on oracles and the holy inner voice that directs his personal affairs (*Apol* 31c–d). Even in the *Crito*, reason is only used to dispose of positions that conflict with the latter (see below). Faith, not reason, is in this sense the basis of Socrates' belief and certainty, and his stance is consistent with his scepticism. In modern terms, his position is a form of mitigated scepticism.

A further aspect of Socrates' mitigated scepticism is his commitment to custom and convention (a commitment that might be criticized on moral grounds). Like the rest of his belief, it is founded on personal conviction coupled with the conclusion that humans cannot justify competing points of view. In the *Euthyphro*, for example, Socrates defends traditional obligations to one's father over the rights of a slave, not by proving them correct, but by refuting Euthyphro's arguments to the contrary. Socrates argues that a true appreciation of our ignorance will make us more humble and less willing to reject conventional obligations. As he puts it at one point, "you [Euthyphro] think that your knowledge of the divine, and of piety, is so accurate that, when those things happened as you say, you have no fear of having acted impiously in bringing your father to trial" (4e Grube). Socrates himself holds that our inability to know what is right should make us less comfortable about rejecting traditional assumptions.[22]

In the *Republic,* Socrates attacks the critique of conventional values propounded by Thrasymachus and the *physis* sophists, and in both the *Republic* and the *Euthyphro* he denounces stories that show disrespect to the gods (*Rep* 2.377c–83c and *Euthyphro* 6). In the *Crito*, he argues that he must obey the laws of the state because it has been like a parent to him (50–54). He disobeyes them only when they contravene traditional laws and virtues (*Crito* 47–48; *Apol* 31–32).[23]

It might seem that Socrates adopts a different outlook in the *Crito*, when he claims that he must obey the laws of Athens even though he has been unjustly tried. But even here his arguments are a critique of others' views (in this case Crito's) rather than an independent argument for justice. In the process, Socrates provides a dubious basis for a defense of traditional moral principles by assuming a series of unlikely propositions: that one wrong can never alleviate another,[24] that his

22. One might equally conclude that there is no reason for *accepting* custom and convention, but it can at least be said that they are the norms most likely to be intuitively appealing.

23. Socrates might seem to be rejecting tradition when he rejects worldly accomplishments, for they play an important role in traditional Greek values. Nietzsche condemns the rejection of these values in the *Twilight of the Idols*. Socratic indifference to worldly accomplishment is, however, a variant rather than the reversal of Greek ideals of strength, for such indifference allows man to cope with any situation (note Alexander's remark that if he were not Alexander, he would be Diogenes). Socrates demonstrates his commitment to strength as an ideal on the battlefield, in his refusal to appeal to pity in the *Apology* (33–34), and in his derogatory suggestion that running from the laws would be behaving "like the lowest menial" (*Crito* 52).

24. Cf. Socrates point, in the *Republic*, that it is permissible to lie if this can minimize another wrong (by preventing someone from carrying out their plan to murder, for example).

refusal to obey the laws will destroy them, that he could not be happy if he escaped, that his son would be worse off, and so on. More importantly, his reasoning begs the very question whether one should accept traditional obligations by justifying duty to the state on the grounds that is analogous to traditional duties to one's parents. It is difficult to know whether Socrates appreciates these problems, though they are unlikely to matter to him; the real basis of his views is a sense of personal conviction.

Equanimity

Despite his fame as a philosopher, the most impressive aspect of Socrates is not his reasoning but his character. Like other early sceptics, he is mainly concerned with the moral, not the scientific (*Mem* 1.1.11, *AM* 11.2; *Apol* 19b–d). Though he rarely discusses his own views in detail, his life and his remarks demonstrate his commitment to equanimity, which places him even closer to the sceptics. When he finally faces death, he says that one should cultivate a state in which one "can be free of all anxiety about the fate of one's soul" (*Ph* 114d). His own success at this is a striking feature of his personality, graphically portrayed in the *Euthyphro*, the *Apology*, the *Crito* and the *Phaedo* (cf. *Mem* 4.8), where he remains unruffled despite an unjust accusation, trial, and execution. As Crito remarks when he comes to tell Socrates that the execution is approaching: "I have been wondering at you, because I saw how comfortably you were sleeping . . . I have often felt before in the course of my life how fortunate you are in your disposition, but I feel it more than ever now in your present misfortune when I see how easily and placidly you put up with it" (43b Tredennick).

Socrates admires Cephalus for his account of old age at the beginning of the *Republic*. Unlike those who bemoan a waning appetite for feasting, drinking, and sex, Cephalus describes it as a liberation from (as Sophocles puts it) a "whole horde of lunatic slave masters" who rule one like a tyrant (*Rep* 1.329d). It is a welcome change precisely because it brings peace of mind. In a manner reminiscent of Democritus, a person can use this peace to counterbalance the frailties and infirmities that accompany old age (cf. Cicero in *On Old Age* 47). Socrates' ability to dispute any view allows him, more generally, to oppose any thought that he is a victim of misfortune. He illustrates his technique when he deals with our ordinary fear of death, declaring that "to fear death, gentlemen, is no other than to think oneself wise when one is not, to think that one knows what one does not know. No one knows whether death may not be the greatest of blessings for a man, yet men fear it as if they knew that it is the greatest of all evils. And surely it is most blameworthy to believe that one knows what one does not know" (*Apol* 29b Grube, cf. 28b–29a). Scepticism about our ability to know death, which we cannot know is bad, thus enables us to accept it with equanimity. We must take seriously the view that it is good, perhaps the greatest good. In the *Phaedo* (114d) Socrates tells us that we should risk a hopeful view, repeating it like an incantation, for it will inspire confidence when we face our end. In consoling Crito, he says that death may take him to a state of heavenly happiness, and that it is only his body that will be burned or buried (115c–16, cf. *Apol* 40c–1a and *Crito* 54b–d).

In many other situations Socrates is able to retain composure or foster it in others by opposing ordinary ways of looking at specific circumstances. When he is kicked and someone expresses surprise at his taking it so lightly, he asks whether he should act like an ass (a donkey) because one has kicked him (D.L. 2.21, cf. 2.35). On another occasion he is said to tell Xanthippe not to feel ashamed of a meagre dinner prepared for guests, "for if they are reasonable, they will put up with it, and if they are good for nothing we shall not trouble ourselves about them" (D.L. 2.34). In these and numerous other cases (cf. *Mem* 2.2, 3.72, 3.13.4–6), Socrates finds a way of arguing that repels ordinary feelings of resentment, misfortune, anger, shame, or disappointment. He manages to retain his equanimity in the most trying circumstances and provides a model for the systematic search for equanimity undertaken by Pyrrho, Arcesilaus, and the later sceptics.

THE MEGARIANS

Socrates' ties to scepticism extend through his followers and their schools. The Megarians are led by Euclid, who combines Socratic and Parmenidean dialectic, maintaining the unity of being and the impossibility of becoming. The Parmenidean critique of time that is a part of scepticism is probably inherited from his school.[25] Its views demonstrate that Parmenidean influence is still a force to be reckoned with, and a number of Megarian philosophers play an influential role in subsequent developments (Sextus mentions Alexinus of Elis, Philo,

25. See Groarke, "Parmenides' Timeless Universe, Again."

Eubulides, and Diodorus Cronus). The most illustrious representative of Megarian philosophy is Stilpo, who is said to teach Pyrrho's follower, Timon. Pyrrho himself may have been a student of Bryson, described as Stilpo's son (D.L. 9.61; *Lex* Pyrrho 2.278). A more likely possibility is Suidas' suggestion that Bryson is a disciple of Socrates or Euclid (*Lex* Pyrrho 2.278 and Socrates 4.404) though he provides, in either case, a link from Socrates to Pyrrho.

MONIMUS AND CYNIC INDIFFERENCE

In addition to Megarian doctrines, Stilpo endorses Cynic moral views. They originate in the views of Socrates' follower Antisthenes, who takes to an extreme the Socratic goal of equanimity, independence, and indifference come what may. Stilpo does not concern himself with material losses, remarking that banishment is not an evil, and that the immoral life of his daughter cannot disgrace him.

The most dedicated Cynics live as beggars, adopting the most severe asceticism, opposing ordinary vanity and desire, and inuring themselves to hardship by embracing it. Slavery or freedom is a matter of indifference to the wise, they hold. Antisthenes' pupil, the Cynic Diogenes of Sinope, is in many ways the most compelling ancient philosopher. Despite the extremes to which he and other Cynics go, it is important to see that they are a part of more general trends that endorse indifference as an ideal to be fostered by antithesis. From Diogenes such views pass to Crates, and then to Zeno and the Stoics, who make indifference to external things a central aspect of their outlook. The Stoics are, however, only one example of such influence: indifference, equanimity, and antithesis are equally important in competing schools. Epictetus' suggestion that we must control our own aims and desires rather than external things (*Ench* 1, cf. *Dis* 7.27 and the frag. in Gel. 29.15–21); Epicurus' concern with long- rather than short-term happiness; Monimus' statement that things are determined by the view we take of them (*Med.* 2.15); and the sceptical attempt to rout disturbing thoughts by adopting an opposing way of looking at them (see below) are part and parcel of the same trends and illustrate the fundamental unity of different schools of thought.

Monimus

The Cynics' ties to scepticism are clearest in Monimus. There is little extant evidence on his views, though Galen classes him (with Zeno,

Anaxarchus, and Pyrrho) as a sceptic (DK A.15), Sextus lists him as one who did away with the criterion of truth (*AM* 7.48), and both Sextus and Meander report his claim that all beliefs are vanity (*tuphos*, "folly," literally "smoke"), "a vain fancy that non-existents are existent" (*AM* 8.5, D.L. 6.83). This is not to say that nothing exists, but that the things we assume to exist do not exist beyond perception (as things in themselves). As we have already seen, Sextus tells us that, like Anaxarchus, Monimus "likened existing things to a scene painting and supposed them to resemble the impressions experienced in sleep or madness" (*AM* 7.88). This implies that sense impressions, like dreams and hallucinations, represent mental states rather than external objects, and that we cannot know the world beyond them.

A similar idealism seems implied by Monimus' dictum that "things are determined by the view we take of them" (*Med* 1.15), for it attacks the notion that there are things and situations which are objectively good and bad. Rather, a situation is good or bad (and fortunate or unfortunate) depending on the view of it that we adopt. Like Democritus, Socrates, and others, Monimus thus suggests that we should be happy with any situation if we take the proper view of things. In adopting such a view, he once again exchanges an objective world of absolutes for a subjective world made up of human responses to particular situations.

THE CYRENAICS: EXTERNAL OBJECTS AND OTHER MINDS

Led by Aristippus of Cyrene, the Cyrenaics are, of all the Socratic schools, the most important representatives of the anti-realist trends that culminate in scepticism. Appealing to traditional oppositions, they hold that the senses cannot be trusted (D.L. 2.93, 95) and that the opposing ways things appear in different circumstances, to different individuals, and to different species show that we cannot judge the nature of external things (*Ad Col* 1120C–E; Aris. in Eus. 764c, D.L. 2.92). The Cyrenaics therefore suspend judgment on the nature of external objects, admitting that they "'appear' (*phainetai*), but refusing to venture further and pronounce the word 'are'" (*Ad Col* 1120D, cf. *AM* 7.190–200). In a move remarkably like the idealist attempt to eschew realist claims, they therefore replace claims that external objects are sweet, hot, or dark, with claims that they themselves are "sweetened," "warmed," or "darkened"—that is, claims that state the nature of their impressions and affections (*pathoi*) but do not assert anything about the external world (*Ad Col* 1120D–F).

Like modern idealists, the Cyrenaics see their endorsement of claims about the affections as a way of ensuring truth (*Ac* 2.20, D.L. 2.92, Eus. 718c, Aris. in Eus. 764c); we can at least know our impressions, and each contains "within itself a manifest character that guarantees its truth." Opinion is, in view of this, free from error when it "keeps within the bounds of our responses," but forever embroiled with itself and falling into conflict when it "strays beyond and meddles with judgements and pronouncements about external matters" (*Ad Col* 1120E–F, cf. 1121C). This anticipates the Pyrrhoneans, though they see an appeal to the affections not as a way to establish truth but merely as a way to deal with practical affairs.

From the point of view of modern epistemology, one important aspect of Cyrenaicism and the other trends we have noted is their emphasis on what distinguishes the perspectives of different individuals. In contrast, modern idealism assumes the unity of human sense impressions. Certainly the ancient emphasis on the individual is, to some extent, fueled by oppositions that are no longer so perplexing. By the time we reach the Cyrenaics, however, they have given rise to real problems that are ignored in modern idealism. In particular, the Cyrenaics see the impossibility of establishing that perceptions correspond to some external world as raising another question: How can we know that other individuals have impressions similar to our own (the problem of other minds)? As Sextus puts it when he describes the Cyrenaics' views:

The affection (*pathoi*) which takes place in us reveals to us nothing more than itself. Hence . . . our affection alone is apparent to us, and the external object which is productive of the affection, though it is perhaps existent, is not apparent to us. And, in this way, whereas we are all unerring about our own affections, as regards the external real object we all err; and whereas the former are apprehensible, the latter is non-apprehensible, the soul being far too weak to discern it, owing to the positions, the intervals, the motions, the changes and a host of other causes [that produce opposing points of view]. Hence they [the Cyrenaics] assert that there exists no criterion common to mankind, but common names are given to the objects. For all in common use the terms "white" or "sweet," but they do not possess in common anything white or sweet. Each man perceives his own particular affection, but as to whether this affection is produced by a white object both in himself and in his neighbour neither the man can affirm without experiencing his neighbour's affection, nor can the neighbour without experiencing that of the man. Since there is no affection common to us all, it is rash to assert that the thing which appears of this kind to me appears to be of this kind to the man next to me as well. For possibly while I am so constituted as to get a feeling of whiteness from that which impresses me from without, the other man has his sense so constructed as to be otherwise affected. So what appears to us is not always common to all. And that we do not, in fact, receive identical impressions, owing to the different constructions of our senses, is obvious in the case of sufferers from jaundice and ophthalmia and of those who are in a normal condition. For just as some have an affection of yellow, others of crimson, it is likely that those who are in a normal condition will not receive identical impressions from the same objects owing to the differing construction of their senses, but the grey-eyed one kind, the blue-eyed another, and the black-eyed a different kind. (*AM* 7.194–98).

It is never mentioned in contemporary discussion, but this is a classic formulation of the problem of other minds. Modern science can explain away some of the antitheses that motivate it, but the basic problem, how we can know that other people have perceptions similar to ours, is still alive today.[26]

In the moral sphere, the Cyrenaics place a similar emphasis on individual affections, maintaining that we have access only to our own feelings, and that nothing is just or base by nature (Aris. in Eus. 764c, cf. *Ac* 2.142). In place of general principles, we should therefore use our feelings as a guide to pleasure, which is the highest good (D.L. 2.91, *Ac* 2.131, Eus. 764a). This notion is, as often noted in ancient and modern commentary, a considerable departure from Socratic virtues, though the latter are still part of the suggestion that we should not let pleasure master us (D.L. 2.75), and that poverty and riches, slavery and freedom, nobility and low birth, and honour and dishonour are all indifferent when one is calculating pleasure (D.L. 2.94). It is a sign of the prevailing trend toward asceticism that Aristippus feels compelled to write two works: *To those who blame him for his love of old wine and women*, and *To those who blame him for extravagant living* (D.L. 2.83–84).[27]

26. An even more fundamental problem is that of solipsism. It does not play a central role in Cyrenaic views, though it is at least recognized by Aristocles when he criticizes the followers of Aristippus, proposing that they cannot know their teacher exists (Eus. 765c). One might give a variety of answers, though the important thing is that a satisfying response to the Cyrenaics requires a *proof* that we can establish the existence and the nature of other minds, not the assumption that this is obviously so.

27. When asked why philosophers go to rich men's houses, but not vice versa, Aristippus replies that philosophers know what they need, but not vice versa (D.L. 2.69). His ability to adapt to circumstance is better depicted by the story that he was taken prisoner by the satrap Artaphernes and asked if he could still be cheerful. He answered, "Yes, you simpleton, for when should I be more cheerful than now that I am about to converse with Artaphernes" (D.L. 2.79).

The Cyrenaics and the External World

Despite those aspects of their views we have already noted, Burnyeat argues that it is a mistake to conclude that the Cyrenaics anticipate modern thinkers. In particular, he denies that they discuss the problem of the external world and maintains that it is "anachronistic" to link their notions of internal feelings and external objects with the modern concept of the external world.[28] According to his account, modern philosophers use the word *external* to mean "external to the mind," while Greek philosophers use the term *ektos* to mean "external to the body." It follows that "one's own body has not yet become for philosophy a part of the external world" and is not an object for sceptical inquiry.[29] "Greek philosophy does not [therefore] know the problem of proving in a general way the existence of an external world. That problem is a modern invention."[30] According to Burnyeat, it is the introduction of the problem of the external world that makes for a more radical modern scepticism that is "substantially new with Descartes."[31] Matson and Rorty suggest a similar analysis when they claim that the ancient world does not distinguish the senses and the body.

Such attempts to preserve the originality of modern discussion fall very far off the mark. To begin with, the notion that the body has a special epistemic status is at odds with the general context in which the Cyrenaics develop their views. To take a few examples, the Parmenidean One, Gorgias' not being, and various kinds of atomism cast as much doubt on the body as on any other object.[32] In keeping with this, the general move to subjective notions of belief relativizes all

28. Burnyeat, "Idealism in Greek Philosophy," p. 40.
29. Ibid., p. 42.
30. Ibid., p. 33.
31. Ibid., p. 49.
32. Burnyeat tries to discount Gorgias' doubts by declaring that they are a rhetorical exercise and therefore not as radical as those of Descartes. This is hardly to the point given that Descartes himself is not committed to his doubts and eventually describes them as "ridiculous" (*Oeuvres*, p. 88; *Philosophical Works*, Haldane and Ross, p. 199). What matters is that Gorgias' arguments are used by the sceptics to establish the conclusion that there are equal arguments for and against the view that anything exists.

Something similar might be said of Burnyeat's analysis of Xeniades' claim that every impression and opinion is false; even if he were correct, it must still be said that the sceptics take his claim at face value, in the process demonstrating that at least *they* take seriously the notion that nothing may exist.

beliefs, and no attempt is made to exempt beliefs about the body. In particular, the Democritean claim that we can only know our subjective responses to the world applies to all impressions, and thinkers such as Democritus, Metrodorus, Monimus, and Anaxarchus cast doubt on all perception. In this regard it is worth noting that the antitheses that motivate such thinkers have to do with dreams and illusions, which can mislead us about the body as much as other objects (see, e.g., *AM* 7.403–4, *Ac* 2.51 and cf. *De A* 404a29, *Ac* 2.89–90).

Doubts about our knowledge of our bodies are explicity raised when Aristocles ridicules the Cyrenaics, declaring that their commitment only to affections makes it impossible for them to say that they feel something by taste with their tongues, by sight with their eyes, or by hearing with their ears. Indeed, "being what they are they cannot even say how many fingers they have on their hands, nor whether each of them is one or more" (Eus. 764d–65c). Epictetus proposes similar criticisms of Pyrrho and the academics, rebutting their views by declaring that "you and I are not the same persons I know very certainly," and that "when I want to swallow something, I never take the morsel to that place [the eye] but to this [the mouth]" (*Dis* 1.27.18, Oldfather).[33]

We can better understand the Cyrenaics if we consider them within the more general context of ancient scepticism. It should in particular be noted that doubts about the external world encompass doubts about the body in later Pyrrhonism. The Pyrrhoneans provide strategies for undermining *any* claim to knowledge and explicitly argue that there is no way to prove the existence of the external world, or of space or place or substance.[34] Sextus contradicts the claim the Greek philosophy conflates the body and the senses when he accepts "the philosophers' view" that humans are constituted of soul and body, the former comprising intellect and sense. At one point he comments, "it is perfectly ridiculous to suppose that the body's substance does not differ from the senses and the intellect" (*AM* 7.291). Using this distinction, he goes on to question the existence of the body, arguing that "the senses do not apprehend the bodily substance" and that the

33. Oldfather: "The accompanying gesture explained the allusion, which was probably to the eye and the mouth, as in 2.20.28. A Cynic like Diogenes would very likely have illustrated his point in a somewhat coarser fashion; and this is not impossible in the present instance."

34. On the arguments regarding the external world and the modes for undermining any claim to knowledge, see chapter 6. (Arguments against space and place and substance are found in *PH* 3.119–35, *AM* 10.6–36 and *PH* 3.38–55.)

intellect cannot, therefore, know that it exists (*AM* 7.300). Essentially the same reasoning is used repeatedly in Sextus' discussion (see *AM* 7.352–58, 294–300, 6.55, *PH* 2.29–33, and the discussion in chap. 6).

That the Cyrenaics adopt a similar view is seen in their use of the term *ektos* in the ordinary sense to mean simply "external" or "outside." They claim we are immediately aware only of our impressions and conclude that we cannot know the nature of the world external to them. Plutarch, in his summary of Cyrenaic views, says every impression contains "within itself a manifest character that guarantees its truth," and is "trustworthy when it testifies *in its own behalf*, but not when it testifies on behalf of *anything* else" (*Ad Col* 1121D). Sextus gives us the same account of the Cyrenaics: they hold that "the affection (*pathos*) which takes place in us reveals to us nothing more *than itself*. Hence . . . our affection *alone* is apparent to us, and the external object which is productive of the affection, though it is perhaps existent, is not apparent to us" (*AM* 7.194, cf. D.L. 2.92). It is in view of this that "the Cyrenaic philosophers assert that only the feelings exist, and nothing else" (*AM* 6.53). The only plausible conclusion is that the Cyrenaics question all objects external to our impressions, presenting the problem of the external world in the modern sense. Claims to the contrary do not pay enough attention to the details or the logic of their arguments, and the usual assumption that the modern problem has no antecedent only demonstrates a widespread failure to understand the details of Greek epistemology.[35]

35. The most plausible way to raise questions about the Cyrenaic rejection of the external world is by referring to Sextus: "Whereas we [the Pyrrhoneans] suspend judgement, so far as regards the essence of external objects, the Cyrenaics declare that those objects possess a real nature which is in apprehensible" (*PH* 1.215). Sextus is here saying that the Pyrrhoneans suspend judgment on the question whether external objects possess a real or unreal nature (i.e., exist or not exist), while the Cyrenaics accept that they exist, maintaining only that their nature is inapprehensible. The problem is that this contradicts the philosophical basis of Cyrenaic views as well as Sextus in *AM* 6.53, 7.194–95. The Cyrenaics says Sextus, hold that "only our affection is apparent to us, and the external object which is productive of the affection, though it is *perhaps* existent, is not apparent to us." The use of "perhaps" (*tacha*) in the latter comment suggests that the external object producing an affection may or may not exist, especially as this is the standard way the Pyrrhoneans use the word *perhaps* (cf. *PH* 1.194–95). Given such remarks, Sextus' testimony in the *Outlines* cannot be accepted, especially as he is trying to separate the Pyrrhoneans from a rival school of scepticism (cf. his farfetched tales about Arcesilaus in *PH* 1.234–35).

Regardless, *PH* 1.215 demonstrates that Greek philosophy considers the problem of the external world even if the Cyrenaics do not; for Sextus there argues that Cyrenaic scepticism is not as radical as Pyrrhonism, which does doubt the existence and not merely the nature of external objects (for more on this point, see chap.6).

PLATO

The philosophy of Plato constitutes a final link between Socrates and the sceptics. He has a little patience for opposition as an end in itself (see, e.g., *Rep* 7.537–9), though his attack on opposition is itself a sign of his concern—a concern reflected in his reductio arguments and the give and take that is a central feature of his dialogues. Even the Platonic forms are questioned in the *Parmenides*. Ultimately, the phenomenal world is rejected precisely because it is full of change and opposition. Indeed, Plato objects to the sophists' notion that such a view is uniquely theirs. "(T)hose who spend their time dealing with antitheses [*logoi antilogikoi*] end as you well know by thinking that they have become the wisest of men and that they are the only ones who have come to understand that there is nothing sound or secure at all either in facts or in arguments, but that all things are simply carried up and down like the Euripus and never stay at any point for any duration of time" (*Phaed* 99d–100c7 Kerferd, cf. *Rep*. 5.479). Here the suggestion that all things are carried up and down like the Euripus is a variant of the sceptical suggestion that things are "no more this than that" (*ou mallon*). As Sextus puts it at one point, "when we say 'Not more' we are implicitly saying 'Not this more than that, up than down'" (*PH* 1.188). Despite his antipathy, Plato agrees with the sophists' and the sceptics' view of the phenomenal world and is himself convinced that it is full of opposites and the antitheses this implies. Not surprisingly, many sceptical currents run through his philosophy and are subsequently stressed when his Academy becomes a school of scepticism. From our perspective, the sceptical interpretation of Plato's views seems strained, though we still grant the importance of opposition to his views: we see him as attempting to transcend it in favour of a more stable ground for knowledge.

THE RISE OF SCEPTICISM

Plato's philosophy takes us back to points that we began with. His whole epistemology is a response to the question how or whether we can overcome the differences between opposing views. By the time the sceptics develop their own response to opposition, the question has a long history that has made it the focal point of Greek epistemology. In a variety of ways, the importance of the problem has already been highlighted in the philosophies of Xenophanes, Heracleitus, Parmenides, Zeno, Empedocles, Anaxagoras, Democritus, Protagoras, Metrodorus, Anaxarchus, the sophists, Socrates, the Socratic schools, and Plato. The ability of philosophers to argue for any view, to push any claim against itself, has been demonstrated time and time again. The relativity of belief and the opposing views of different individuals and different species are a topic of discussion long before the sceptics. Commonsense views of the world are discredited by the pre-Socratics and philosophy is characterized by competing cosmologies.

Within the moral sphere, Democritus and his followers advocate opposition to further equanimity. Socrates has demonstrated the method in his life. The emphasis on opposition has been noted even in drama, in the debate between justice and injustice in Aristophanes' *Clouds*, and in Euripides' *Antiope*, where it is written that "if one were clever at speaking, then in every case one could establish a contest of two-fold arguments" (frag. 189N Kerferd). The profession of varying kinds of ignorance has been espoused by Metrodorus, Democritus, Gorgias, Socrates, Monimus, and others. Xeniades of Corinth goes further, maintaining that "every impression and opinion is false" (*AM* 7.53, cf. 48).

These general trends, and not specific sceptics, best account for the rise of scepticism. Faced with the oppositions that characterize Greek philosophy, in thinkers such as Heracleitus, Protagoras, and Democritus, in the battles between the schools, in debates that pit reason against common sense, and in frequent and impressive rhetorical displays, they draw the conclusion that humans cannot decide between a view and its antithesis, and cannot establish realist truth. Considered in the context of its intellectual milieu, Greek epistemology would be more of an enigma if there were no schools of scepticism.[36]

Scepticism is not, however, entirely negative, and its positive basis for belief is also anticipated by earlier philosophers. It is found in the corollary of the conclusion that humans cannot objectively decide between opposing views—that one must endorse a more subjective way of choosing beliefs. Xenophanes makes the earliest moves in this direction when he endorses conjecture. Parmenides accepts opinion (*doxa*) as opposed to truth. Subjective determinants of belief are also recognized by Heracleitus, though the move toward an anti-realist

36. There are many circumstantial facts that raise interesting possibilities about influences on specific sceptics, but there seems no way to establish their significance. Pyrrho, for example, lives in Elis, the home of the school founded by Socrates' follower Phaedo and the home of the sophist Hippias.

anti-realist notion of belief is more clearly seen in Empedocles and Anaxagoras, who emphasize the subjective limits of perception. Their claim that human beliefs are relative to subjective states gives rise to Democritus' rejection of the notion that the senses are mirrors of the external world, and to his consequent adoption of beliefs defined in terms of a subjective interaction with the world. The idealist trends in Democritus' thought are carried further by his followers and their associates; ancient versions of idealism are found in Metrodorus, Anaxarchus, and Monimus. Protagoras eliminates objective truth altogether, replacing it with a notion of truth relative to specific individuals. Socrates combines his composure with a mitigated scepticism that accepts custom and convention.

It has already been suggested that the sceptics' tendency toward anti-realism anticipates modern trends, though this anticipation is already clear in many of their predecessors, who are often even closer to the anti-realists in interpreting subjectively based beliefs in a way that secures truth. The pessimism of the sceptical side of philosophers such as Democritus, Metrodorus, Anaxarchus, and Monimus has misled modern commentators; they fail to see that such philosophers give up on realist truth, but that this is coupled with an attempt to define anti-realist (in particular, idealist) notions of belief. In this respect the Cyrenaics are particularly noteworthy, interpreting their claims as claims about sense impressions in order to defend their truth. Protagoras, Euthydemus, and Dionysodorus go further, redefining truth in a subjective way that makes it attainable. The emphasis on the individual distinguishes such thinkers from modern anti-realists, but their ideas still represent an important analogue of modern anti-realism (they are *more* sensitive to the problem of other minds). The fact that the sceptics' predecessors are almost entirely ignored in contemporary epistemology shows how much we have failed to appreciate some central aspects of Greek philosophy.

Given that some presceptical thinkers anticipate anti-realism even more than sceptics do, one might ask why we should focus on the latter. Because it is scepticism, not its antecedents, that offers the most in-depth critique of realism and the most plausible alternative to realism. Indeed, sceptical understanding of the problems with the ordinary assumption that humans can attain objective truth far surpasses anything in early (and perhaps later) modern thought. Earlier Greek philosophy is in this sense only the beginning of a discussion of the limits of belief that reaches its maturity in the later schools of scepticism.

IV

Pyrrho and Early Pyrrhonism

The most important school of ancient scepticism originates with Pyrrho. According to our sources, he is given a bad start by Metrodorus (Eus. 765c), studies with Anaxarchus in Alexander's court, and admires Democritus above all others (D.L. 9.67). Such influences are very much in keeping with the details of his philosophy, which is a natural extension of the anti-realist side of Democritean thinking (Indian influence is also to be granted, but its importance has been greatly exaggerated).[1] The standard prejudices suggest that Pyrrho

1. There is some initial plausibility to the suggestion (see Flintoff) that we can make sense of Pyrrho's conclusions by taking seriously the possibility that he is influenced by Indian philosophy. If he adopts a view similar to ancient Buddhism, for example, this would explain both his views and some of his apparent inconsistencies (see below), since Buddhism eliminates all individuality and duality, establishing that things are indeterminate and unmeasurable and that beliefs are neither true nor false. All distinctions are eradicated and no category is more applicable than its opposite.

We shall see, however, that there is a more plausible way around Pyrrho's apparent inconsistency. For the moment, it should be said that he is influenced by Indian philosophy, but not to the extent that has been put forth. Indeed, the influence reported by Diogenes Laertius (9.61, 63) is quite minimal. More impressive is the Pyrrhoneans' repeated use of the Indian argument called the quadrilemma. Its uniqueness is its explicit consideration of the possibility that (1) things both are and are not and (2) neither are nor are not—possibilities Pyrrho clearly countenances. This can however be easily explained without reference to Indian thought. Possibility (1) is an expression of Protagoras' view of truth, which concludes that things both are and are not, while (2) can be seen as an elaboration of Xeniades' and Gorgias' (even Parmenides') view that all claims are false. Taken together, these radical views play a central role in sceptical (and, for the most part, only sceptical) discussion and this is what best accounts for Pyrrho's views. From a Greek perspective, his quadrilemma is a natural culmination of an emphasis on the equality of the competing views of different individuals—an equality which countenances the claim that *all* views are true, or all false (cf. D.L. 9.91). (Cont'd p. 82)

and his followers adopt an unmitigated, self-defeating scepticism. We shall see that it is a mitigated scepticism that provides a plausible response to the problems already noted.

THE ARGUMENTS FOR EARLY PYRRHONISM

We have no exact account of the arguments Pyrrho used, though the considerations that motivate the earlier Pyrrhoneans can be gleaned from Sextus, Philo, and Diogenes Laertius. In general, Pyrrhonean arguments hold that it is impossible to choose between opposing views, and appeal to various antitheses to show this to be the case. One important source of opposition is pre-Pyrrhonean philosophy. The kind of opposition it makes possible is seen in Sextus' discussion of the "instruments" that allegedly allow us to gain knowledge (*PH* 2.48–69). Considering first the senses, he argues that it is impossible to know whether we should follow Protagoras and declare all the appearances (*phainomena*) true; or most philosophers and declare some true and some false; or Xeniades, Gorgias, and others and declare them all false. Turning next to the intellect, Sextus claims that Gorgias' arguments show that nothing exists, and that we cannot know that the intellect exists much less apprehends reality. Indeed, we will be unable to discover truth even if we grant that the intellect exists, for different intellects judge differently and we cannot choose between the views of

---

Those authors who stress the affinities between Pyrrho's views and Indian philosophy have made too much of very general similarities that characterize both Greek and Indian philosophy (but not because of their influence on one another). We have, for example, already seen that Greek thought emphasizes opposition, the rejection of ordinary distinctions, the folly of human desire, and indifference to external circumstances well before Pyrrho goes to India (it is no doubt in view of this that he is so impressed by Indian asceticism). His favourite authors are Democritus and Homer, and the Democritean tradition and the philosophies close to it are most evident in his thinking. Most importantly, the Democritean attempt to oppose disquiet with argument by establishing the conclusion that one should be content—not meditation followed by mystical enlightenment—is the basis of Pyrrho's equanimity.

Buddha's eightfold path is not an analogue of Pyrrhonism, for Buddha is not a philosopher in the sense that Pyrrho is. Buddha does reject metaphysical pursuit in favour of a religious life, but there is no evidence that this is a conclusion deduced from philosophical considerations (on the contrary, it seems clear that he follows a different path to enlightenment). In light of this Buddha can accept contradictory conclusions without qualm. In contrast, Pyrrhonism is a concerted philosophical attempt to avoid contradiction—both by suspending judgment when one is faced with equal yet opposing views and by accepting appearances in everyday affairs.

Gorgias and Heracleitus. It follows that the only way to judge reality is by using both the senses and the intellect, but this too is problematic, for they do not resolve the oppositions in Heracleitus, Democritus, and Gorgias. According to Sextus, we are left with no instruments with which to judge the truth, and no way to prove or disprove Gorgias' claim that nothing at all exists.

Other early arguments establishing sceptical conclusions more directly are collected and systematized in the modes Aenesidemus attributes to the earlier Pyrrhoneans. To a great extent, these arguments are an elaborate presentation of the kinds of antitheses in earlier philosophy, and demonstrate the relativity of belief by contrasting the views that characterize or are produced by different species,[2] cultures, individuals, circumstances,[3] senses, and so on. The Pyrrhoneans' general strategy is summarized in Sextus' introduction to the older modes, which explains that they induce a suspension of judgment (*epoche*) on the question what is ultimately true by demonstrating that beliefs are relative (*PH* 1.38–39), and that we cannot "state what is the nature of each of the objects in its own real purity, but only what nature it appears to possess in its relative character" (*PH* 1.140). We must, therefore, suspend judgment on "the real nature of external objects" (*PH* 1.163).[4] Because all the modes demonstrate the relative nature of belief, Sextus calls the mode of relativity the fundamental mode.

The force of the Pyrrhoneans' early arguments has been underestimated, primarily because commentators have failed to recognize them as an attack on realist truth.[5] (Once recognized, this is obvious, both in Sextus' discussion and in the arguments themselves.) In many cases, the arguments have lost their original force, though even then they are founded on more basic issues not easily evaded. Consider the fourth in Sextus' collection. It contrasts the different states of

2. Cf. Pyrrho's fondness for Homer "because he likened men to wasps, flies and birds" (D.L. 9.67, Aris. in Eus. 763b).

3. The filings of a goat's horn appear white when viewed by themselves but black when combined with the substance of the horn (silver filings appear black by themselves but white when united), while objects seem precious or inconsequential depending on their abundance (gold is much more valuable than water, but water much more important for our lives; water itself is more valuable in cultures where it is scarce).

4. On the nature of external objects, see chapter 6.

5. Cf. Striker: "It may be that the apparent neglect of the Tropes by recent scholars is due, as one colleague has suggested to me, to the fact that they are quite bad arguments. I suppose they are . . . " ("The Ten Modes of Aenesidemus," p. 96).

awareness we have in different sets of circumstances, arguing that one cannot decide which circumstances are the most reliable guide to truth: "For example, objects impress us as dissimilar depending on our being in a natural or an unnatural state, since people who are delirious or divinely possessed think that they hear spirits, while we do not ... The same cloak appears orange to people with a blood suffusion in the eye, but not to me; and the same honey appears sweet to me, but bitter to people with jaundice" (*PH* 1.101–3 Annas and Barnes).[6] Other circumstances in which we view things in opposing ways occur when we are awake and asleep, young and old, hungry and sated,[7] drunk and sober,[8] brave and afraid, distressed and relaxed, and influenced by love or hate.[9]

It is natural to protest that the impairment of our faculties (when dreaming, drunk, sick) is what produces many of the claims the Pyrrhoneans here oppose to ordinary views, but they have an answer. "If anyone says that it is the mixing of certain humours that produces inappropriate appearances from existing objects in people who are in an unnatural state, we should tell him that, since healthy people too have mixed humours, it is possible that these humours are making the external existing objects appear different to the healthy, while they are by nature the way they appear to people in so-called unnatural states. For to grant one lot of humours, but not the other, the power of changing external objects has as air of fiction ... " (*PH* 1.102–3). As Sextus here points out, the claim that unnatural physical states distort perception assumes that physical states affect perception; it is ad hoc to claim this and then deny that it is possible in more ordinary circumstances. Those who say that they perceive the truth in such circumstances are, like anyone else, influenced by circumstances and the states they induce and are not, therefore, "impartial judges" of either their states or objective truth and falsity (*PH* 1.113).

6. One finds versions of the same mode in Diogenes Laertius (9.82) and Philo (178–80). Laertius' version alludes to a famous incident in which Pericles' favourite slave is injured after falling off the top of the Acropolis. An herb revealed to Pericles in a dream cures him. Annas and Barnes (*The Modes of Scepticism*, p. 84) wonder how "Pericles' slave on the roof-top" provides evidence for the fourth mode, but it is not difficult to think of a connection. One of the effects of the fall is probably a delirium cured by the herb; this delirium represents yet another set of circumstances in which a view of the world opposes ordinary notions.

7. Plain food is agreeable to the hungry but not to the full.

8. Those who are drunk approve actions they would not approve when sober.

9. Some have ugly lovers whom they believe attractive.

The basic issues underlying the Pyrrhoneans' early arguments are clearer in later Pyrrhonism, though we shall leave it for chapter 6.[10] For the moment, suffice it to say that early Pyrrhonism is founded on a sceptical attack on realist truth that encompasses traditional antitheses and propounds, in a more sophisticated way than is usually imagined, the subjectivity of belief. According to Pyrrho, it follows that things are by nature equally indifferent, unmeasurable, and undecidable; that nothing can be shown honourable or dishonourable, just or unjust; and that we must abstain from judgments and opinions, saying of each thing that it no more is than is not (Aris. in Eus. 758c–d, D.L. 9.61). Accepting such an outlook, the early Pyrrhoneans refrain from assertions about what is true (thus practicing *aphasia*), denying the mind's movement in either direction (D.L. 9.70) and admitting that there is no way to choose between opposing claims (ibid).

PYRRHONISM AS A PRACTICAL PHILOSOPHY

Evidence for the claim that early Pyrrhonism is an umitigated scepticism is found in a few lines of Diogenes Laertius derived from a book written by Antigonus of Carystus. They refer to some ancient stories that attribute to Pyrrho a rampant and unbridled scepticism that left "nothing to the arbitrament of his senses" and refused to acknowledge "all risks as they came, whether carts, precipices, dogs or what not" (D.L. 9.62). The founder of scepticism is, according to this account, saved from harm by a group of followers who accompany him (and who have, one must suppose, little time for other occupations).

There would be little reason to take such stories seriously if they did not represent the standard view of scepticism. Incredible accounts of any ancient thinker must be taken with a grain of salt (cf. Aristophanes on Socrates, and Diogenes Laertius' discussion of all the ancient thinkers), and there are special problems in the case at hand. To begin with, the stories are not in keeping even with the negative side of Pyrrhonism, for it is always forwarded as a defense of practical concerns. In this respect it is analogous to modern attacks on metaphysics, for the Pyrrhoneans see their scepticism as a means of doing away with the useless speculation of their contemporaries. Instead of solving practical problems, such speculation encourages

10. Sextus does discuss the problem of the criterion in conjunction with the fourth mode (*PH* 1.114–17), but this seems a digression on his part and is not formalized until later modes.

metaphysical fancy, verbal quibbling, paradox, and confusion, and leads to dogmatism and conceit.

Sextus expresses the Pyrrhonean attitude in his discussion of antisceptical philosophers, whom he refers to as the dogmatists. Along with many other commentators, Annas and Barnes suggest that this translation of the Greek creates a tone not found in the sceptics, but this is not the case.[11] The extant information that we have on the Pyrrhoneans shows quite clearly that they make no bones about their attitude to dogmatists, calling them "rash . . . self-loving . . . fools" and "conceited braggarts," and repeatedly accusing them of pride, vanity, and dogmatism in the modern sense (see, e.g., *PH* 1.62, 90, 177; 2.193–94, 205–6, 229, and3.280–81).[12] As Diogenes Laertius writes, "They declared the dogmatic philosophers to be fools, observing that what is concluded *ex hypothesi* [i.e., founded on unquestioned assumption] is properly described not as inquiry but assumption, and by reasoning of this kind one may argue even for impossibilities" (D.L. 9.91). Pyrrho "was, as Timon says, most hostile to Sophists" (D.L. 9.69), while Timon himself scorns and lampoons anti-sceptical philosophers (D.L. 9.111). The tone of the Pyrrhoneans' rejection of the views of other thinkers is heard in Sextus' critique of dialectic, which attacks arguments that would have been familiar to the earlier Pyrrhoneans; Sextus complains that they deal with silly arguments and paradoxes, and not with anything of practical significance.

As regards sophisms the exposure of which is useful, the dialectician will not have a word to say, but will propound for us arguments such as these—"If it is not so that you both have fair horns and have horns, you have horns; but it is not so that you have fair horns and have horns; therefore you have horns." "If a thing moves, it moves either in the spot where it is or where it is not; but it moves neither in the spot where it is (for it is at rest) nor in that where it is not (for how could a thing be active in a spot where it does not so much as exist?)" "Either the existent becomes or the non-existent; now the existent does not become (for it exists); nor yet does the non-existent (for the becoming is passive but the non-existent is not passive); therefore nothing becomes." "Snow is frozen water; but water is black; therefore snow is black." And when he has made a collection of such trash he draws his eyebrows

11. *The Modes of Scepticism*, p. 2. See also Rescher, *Scepticism*, Johnson, *Scepticism*, and Barnes, "Ancient Scepticism and Causation."

12. The suggested alternatives to the word *dogmatist* (*cognitivist*, Rescher and Johnson; *believer*, Barnes) are based on a translation of *dogma* ("belief") that does not recognize the sceptical acceptance of anti-realist notions of belief.

together, and expounds Dialectic and endeavours very solemnly to establish for us by syllogistic proofs that a thing becomes, a thing moves, snow is white, and we do not have horns, although it is probably sufficient to confront the trash with the plain facts, smashing up their positive affirmation with equal contradictory evidence derived from the appearances. (*PH* 2.241–44)[13]

The conundrums Sextus mentions here are propounded by Parmenides, Zeno, Gorgias, Anaxagoras, and the Megarians; Pyrrho and his followers would have known them well. Instead of continuing the philosophical tradition that focuses on such problems, the Pyrrhoneans repudiate them, turning their efforts toward the practical goal of happiness. As Timon says, "I do not care for these wafflers, nor for any other, not for Phaedo, whoever he was, nor for quarrelsome Eucleides, who implanted a frenzied love of contentiousness in the Megarians" (D.L. 2.107 Long and Sedley).

Pyrrho himself is, like Socrates, very much a moralist who rejects science for the goal of equanimity. According to Ascanius of Abdera, he adopts a most noble philosophy (D.L. 9.61). According to others, he does not "inquire into such things as these: what breezes circle Hellas; to what end, and from what quarter each may chance to blow" (D.L. 9.65, cf. 69); Pyrrho is "quite oblivious to all sweet-voiced Science's tales" and perseveres in "great comfort and calm; ever devoid of care, uniformly free from distraction" (*AM* 11.1).

EQUANIMITY AND INDIFFERENCE

It is not his arguments but Pyrrho's psychological goal of equanimity that marks early Pyrrhonism and sounds as the recurrent theme in ancient discussions of his views. Timon writes, "This Pyrrho, this my heart is fain to know, whence peace of mind to thee doth freely flow; why among men thou like a god dost show" (D.L. 9.65). Pyrrho's philosophy is thus an answer to the practical search for happiness, though he denies the usual assumption that it can be attained by cultivating wealth and ordinary pleasure. The latter are not necessarily incompatible with

---

13. Cf. *PH* 2.211, where Sextus ridicules the pride philosophers take in definitions. He asks how silly it would be if he were to use them to ask someone whether he had met a man riding a horse and leading a dog: "O rational mortal animal, receptive of intelligence and science, have you met with an animal capable of laughter, with broad nails and receptive of political science, with his hemispheres seated on a mortal animal capable of neighing and leading a four-footed animal capable of barking?"

Pyrrhonean equanimity (as demonstrated by Timon's life), but it is committed to an indifference to external circumstances that makes it possible to accept any fortune or misfortune, making one invulnerable to fate.

Sextus describes the Pyrrhonean goal of equanimity in a passage that he illustrates with an incident said to befall Alexander's court painter, Apelles (an incident that must have originated in Pyrrho's stay in Alexander's court). Thus:

The Sceptic, having set out to philosophize with the object of passing judgement on the sense-impressions and ascertaining which of them are true and which false, so as to attain quietude (equanimity) thereby, found himself involved in contradictions of equal weight, and being unable to decide between them suspended judgement; and as he was thus in suspense there followed, as it happened, the state of quietude (*ataraxia*) in respect of matters of opinion . . .

The Sceptic, in fact, had the same experience which is said to have befallen the painter Apelles. Once, they say, when he was painting a horse and wished to represent the horse's foam, he was so unsuccessful that he gave up and flung at the picture the sponge he used to wipe the paints off his brush, and the mark of the sponge produced the effect of a horse's foam. So, too, the Sceptics were in hopes of gaining quietude by means of a decision regarding . . . the objects of sense and thought, and unable to effect this they suspended judgement; and they found that quietude, as if by chance, followed upon their suspense, even as a shadow follows its substance. (*PH* 1.26–29)

The rejection of the kinds of questions that preoccupy philosophers is, on this account, a prerequisite for equanimity, though scepticism about what is good and bad also underlies it. As Socrates and Democritus have already demonstrated, such scepticism calls in doubt the claim that anything is bad, and thus promotes indifference to external circumstances. Sextus explains that

the man who opines that anything is by nature good or bad is forever being disquieted: when he is without the thing which he deems good he believes himself to be tormented by things naturally bad and he pursues the things which are, as he thinks, good; when he has obtained them he keeps falling into still more perturbations because of his irrational and immoderate elation, and in his dread of a change of fortune he uses every endeavour to avoid losing the things which he deems good. On the other hand, the man who determines nothing as to what is naturally good or bad neither shuns nor pursues anything eagerly; and, in consequence, he is unperturbed. (*PH* 1.28)

Here uncertainty over what is good and bad keeps one from immoderate disappointment or elation. A similar way of opposing unhappiness is demonstrated in Pyrrho's fondness for Homer's verse: "Ay, friend, die thou; why thus thy fate deplore? Patroclus, thy better, is no more" (D.L. 9.67). Such sentiments hold unhappiness at death in check by reminding us that those who are more deserving have suffered a similar fate; it is unclear that we are badly done by (as Democritus says, we can thus retain our contentment by dwelling on those worse off than ourselves). The possibility of eliminating unsettling thoughts by doubting them explains Pyrrho's remark that anyone who wishes to be happy must ask after the nature of things, must understand that they are equally indifferent, unmeasurable, and undecidable, and must refrain from judgment and assertion (Aris. in Eus. 758c–d).

Perhaps in answer to claims that Pyrrho's asceticism is too severe, the later Pyrrhoneans qualify their account of *ataraxia* by stating that they are not "wholly untroubled" (for they are at times cold, thirsty, and sick), adding that they moderate their feeling even in unavoidable misfortune, and that this makes them better off than others. Pyrrho may adopt a stronger view; it is said that he maintained the same composure at all times (D.L. 9.63) and did not so much as frown when septic salves and surgical and caustic remedies were applied to a wound that he sustained (D.L. 9.67). Elsewhere he exhibits indifference: when he rebukes a follower who treats him too lavishly (*Deip* 419d–e); in his fondness for all the passages of Homer that "dwell on the unstable purpose, vain pursuits, and childish folly of man" (D.L. 9.67); and in the statement that, discovered talking to himself (perhaps constructing antitheses to sustain *ataraxia*), he is training to be good (D.L. 9.64).

Pyrrho's follower Eurylocheus is noted by Diogenes Laertius precisely because he "fell short of his professions," failing to retain his composure and on one occasion becoming so angry that he seized a spit and chased his cook into the market (ibid 9.68). Pyrrho himself must have had more success controlling his emotions, for he is highly respected by philosophers like Timon, Nausiphanes, and Epicurus (ibid 9.64), and by his fellow citizens, who erect a statue in his honour (Pausanias),[14] make him a high priest, and on his account exempt philosophers from taxes (D.L. 9.64).

14. In his description of the Eleans' Corcyrean portico, he writes: "Down the centre of it the roof is supported, not by pillars, but by a wall, beside which on either side have been dedicated statues. On the side towards the market place stands a statue of Pyrrho, son of Pistocrates, a sophist who never brought himself to make a definite admission on any matter. The tomb also of Pyrrho is not far from the town of the Eleans" (6.24.5 Jones).

Reputedly Pyrrho lived a life of honourable poverty with his sister Philista, "now and then even taking things for sale to the market, poultry, perchance, or pigs, and he would dust the things in the house, quite indifferent as to what he did. They say he showed his indifference by washing a porker" (D.L. 9.66). This indifference is not to the senses, as in unmitigated scepticism (indifference that would make Pyrrho a comic character rather than a moral hero); rather it encompasses a willingness to accept any circumstance with composure. Indifference to the senses (and the complete rejection of speech that some authors associate with *aphasia*) would be incompatible with the activities mentioned here and in numerous other anecdotes that show him accepting his senses without pause or explanation (see, e.g., Eus. 761a, D.L. 9.63 and below).[15]

Pyrrho's aim of equanimity is itself at odds with the suggestion that he is an unmitigated sceptic, for someone who ignores precipices, trees, and moving carts is unlikely to attain the state of mental peace that is the aim of Pyrrho's life. Such an attitude is rather bound to bring calamity, and one must wonder how Pyrrho could adopt it and survive his reported ninety years. More in keeping with his moral goals is the figure we find portrayed in another anecdote: "When his fellow passengers on board a ship were all unnerved by a storm, he kept calm and confident, pointing to a little pig . . . that went on eating, and telling them that such was the unperturbed state in which the wise man should keep himself" (D.L. 9.68). Hallie remarks:

Pyrrho did not strip himself, or try to do so, of his sensibilities; he was solicitous of the feelings of his fellow passengers enough to give them a . . . demonstration, and he advocated a life imitative of a pig calmly eating rather than imitative of an ascetic trying to act as if he had no body. This . . . story exemplifies the old Greek notion of moderation, or *metriopatheia*, which is a commonsensical notion having to do with keeping our passions under control when confronted with natural forces that are beyond our control. It is a very different matter from the extinction of all awareness, all human sympathy. It is consistent with living a life in a community of men; in fact it is quite useful for such a life. And the more or less "known" facts of Pyrrho's life attest to the success with which he lived in . . . Elis. ("A Polemical Introduction," pp. 12–13, cf. *PH* 1.25, 3.236 and *AM*, 11.155, 161)

---

15. Anecdotes are noticeably absent of the followers who are said to keep him from harm.

Rather than being an enigma, Pyrrho's reputation is on this account entirely understandable; it is built upon a strength of character that comes of the sceptical rejection of unsettling beliefs. As he might have noted in the case at hand, unsubstantiated claims (that the storm will not abate, that the ship will be destroyed, that death in these circumstances is a terrible fate, that it is unfair that one should die) are the cause of fear and panic. Scepticism can, by showing their unsubstantiated nature, help ensure composure.

Burnyeat, Zeller, and Maccoll defend the claim that Pyrrho wished to strip himself even of his senses. They appeal to a famous incident: "When a cur rushed at him and terrified him, he answered his critic that it is difficult to completely strip oneself of one's humanity, but that one should strive with all one's might against facts, by deeds if possible, and if not, in word" (D.L. 9.66, cf. Eus. 763). The assertion that this shows Pyrrho rejects the senses does not, however, sit with so many other anecdotes demonstrating his reliance on them. What is special about the incident in question is not Pyrrho's use of sense perception, but his terror and his failure to retain peace of mind; the departure from the equanimity he espouses gives rise to criticism. His excuse, that he is only human, means that it is difficult to strip oneself of human fears and frailties, and that we must strive against them (and the facts that produce them) by deeds and, if not, then at least in what we say.[16]

Philosophers who regularly marvel at Socrates' composure have failed to see that Pyrrho practices the same. Sometimes they interpret Pyrrhonism as the abandonment of moral goals and moral striving. Though granting them the acceptance of custom and convention, Burnyeat says that the Pyrrhoneans do not identify with the traditional values they adopt; rather they accept them in the nonchalant way that we might toss a coin.[17] In fact, indifference to external circumstances means that the Pyrrhoneans are (as Sextus says at *AM* 11.164–66) more willing to suffer punishment, pain, and persecution in trying to be virtuous. Their ideal of *aphasia* in misfortune is exemplified by Praylus of the Troad, a man of "such unflinching courage" that, although unjustly accused and condemned, "he patiently suffered a traitor's death without deigning to speak one word to his fellow citizens" (D.L. 9.115). Even in more mundane circumstances, Pyrrhonism is not the

16. On another occasion, Pyrrho justifies his anger over how his sister has been treated by replying to the man who blamed him, "It is not over a weak woman that one should display indifference" (D.L. 9.66).
17. "Can the Sceptic Live His Scepticism?" pp. 131–32.

rejection of moral striving, for it requires a constant struggle against anger, impatience, disappointment, jealousy, shame, and other human weaknesses. Anyone who has tried to retain equanimity in the midst of calamity or pain must see that this is no easy matter.[18]

APPEARANCES

Pyrrho's statement that we should refrain from assertion (practicing *aphasia*) means that we should resign ourselves to our inability to know what is true in the realist sense. We have already noted that this leaves room for anti-realist conceptions of belief, though this has not been appreciated in the secondary literature. Instead of claiming that the Pyrrhonean is a man who can see "no reason to believe *p* rather than *not-p*,"[19] Burnyeat should, for example, say that the Pyrrhonean can see no reason to believe *p* rather than *not-p* in the realist sense, especially as Burnyeat grants the realist character of Greek truth.

We have no detailed account of the belief that Pyrrho adopts in day to day affairs, though it is probable that he accepts appearances (*phainomena*) as a subjective guide to life. This is in keeping with his Democritean heritage and with the views of his teachers Metrodorus and Anaxarchus, his follower Timon, and later Pyrrhonism. His belief in scepticism can be seen as yet another appearance he accepts (an inability to know realist truth appears to be the lot of humankind).[20] According to Aenesidemus, Pyrrho determines nothing dogmatically and guides himself by apparent facts (D.L. 9. 106).[21]

Certainly this is the outlook of Pyrrho's most famous student, Timon of Phlius. None of the details of his active life—his literary works, his fondness for wine and gardens, and the anecdotes about him—are compatible with an unmitigated scepticism, though he expresses the

---

18. He is not a sceptic, but Thoreau has something similar in mind when he writes: "Let us spend one day as deliberately as Nature, and not be thrown off the track by every nutshell and misquito's wing that falls upon the rails. Let us rise early and fast, or break fast gently, and without perturbation; let company come and let company go, let the bells ring and the children cry,—determined to make a day of it. Why should we knock under and go with the stream?" (*Walden*, p. 70).

19. See Burnyeat, "Can the Sceptic Live His Scepticism?" pp. 131–32.

20. This might seem to contradict his conclusions, but the apparent contradiction is explained below.

21. Cf. 103 and 62 ("it was only his philosophy that was based upon suspension of judgment, and he did not lack foresight in his everyday acts").

goals of indifference and tranquillity in his remark that "desire is absolutely the first of all bad things," (Athenaeus 337, Long and Sedley). He would stop his writing when disturbed, "his earnest goal being to maintain his peace of mind" (D.L. 9.113).[22] He makes his practical affairs compatible with scepticism by accepting appearances and the impressions (*phantasiai*, both sense impressions and impressions more generally)[23] they incorporate, all the while suspending judgment on the question what is true in realist terms. "That honey is [in itself] sweet I do not affirm," he says, in answer to a standard opposition, "but I agree that it appears so" (D.L. 9.105, Long and Sedley). Indeed, "the appearance is [accepted as] omnipotent wherever it goes" (*AM* 7.30, D.L. 9.105). Both Timon and Pyrrho therefore live by custom and by nature (Aris. in Eus. 759d, 762a and D.L. 9.61, 105), for things appear right and wrong and true and false depending on natural necessity and cultural convention.

The Pyrrhonean notion of appearances shows up in later Pyrrhonism, which adopts Timon's dictum that appearances are omnipotent (*AM* 7.30, D.L. 9.103–5), employs his example (honey appears sweet), and accepts nature and convention as a basis for practical affairs (see *PH* 1.19–24 and *AM* 11.20, where Timon's remarks contain the first indication of a practical criterion).[24] According to Diogenes Laertius, the Pyrrhoneans in general claim that they do not accept an unmitigated scepticism: "We recognize that it is day and that we are alive, and many other apparent facts in life," suspending judgment only on those (realist) claims "about which our opponents argue so positively, claiming to have definitely apprehended them" (D.L. 9.103). Sextus concurs, maintaining that the Pyrrhoneans do not overthrow appear-

---

22. In all likelihood, by constructing antitheses that oppose disturbing thoughts.

23. See Burnyeat, "Can the Sceptic Live His Scepticism?" pp. 126–27. The important point is that while *phainomena* and *phantasiai* are often used to refer to sense impressions, they may refer to impressions produced in other ways (to the impression, e.g., shared by all opponents of Protagoras, that not every impression is true, *AM* 7.390). Stough has taken exception to Burnyeat's account of *phantasiai* ("Sextus Empiricus on Non-Assertion," fn. 6), but it seems arbitrary to set it apart from appearances, especially as that would not be in keeping with the Stoic use of the term *phantasiai*. Diogenes Laertius comments: "According to them some presentations [*phantasiai*] are data of sense and others are not; the former are the impressions conveyed through one or more sense-organs; while the latter, which are not data of sense, are those received through the mind itself, as in the case of incorporeal things and all the other presentations which are received by reason" (7.51).

24. See Stough, *Greek Scepticism*, p. 25.

ances, and that those who say so seem unacquainted with "the statements of our School" (*PH* 1.19). He goes on to invoke Timon's example, saying that the sceptic grants that honey appears sweet, confining doubt to the question whether it is sweet "in its essence" (cf. *PH* 1.213).

PYRRHONISM AND IDEALISM

Like other kinds of scepticism, early Pyrrhonism is distinguished from idealism by its unwillingness to grant our knowledge of our own impressions (and, therefore, appearances). Such doubts are not explicitly discussed in the extant evidence, but they are implied by Pyrrho and Timon's strident rejection of all opinion, and by their failure to exempt claims about what appears to be the case from their sceptical conclusions (they *accept* such claims in the pursuit of practical affairs, but not because they can be proved true). This aspect of Pyrrhonism surfaces in later Pyrrhonism, where Sextus carefully avoids the claim that humans can know appearances. The Pyrrhoneans, he argues, do not overthrow sense impressions and do not doubt the appearance itself, for "no one, I suppose, disputes that the underlying object has this or that appearance; the point in dispute is whether the object is in reality such as it appears to be" (see *PH* 1.19–22). This means only that the Pyrrhonean refrains from disputing appearances, not that they are indisputable. "Even if we do actually argue against them directly, we do not propound such arguments with the intention of abolishing appearance, but by way of pointing out the rashness of the Dogmatists; for if reason is such a trickster as to all but snatch away the appearances from under our very eyes, surely we should view it with suspicion in the case of things non-evident [things beyond appearances] so as not to be rash in following it" (*PH* 1.20). Appearances are to be accepted and adhered to, not because humans can establish their true nature, but because they need a basis for practical affairs. The acceptance of appearance thus represents a move to mitigated scepticism rather than to idealism, though the Pyrrhoneans interpret appearances as subjective determinants of belief, thus accepting them in an anti-realist sense.

THE CONSISTENCY OF EARLY PYRRHONISM

While this suggests that early Pyrrhonism encompasses a perspective compatible with belief and practical affairs, there is a problem with the way Pyrrho expresses his conclusions. His philosophy seems to permit only the conclusion that certain things *appear* to be the case, but Timon tells us that he holds that things *are* by nature equally indifferent, unmeasurable, and undecidable; that claims *are* neither true nor false; and that each thing *is* no more real than not (Aris. in Eus. 758c–d).[25] According to Diogenes Laertius, for Pyrrho "there *is* nothing truly existent . . . for each thing *is* no more this than that" (D.L. 9.61). Taken at face value, such claims are even contradictory; they suggest that nothing is true or false, but that they themselves are true; that things are indeterminable, but that this can be determined; that things are no more this than that, but that they are as Pyrrho says.

We can easily avoid this contradiction by interpreting Pyrrho's claims as claims about appearances, and by assuming that he uses ordinary assertions to express appearances. This aligns his philosophical pronouncements with his mitigated scepticism and is in keeping with Pyrrhonean arguments, which make things *appear* indeterminate, neither true nor false, and no more this than that (for any claim can be opposed). That this is the correct interpretation of Pyrrho's claims is suggested by later Pyrrhonism, which explicitly uses ordinary language and the verb "to be" (*einai*) to indicate appearances. Sextus writes at the beginning of "Against the Ethicists," that

it will, perhaps, be fitting to explain first that the word "is" (*esti*) has two meanings, one of these being "really exists" (as, at the present moment, we say "it is day" for "day really exists"); and the other "appears" (as some of the mathematicians are frequently in the habit of saying that the distance between two stars "is" a cubit's length, this being equivalent to "appears to be but is not really"; for perhaps it is really "one hundred stades" but appears to be a cubit owing to its height and owing to the distance from the eye) . . . [A]s the element "are" is twofold in meaning [in sentences of the form "X are Y"], we insert the "are" as indicative not of real existence but of appearance. (*AM* 11.18–19)

The same point is made repeatedly when Sextus discusses the Pyrrhoneans' standard ways of announcing sceptical conclusions (*PH* 1.187–209). He gives a similar account of Pyrrho's formula *ou mallon* ("no more this than that"), and distinguishes between the two meanings of "to be" in conjunction with the eighth mode (the mode of relativity), which he attributes to the earlier Pyrrhoneans (*PH* 1.135).

That Pyrrho and his followers are aware of the question of inconsis-

25. Other than a poem written for Alexander of Macedon (*AM* 1.282), Pyrrho apparently wrote nothing, so this is as close to his views as we can get.

tency and adopt an interpretation of their sceptical assertions to avoid it seems confirmed by Timon, who maintains (in the *Pytho*) that the phrase "no more this than that" does not make or determine any claims about absolute reality, and only signifies the withholding of assent" (D.L. 9.76). Similarly, Aristocles says, Timon holds that the Pyrrhonean claim "no more this than that" can be understood as the question, "Why yes, why no, why the question 'why' itself?" (Eus., 759c). According to Sextus, Timon maintains that he describes (and questions)[26] every fact as good, bad, or indifferent depending on appearance (*AM* 11.20, cf. 140).

On this reading, the early Pyrrhoneans (like Protagoras, Metrodorus, and the Cyrenaics before them) recognize that they need an interpretation of their own claims to make them consistent with their outlook. Combined with the notion that appearances are omnipotent, Timon's remark that he does not move beyond the customary suggests that appearances rule not merely the sceptic's, but everyone's, claims about what is the case (D.L. 9.105). If this is his view, then ordinary claims in practical affairs are about appearances and the Pyrrhoneans merely recognize their real nature, in the process anticipating modern anti-realism, for it too proposes an anti-realist interpretation of ordinary language. For our purposes, the important point is that the Pyrrhonean appeal to appearances preserves the consistency of Pyrrhonism, undermining the standard charges brought against it. They serve, like the standard view of Pyrrho, as an indictment of ourselves rather than of the sceptics.

TOWARD LATER PYRRHONISM

From the time of Timon until the death of Sextus in A.D. 210, there extends a long (and perhaps fragmented) succession of Pyrrhonean philosophers.[27] Little is known about their lives and works, though there is no reason to think that they differ greatly from

26. The remark is ambiguous (see Stough, *Greek Scepticism*, p. 25).

27. According to Hippobotus and Sotion (D.L. 9.115–16), the Pyrrhonean tradition incorporates the following succession of philosophers: Pyrrho, Timon, Dioscurides of Cyprus, Nicolochus of Rhodes, Praylus of the Troad, Euphranor of Seleucia, Eubulus of Alexandria, Ptolemy, Sarpedon, Heraclides, Aenesidemus of Cnossus, Zeuxippus, Zeuxis of the angular foot, Antiochus of Laodicea on the Lycus, Theiodas of Laodecia, Menodotus of Nicomedia, Herodotus of Tarsus (son of Arieus), Sextus Empiricus, and Saturnis called Cythenas. One important Pyrrhonean not in this list is Agrippa, to whom Sextus ascribes five modes.

the Pyrrhoneans we know. The most significant change in Pyrrhonism is a move toward a more systematic and comprehensive treatment of the different themes already found in early Pyrrhonism. Appearances remain the focal point of the Pyrrhoneans' positive philosophy. Aenesidemus, Zeuxis, Antiochus of Laodicea, and Appellas are all said to accept them as their guide to life (D.L. 9.106). According to Philostratus, Favorinus concedes, in his books on Pyrrho, the Pyrrhonean ability to make legal judgments (491).

The most complete account of Pyrrhonism is found in the works of Sextus. He propounds a more sophisticated version of the views we have already seen in early Pyrrhonism. Before we turn to the details of his views we must, however, discuss the Academy, for it becomes the major school of scepticism in the interlude between Timon's death and the resurrection of Pyrrhonism as a major force at the beginning of the first century B.C. Here too we find a mitigated outlook that contradicts the standard view of ancient scepticism.

V

Scepticism in the Academy

Academic scepticism (and the "New" Academy)[1] begins with Arcesilaus. Born in Pitane in Aeolis, he is said to have studied mathematics, poetry, and philosophy, and to have become the head of the Academy when Crates died in 262 B.C. Timon asserts that he mixed "sound sense with wily cavils."Anecdotes point to a keen intellect and a sharp tongue.[2] Plutarch describes him as "the best loved" philosopher of the time (*Ad Col* 1121F).

To understand how scepticism beomes a part of the Academy, we must recall that many ancient thinkers see Plato differently than we do. Rather than stress his commitment to reason and transcendental truth, they interpret him as a sceptic, citing his use of dialectic, his account of Socrates, and the indeterminate nature of many of his dialogues (cf. chap. 3). Cicero, for example, says that Plato is a sceptic because he argues pro and contra, states nothing positively, inquires into everything, and makes no certain statements (*Ac* 1.46). It must have been a similar interpretation that allowed Arcesilaus to initiate the sceptical phase of the Academy.

1. The history of the Academy is sometimes more finely divided, and it is possible to distinguish the Middle or Second Academy of Arcesilaus from the New or Third Academy beginning with Carneades. Here, it is more convenient to treat the sceptical phase of the Academy as a unity, distinguishing Arcesilaus and Carneades where this is necessary or appropriate.

2. When asked why pupils from all the schools went to Epicurus but converts were never made of Epicureans, he replies that "men can become eunuchs, but a eunuch never becomes a man" (D.L. 4.43). On another occasion: "When some one of immodest life denied that one thing seemed to him greater than another, he rejoined, 'Then six inches and ten inches are all the same to you?'" (D.L. 4.34).

Despite his allegiance to Plato Arcesilaus has an outlook similar to Pyrrho's, and it is likely that he was influenced by early Pyrrhonism as well as other philosophical developments.[3] Like Pyrrho, he provides a positive basis for belief, though his philosophy is distinguished by the rivalry between the Academy and the Stoa and by his consequent emphasis on a critique of Stoic epistemology.

After Arcesilaus, the leadership of the Academy passes to Lacydes, to Telecles and Evander, and then to Hegesinus (D.L. 4.60). Little is known about their views, though they apparently preserve Arcesilaus' teaching. The next head of the Academy is Carneades, the leader of the "Third" Academy and the founder of the most sophisticated form of academic scepticism. Like Arcesilaus, he attacks the Stoics and provides a positive basis for belief. According to Diogenes Laertius, he "studied carefully the writings of the Stoics and particularly those of Chrysippus, and by combating these successfully he became so famous that he would often say, 'Without Chrysippus,where should I have been?'" (D.L. 4.62).[4] The last head of the sceptical Academy is Carneades' follower and companion, Clitomachus. The school then passes into the hands of Philo of Larissa, who institutes a more dogmatic way of thinking and thus ends its scepticism.[5]

The traditional view of academic scepticism can be illustrated with an anecdote related by Numenius (Eus. 734–36). It tells how the servants of Lacydes steal from him in so clever a fashion that he concludes the truth about his stores cannot be known and goes to study with Arcesilaus. Even when their culpability comes to light, they continue to steal, seeking advice from the Stoics and defending themselves by claiming that one cannot know what has happened to the stores. This eventually forces Lacydes to reject his scepticism in practical affairs. Bayle comments:

3. As Zeller puts it in reference to Pyrrho's probable influence on Arcesilaus, "it is not in itself probable that the learned originator of this line of thought in the Academy should have ignored the views of a philosopher whose work had been carried on in Elis in his own lifetime, and whose distinguished pupil [Timon], a personal acquaintance of his own, was then working at Athens as a prolific writer" (*Stoics, Epicureans and Sceptics*, p. 528). Close ties are suggested by Timon, Ariston, Numenius, and Sextus (D.L. 4.33, *PH* 1.232–33 and Num. in Eus. 729c, 731a–b).

4. Academic arguments are nonetheless applicable to the views of all the major schools, and Sextus writes that Carneades' arguments are arrayed "not only against the Stoics, but against all his predecessors" (*AM* 7.159, cf. *Ac* 2.7).

5. On the philosophy of the Academy after Clitomachus, see Dillon, *The Middle Platonists*, and Tarrant, *Scepticism or Platonism?*

This is a pretty story, and if it were put into the hands of La Fontaine, he could make it most diverting. But who does not see that it was fabricated by a pious fraud of the Stoics? This method is used at all times in all countries. Men have always tried, and still try, to ridicule the doctrine and the person of their adversaries' views. This passion has been followed so blindly against the . . . sceptics that not only good faith, but probability as well has been set aside. For the sceptics have never denied that in the ordinary course of life men have to conduct themselves by the testimony of the senses. The sceptics have only denied that it was certain that the absolute nature of the objects is entirely such as it appears. (123 Popkin)

Bayle's scepticism is all the more appropriate given that Numenius is not a reliable guide to scepticism and colours his anecdotes (Diogenes Laertius relates essentially the same story without making it a critique of scepticism in 4.59).[6] His attitude to scepticism can be seen in his claim that Carneades enslaved men's souls and was, after Arcesilaus, "evil upon evil" (Eus., 737d). A more sympathetic look at academic scepticism shows that it cannot be so easily dismissed.

THE ARGUMENTS FOR ACADEMIC SCEPTICISM

Cicero's assertion that the New Academy attains its goals "by arguing on both sides" (*Ac* 1.45–46, cf. 2.8), and his description of the teaching practices of the Academy, which focus on opposing arguments (see *De Fin* 2.2, quoted below), show the importance of antithesis in academic arguments. According to Diogenes Laertius, Arcesilaus was the first in the Academy "to argue on both sides of a question" and the first "to suspend his judgement owing to the contradictions of opposing arguments" (D.L. 4.28). Carneades is famous for his antithetical arguments in Rome, where he speaks with equal eloquence for justice and against it. (Some have argued against the academic commitment to *equal* opposition, but I shall take issue with their views as I proceed.)

Before we turn to the academics' central arguments, it is important to see that they are forwarded against a multifarious background of other arguments casting doubt on the human ability to establish truth. Our most complete example of an extended academic argument is Cicero's *Academica*. Three themes it develops are the limits of perception, the impossibility of resolving paradox, and the evidence for

6. Numenius has a tendency to colour his discussion, as is evident if one compares his and Laertius' account of Mentor's expulsion from the·Academy (Eus. 736 d, D.L. 4.64).

scepticism in the views of earlier philosophers. In developing the first, Cicero attacks the weakness of the sense of sight, noting that it is subject to illusion (the oar, the pigeon's neck, the ship);[7] that we cannot see great distances; that certain birds have better eyesight; that the sun looks "about a foot in diameter"; and that we cannot distinguish twins, eggs, hairs, grains, or the different markings of a seal (*Ac* 2.79–85).[8] To demonstrate the impossibility of resolving paradox, he invokes the liar, proving that some propositions are neither true nor false (the proposition "I am lying" can be neither), and the *sorites*, which undermines ordinary distinctions by appealing to small differences that cannot be distinguished.[9] When Cicero invokes the views of earlier philosophers, he enumerates a staggering list of thinkers, arguing that we cannot choose between them. Appealing to the authority of Xenophanes, Parmenides, Anaxagoras, Democritus, Metrodorus, Socrates, Plato, and the Cyrenaics, he tells Lucullus that "the views we hold are ones that you yourselves admit to have been approved by the noblest of philosophers" (*Ac* 2.72, cf. 72–76, 129–34, 142–44).

One argument that merits special comment is the academic version of Descartes' famous reasoning in the first chapter of his *Meditations* (*Ac* 2.47–48). Though Burnyeat, Popkin, Matson, and Descartes[10] say that there is something new in his proposal that humans may be deceived by supernatural deception (a hypothesis Beck has called "the most daring metaphysical supposition the human mind can invent"),[11] the academics argue similarly; indeed, their suggestion that God may deceive us could well be the source of Descartes' argument.[12] Taken within the broader context of the *Academica*, the argument cites (as does Descartes) dreams, illusions, madness, and supernatural deception as grounds

7. The oar looks bent in water, the pigeon's neck seems to change in colour, and land appears to move to someone on board a ship.

8. These limits to perception form the basis of Carneades' claim that God must have additional kinds of sense perception (*AM* 9.140).

9. He states that "if we are asked by gradual stages, is such and such a person a rich man or a poor man, famous or undistinguished, are yonder objects many or few, great or small, long or short, broad or narrow, we do not know at what point in the addition or subtraction to give a definite answer" (*Ac* 2.92–93, cf. 93–94). A more popular version of the argument reasons that taking one hair from the face of a bearded man will not take away the beard, and therefore if we remove hairs one by one, the beard remains (for we take, at each stage, one hair from a man who was previously said to have a beard).

10. See chapter 1.

11. Beck, *The Metaphysics of Descartes*, p. 71.

12. As is suggested by Gouhier (*La Pensée metaphysique de Descartes*, p. 35), Robin (*Pyrrhon et le scepticisme grec*, pp. 89–90), and myself (see fn. 13 below).

for doubt. It is impossible to discuss the details here (the reader is referred to my account elsewhere),[13] though, it should be noted commentators are mistaken when they maintain that the argument only raises doubts about sense impressions (it questions all belief),[14] or that it does not suggest that *all* impressions are possibly mistaken (the "whole totality" is, at least implicitly, called in question).[15] Rather than endorse a weaker version of Descartes' reasoning, the academics push doubt further by rejecting clear and perspicuous impressions as guarantees of truth,[16] and by questioning God's beneficence. The latter undermines Descartes' suggestion that God's goodness makes impossible supernatural deception.[17]

13. Groarke, "Descartes' First Meditation."

14. In *Descartes against the Sceptics*, E. M. Curley suggests that (unlike Descartes) the academics do not raise doubts about the "eternal" truths of logic and geometry, but this seems mistaken. In a general way, the academics raise such doubts whenever they appeal to paradoxes such as the liar, which they use to cast doubt on the basic truths of logic. In the specific argument in question, the academics reason that man cannot know the truth of *visa*, a term Cicero uses to translate *phantasiai*. We have already seen that *phantasiai* include the impressions that result from purely rational deduction, however, and are not confined to sense impressions (see again D.L. 7.51). Cicero makes the same point in the *Academica* (2.42). In keeping with this, the impressions God is said to send include messages in oracles, auspices, and sacrifices, and they encompass more than sense impressions (i.e., moral commands, religious truths, and predictions about the future).

15. According to Burnyeat ("Idealism in Greek Philosophy," p. 47), the academics do not go as far as Descartes because they do not suggest that "the whole totality" of our impressions may be false. Two things must be said in answer to this suggestion.

First, that it is not in keeping with the spirit of Greek philosophy, in which doubts about the totality of our ordinary beliefs are commonplace (in, e.g., the views of Gorgias, Xeniades, Parmenides, and the Pyrrhoneans). Burnyeat dismisses Gorgias' arguments as mere rhetorical display, but the same might be said of Descartes, who is not committed to his doubts and eventually calls them "ridiculous" (*Oeuvres*, p. 88; *Philosophical Works*, Haldane and Ross, p. 199). The important point is that Gorgias' arguments (and even Xeniades' views) raise questions about all beliefs and are taken seriously by sceptics.

Second, it must be said that Burnyeat's argument is founded on an artificial distinction between individual impressions and groups of impressions. The distinction collapses once we recognize that the impression that a group of impressions is not mistaken is *an* impression and thus called in question by the academics' universal questioning of (single) impressions. We should note in this regard that many of the individual impressions discussed by the academics are impressions that some group of impressions (in dreaming, for example) are veridical.

16. Typically, by using the academic argument we discuss below.

17. Thus they suggest that God is beyond the virtues (*DND* 3.38–39) and at least consider the possibility that he is not bound by moral law, for nothing is above him (*AM* 9.176). More generally, it is to be noted that the Greek account of the gods leaves more room for doubting their goodness than does Christianity, and that this makes a more serious scepticism possible (something similar can be said of al-Ghazali's scepticism in Islamic thought).

The central academic argument is typically (though not always)[18] forwarded as an attack on the Stoic claim that humans can use the *phantasiai kataleptikai* (the "cognitive" impressions, characterized by their clear and compelling nature) as a criterion of truth. In answer to this, both Arcesilaus and Carneades[19] argue that any such impression can be paired with an equally compelling impression which is false, and that no impression can, therefore, be certain. As Cicero puts the point, "Some impressions are true, others false; and what is false cannot be perceived [as true]. But a true impression is invariably of such a sort that a false impression . . . could be of exactly the same sort; and among impressions of such a sort that there is no difference between them, it cannot occur that some are capable of being perceived and others not. Therefore, there is no impression that can be perceived "(*Ac* 2.40–41, cf. 77–78, 83 and *AM* 7.252).

The academic claim that an apparently true impression can always be paired with a false impression of "exactly the same sort" is backed by an appeal to a set of clear, distinct, convincing, but ultimately false impressions experienced in dreams, illusions, and cases where convictions turn out to be mistaken. The key point is that these impressions demonstrate our beliefs to be convincing for subjective reasons, and not because they are true from a realist point of view. As Carneades recognizes,

the impression is an affection of the living creature which reveals both itself and the other object . . . When we look at an object we put our sense of sight into a certain condition, and not in the same condition that it was in before we looked; and owing to such an alteration we perceive, in fact, two things, one the alteration itself, which is the impression, and, secondly, that which produced the alteration, which is the visible object. And similarly in the case of the other senses. So then, just as light shows both itself and all things within it, so also the impression, which is the primary factor in the cognition of the living creature, must, like light, both reveal itself and be indicative of the evident object which produced it. But since it does not always indicate the true object, but often deceives and, like bad messengers, misreports those who dispatched it, it has necessarily resulted that we cannot admit every impression as a criterion of truth, but—if any—only that which is true. So then again, since there is no true impression of such a kind that it cannot be false, but a false impression is found to exist exactly resembling every apparently true impression . . . [it is impossible to establish a criterion of truth]. (*AM* 7.161–64)

18. Sextus presents a version aimed "at all of Carneades' predecessors" (*AM* 7.159, cf. 166).

19. See *Ac* 2.77–78, and *AM* 7, where the argument is attributed to Arcesilaus at 153–54 and to Carneades at 159 and 164 (cf. Eus. 736d).

Cicero makes the same point in his account of the academic version of Descartes' argument for scepticism, suggesting that "the mind is capable of entirely self-originated motion" and that it is therefore possible to have false impressions that are indistinguishable from true ones. It is "just as if people . . . shiver and turn pale either of themselves or as a result of . . . some terrifying external object, with nothing to distinguish between the two kinds of shivering and pallor, and without any difference between the internal state of feeling and the one that came from without" (*Ac* 2.48). Here the problem is that we have no way of telling when the subjective aspects of perception reflect truth.

ACADEMIC ARGUMENTS, PROBABILITY, AND EQUAL OPPOSITION

According to Striker, the academics' central argument is weaker than the arguments put forth by the Pyrrhoneans and can be used to distinguish the two philosophies. For while the Pyrrhoneans are said to establish the equal force of opposing points of view (*isostheneia*), the ability to pair any apparently true impression with an equally convincing false impression shows only that "we can never be *certain* that a given impression is true."[20] If a cognitive impression is, for example, false only rarely (say, ten percent of the time), it will be possible to pair it with a false impression, though it will still be (90 percent) probable, and it follows that there will not be equal evidence for it and against it. Striker concludes that there is a fundamental difference between academic and Pyrrhonean ways of arguing.

It is, however, unlikely that the academics would accept the conclusion that their scepticism leaves room for the probability of belief. Before we see why, we should note two other problems that undermine Striker's argument. The first is textual evidence that clearly links the academics and their central argument with the idea of equal opposition (the texts said to contradict it are, we shall see, compatible).[21] Cicero, for example, says that Arcesilaus convinced his hearers "by arguing against the opinions of all men so that when equally weighty reasons were found on opposite sides of the same subject, it was easier to withhold assent" (*Ac* 1.45–46). Arcesilaus' belief in equal opposition is also reported by Plutarch (*Ad Col* 1124A), Eusebius

20. Striker, "Sceptical Strategies," p. 59.
21. The claim that the Academics do not make "everything as uncertain as whether the stars are even or odd in number" has to do with the Academics' *response* to sceptical conclusions (see below and cf. Striker, ibid., p. 60).

(726d), and Sextus (*PH* 1.232, cf. Eus. 731b). According to Hippolytus, the academic school uses the Pyrrhonean formula "no more this than that" to express its scepticism (*Haer* 1.23.3). The formula is associated with Carneades, and with his and Arcesilaus' central argument when Numenius says that "having taken on one side something false but like the truth and on the other a like thing apprehended by the cognitive impression, and having balanced them against each other, he [Carneades] granted neither the true nor the false, or no more the one than the other [*ou mallon*] . . . " (Num. in Eus. 738a DeLacy). Given such conclusions, the academics are attacked by Cicero's antagonist in the *Academica*, who asks how they can be confident of their own doctrines when they "loudly proclaim that they are no more true than false" (*Ac*, 2.43). Any lingering doubts about the intended nature of the central academic argument should be eliminated by Sextus, who uses it when he himself attacks the Stoics, though he is, as always, establishing equal opposition (*AM* 7.402–22).

To see why the ancient sceptics take the academics' argument to establish equal opposition, we must consider the context in which the argument develops. Here we find the second problem with Striker's account, for it employs a modern notion of probability that plays no role in the sceptic-dogmatist debate. None of the ancient sceptics claim to establish the equal *probability* of opposing arguments; this notion is, in general, foreign to ancient ways of thinking.[22] The establishment of equal probability would require an enumeration that determines how frequently certain beliefs are true, but this is not how the sceptics proceed. On the contrary, their attempt to establish equal opposition is

22. The notion that *isostheneia* means "equal probability" confuses a vague notion of plausibility with a modern mathematical notion that has a precision and objectivity foreign to ancient thought. The idea that Homer is the first sceptic because he gives different views at different times, is never definite or dogmatic, and grants the equal value of contradictory sayings (D.L. 9.71, 73–74) suggests how loose ancient accounts of equal evidence are. For the most part, the sceptics and their adversaries judge arguments by their rhetorical force, not by some objective measure of probability. Within scepticism, this is reflected in the sceptics' rhetorical ability (see Eus., 731–733, 736–738 and D.L., 4.37, 62, where we read that "every opinion of Carneades was victorious," that "in persuasiveness" Arcesilaus "had no equal," and so on). Elsewhere the emphasis on the psychological force of arguments is seen in the sceptics' psychological goal of equanimity (on this aspect of academic scepticism, see below). At the end of the *Outlines*, Sextus admits the sceptic may "purposely propound arguments that are lacking in persuasive power" if they are sufficient to deal with milder cases of "the dogmatists' ailment, self-conceit" (*PH* 3.280–81). Weaker arguments can be used in such a case because they produce the required psychological effect.

(and is only) the attempt to answer specific arguments the dogmatists provide for the proposal that truth can be established.[23] Understood this way, the academic argument is a case of equal opposition, for it undermines (and is in this sense equal to) Stoic epistemology, which is founded on the idea that we can establish certain knowledge by appealing to cognitive impressions. As Sextus says repeatedly, the crux of the argument is the demonstration that cognitive impressions and the false impressions the academic pairs them with are equal (*isos*) in the sense that they are equally striking and self-evident; this undercuts the infallibility of cognitive impressions. Questions about probability are beside the point because it is not invoked by the Stoics (even when they respond to academics)[24] and has no place in their epistemology.

Their goal being the refutation of dogmatists, the academics never do discuss the possibility of a probabilistic justification of belief. The thinkers they take issue with do not propose one. The academics are in this sense very much a part of their intellectual milieu. Like other ancient thinkers they assume that knowledge is tied to certainty, maintaining only that there are no impressions incapable of being false (see, e.g., *Ac* 2.99), and casting their conclusions in the most general terms, saying we cannot perceive truth and have no criterion of truth (see *Ac* 2.40–41, 77–78, 83, *AM* 7.402–22, cf. *Ac* 2.15), slipping between talk of truth and certain truth without pause or mention (see ibid., *Ac* 1.45, 2.43–44 passim).

It would be a mistake to conclude that academic arguments are passé, or that their conclusions can be refuted by arguing that cognitive impressions are probable in the modern sense. The only way to establish the probability of such impressions would be by enumerating true instances of them, showing that they are more frequent than false ones. Putting aside procedural problems (how does one count and distinguish kinds of impressions? how does one ensure a random sample of them?), the academics are unlikely to accept the impression that such arguments depend on (the impression that particular impressions are true or probably true). The problem is that they are subjective and may, as Carneades suggests, misreport the facts;

23. Cicero's Cotta says he finds it "much easier to prove a thing false than to prove it true" (*DND* 1.57), and proceeds to criticize Stoic and Epicurean arguments (not by constructing independent arguments for scepticism). The same strategy is adopted by Carneades (*DND* 3.44) and institutionalized in the Academy, where lectures always *disprove* hypotheses advanced by others (*De Fin* 2.2, quoted below). As Cicero says, "Our habit is to put forward our views in conflict with all the [other] schools" (*Ac* 2.7).

24. Not by appealing to probable truth, but by arguing that one can discern a difference between cognitive and noncognitive impressions.

especially as this can be the case with the most compelling impressions. The gods may have deceived us. Our perception or memory may be weak. Reason may confuse us, as it does in the face of paradox and dialectic. More generally, we may be mistaken or deluded. (As modern thinkers put it, people have turned out to be mistaken about things they thought they saw "as clearly as the sun".)

A probabilistic justification of belief cannot, therefore, provide a way around academic argument, for it must be founded on claims or observations that the academics (and even more clearly, the later Pyrrhoneans)²⁵ will not grant. Therefore, Striker is mistaken at least in principle when she suggests that the academics only undermine the certainty of belief. Underlying her analysis is a failure to recognize academic scepticism as an attack on realist truth. Seen in this light, the academic thesis that belief is subjective undermines any attempt to enumerate objectively true belief, for *all* belief is subjective. It is not certainty and probability, but objectivity and subjectivity, which form the crux of the sceptic-dogmatist debate. No amount of subjective evidence can ever bridge the gap between the two, and no such evidence can provide a basis for objective probability.

ACADEMIC EQUANIMITY

We have already seen that both the academics and the Pyrrhoneans believe in equal opposition. A second use of argument showing the continuity of their views is the use of antithesis as a basis for the moral goal of equanimity. This side of academic scepticism is particularly clear in Arcesilaus, who holds that scepticism aims at happiness (*eudaimonia*, *AM* 7.158) and "says that the End (*telos*) is a suspension of judgement [on the question whether any claim is true]—which is accompanied, as we [the Pyrrhoneans] have said, by quietude (*ataraxia*)" (*PH* 1.232).²⁶ This implies a commitment to equanimity, as does

25. Given their mode of circularity, discussed in chapter 6.

26. According to Couissin, Sextus is here *contrasting* the views of Arcesilaus and the Pyrrhoneans, "for whom *epoche* is only a means, the end being *ataraxia*" ("The Stoicism of the New Academy," p. 33). Such a fine distinction does not, however, accord with the loose character of the Pyrrhoneans' discussion (cf. *PH* 1.35, 191). They hold that *ataraxia* follows *epoche* "like its shadow" and therefore they do not treat them as distinct; sometimes they cite *epoche* or the practical criterion (and not *ataraxia*) as the end of scepticism (see D.L. 9.107, *PH* 1.30, 1.231). Above and beyond this, the sentence in question is the second of three that explain why Arcesilaus' views are "almost identical" to Pyrrhonism, and we cannot suppose that it includes a contrast that has not been announced.

Arcesilaus' remark that "most people . . . think it right to examine poems and paintings and statues of others with the eyes of both the mind and the body, poring over them in minute detail, whereas they neglect their own life, which has many not unpleasing subjects for contemplation, looking ever to externals and admiring the repute and the fortune of others, as adulterers do other men's wives, yet despising themselves and their own possessions" (*Tranq* 470A–B). Elaborating themes that hark back to Democritus, Arcesilaus here criticizes our tendency to focus on the good fortune of others, which cultivates unhappiness. Instead, we should focus on the pleasing aspects of our own lives, ensuring our contentment by opposing discontent. It is folly to fear death (*Cons ad Apoll* 110) because this too entails unhappiness.

In an anecdote related in Plutarch's essay "On the Control of Anger," Arcesilaus gives a dinner and discovers that his slaves have forgotten to buy bread for friends and foreign guests. "In such a predicament which one of us would not have rent the walls asunder with outcries? But Arcesilaus merely smiled and said, 'How lucky it is that the wise man takes to the flowing bowl!'" (461E)—meaning that the bread not being there, the time for wine and conversation would come that much sooner. Here we have a clear case of equanimity by antithesis.

The extant accounts of Carneades' philosophy stress his ability to argue rather than his indifference to external circumstances, though he does say we should live a life of moderation (*Non Epic* 1089C) and he uses antithesis as a way to mental equilibrium. According to Plutarch, Carneades held that we should oppose the expected with the unexpected, always reminding ourselves of the latter because it causes grief when it catches us off guard (*Tranq* 474F–75A). According to Cicero, he criticizes Chrysippus for his approval of a passage where Euripides recounts the pain of life, saying that Chrysippus' endorsement promotes depression; the passage should rather be used "to bring comfort to the ill-disposed from the recital of the evils of others" (*Tus Dis* 3.59–60). Here we have a classic example of antithesis: Carneades opposing personal dissatisfaction by arguing that we are fortunate in comparison with others. Elsewhere, Carneades argues in a famous speech that the wise man will not be distressed at the fall of his own country—a speech meant to help Clitomachus bear the destruction of his native city, Carthage (*Tus Dis* 3.54). Whatever the effect on Clitomachus, Diogenes Laertius suggests that Carneades had some difficulty living up to his own ideals when he himself was faced with death.[27]

27. Suffering from disease, he is said to try to emulate Antipater's constancy and drink poison, but to back down and ask for a honeyed draught instead (D.L. 4.64–65).

ARCESILAUS AND NATURAL BELIEF

Arcesilaus combines his attack on dogmatism and his idea of equanimity by espousing subjectively defined belief. According to Sextus, he acknowledges that happiness requires the ability to act in certain ways, and proposes the "reasonable" (the *eulogon*) as a criterion for determining conduct (*AM* 7.158). The reasonable is that which is in keeping with our nature.[28] One might compare Arcesilaus' views to Hume's suggestion that human nature makes it impossible to reject eating, walking, and talking, especially if our goal is happiness (though Arcesilaus probably defines nature in terms of the individual). It would be "unreasonable" to do otherwise, and Arcesilaus suggests that we should act accordingly. This implies an acceptance of that which appears to be the case, for it is a function of our nature.[29] Arcesilaus still denies that we can prove appearances are true and thus adopts a mitigated scepticism rather than the view that we can establish principles that govern human nature. On the contrary, such speculation undermines what naturally seems to be the case, making ordinary beliefs appear equally true and false.

Arcesilaus' commitment to anti-realist belief is seen most clearly in Plutarch (whose account is *not* at odds with that of Sextus).[30] Asking what happens "when we question the objects and images of sense and wonder whether they are true or false" (*Ad Col* 1123F), Plutarch answers that the follower of Arcesilaus is made of flesh and "ruled by the laws of his nature" (1122D–E), and therefore accepts impressions and impulses without assenting to the truth of any claim. Here as elsewhere, "truth" means realist truth. According to Plutarch, Arcesilaus thus suggests that we can accept impressions and inclinations while suspending judgment on the question whether they encompass realist truth:

The soul has three movements: sensation [*phantasiai*], impulse [*horme*], and assent [*sunkatathesis*].
Now the movement of sensation cannot be eliminated, even if we would;

---

28. Cf. Tsekourakis, *Studies in the Terminology of Early Stoic Ethics*, pp. 25–30. The Stoics also use the term to indicate a proposition that is more likely true than false (see D.L. 7.76), though this meaning is not in keeping with Arcesilaus' scepticism.

29. It is our personal (one might say "natural") affinity with our own culture that allows Arcesilaus to accept custom as a basis for moral judgment.

30. Plutarch does not use the word *eulogon*, but too much is made of this. It is not even clear that Arcesilaus uses it as a technical term. What matters is that the accounts of Arcesilaus' belief remain essentially the same in Plutarch and in Sextus.

instead, upon encountering an object, we necessarily receive an imprint and are affected.

Impulse, aroused by sensation, moves us in the shape of an action, directed towards a suitable goal . . . a kind of casting weight has been put in the scale of our governing part, and a directed movement is set afoot. So those who suspend judgment about everything do not eliminate this second movement either, but follow their impulse, which leads them naturally [*physikos*] to the good presented by sense.

Then what is the only thing that they avoid? That only in which falsity and error can arise, namely forming an opinion and thus interposing rashly with our assent, although such assent is a yielding to appearance that is due to weakness and is of no use whatever. For two things are requisite for action: sense must present a good, and impulse must set out for the good presented; and neither of these conflicts with suspension of judgment. For the argument detaches us from opinion, not from impulse or sensation. So, once something good for us is perceived, no opinion is required to set us moving and keep us going in its direction; the impulse comes directly, and is a movement initiated and pursued by the soul.(*Ad Col* 1122B)

According to this account, it is possible to act on impressions and impulses without asserting that impressions correspond to ultimate reality. Modern anti-realists propound analogous notions of belief when they reject claims to realist truth.

Most commentators (among them, Couissin, Striker, Burnyeat, and Sedley) deny that Arcesilaus is committed to everyday affairs and natural belief on the grounds that this would be incompatible with sceptical conclusions. In answer to their views, it is enough to note the realist nature of the truth that Arcesilaus attacks, which leaves room for an anti-realist acceptance of that which appears to be the case, understood as subjective and possibly mistaken. There is in addition no good reason for rejecting Sextus' and Plutarch's accounts of Arcesilaus (too much has been read into the overlap between early academic and Stoic terminology),[31] especially since a rejection of all belief is, as

31. Such overlap is to be expected given the intense rivalry between the schools, their arguments, their common intellectual milieu, and the apprenticeship of their respective leaders, Arcesilaus and Zeno of Citium, under Polemo (see Num. in Eus. 729b, 731c). The latter is particularly significant, for Cicero explicitly states that Zeno's belief about the chief good being based on natural instinct is borrowed from Polemo (*De Fin* 4.45), and that the Academy's appeal to human nature is a constant through its history (*Ac* 1.19).

Even if Arcesilaus did borrow the *eulogon* from Stoic sources (and not vice versa, or from some common source), crosspollination is only natural. It does not prove that Arcesilaus is disingenuous in his espousal of the reasonable (recall Pyrrho and

Arcesilaus himself reputedly says, incompatible with happiness. The routine dismissal of Greek accounts[32] is peculiar: it is motivated by a desire to make Arcesilaus' views consistent, but leaves him no consistent way to accept quotidian affairs—affairs in which he participates without pause, hesitation, or embarrassment.

THE CONSISTENCY OF ARCESILAUS' OUTLOOK

Arcesilaus' appeal to reasonable beliefs makes his scepticism compatible with daily life, though there remains a question: How does he align his philosophical belief in scepticism with the suspension of judgment it implies? He cannot consistently maintain that scepticism is absolutely true.[33] According to Cicero, he therefore says "that there is nothing that can be known, not even that residue of knowledge that Socrates left himself—the truth of this very dictum . . . nor is there anything that can be perceived or understood, and for these reasons . . . one should neither profess nor affirm nor give approval with assent to anything" (*Ac* 1.45). This leaves no room for the truth of sceptical conclusions, and suggests that Arcesilaus approaches scepticism in the same way he approaches everyday life—suspending judgment on the question whether it is true in the realist sense, but accepting it as in keeping with natural impressions (for sceptical conclusions appear to be correct).

In answer to this account, one might point to a number of commentators who apparently hold that Arcesilaus propounds an inconsistent scepticism. Sextus says that Arcesilaus suspends judgment on *all* questions, refuses to make *any* claims about that which is the case, and yet treats his sceptical claims as "statements of real facts, so that he asserts that suspension of judgement in itself really is good and assent bad" (*PH* 1.233). In contrast, "we [the Pyrrhoneans] make . . . [sceptical]

Protagoras' adoption of Democritus' *ou mallon*, and Arcesilaus' adoption of the Pyrrhonean goal of *epoche*). Rather than Striker's "obvious parody" Arcesilaus' proposition that right action or *katorthoma* can be based upon the *eulogon* (*AM* 7.158) is quite in line with sceptical notions of virtue, which stress personal goals of contentment, independence, and equanimity (even when one must suffer for virtuous action). Equanimity in particular is not compatatible with the attempt to thwart one's own essential nature.

32. Note Striker's remark, "I can see *no* reason to take this [Arcesilaus' espousal of the *eulogon*] as his own view" (my emphasis, "Sceptical Strategies," p. 66).

33. Especially as the charge of inconsistency is a standard criticism of the academics and other sceptically inclined philosophers (see, e.g., *Ac* 2.43–44). Plato, who was studied with great care by Arcesilaus, discusses the problem in connection with Protagoras.

statements not positively but in accordance with what appears to us"(ibid). Elsewhere Sextus makes a similar distinction between academic and Pyrrhonean scepticism: the academics, he says, assert that truth cannot be apprehended, while the Pyrrhoneans keep looking, admitting that it is possible their conclusions are mistaken (*PH* 1.3).

Such evidence may seem to point to inconsistency, but Sextus says only that Arcesilaus differs from the Pyrrhoneans, and his claims can be made compatible with scepticism. All Sextus says is that Arcesilaus does not follow the Pyrrhoneans and interpret the verb "to be" to mean "appears to be"; thus he makes statements about that which really is the case and does not limit himself to statements about appearances. This does not amount to inconsistency, however; one can make such statements and still be sceptical by offering them as provisional hypotheses that appear true (because they are in keeping with our nature), suspending judgment on their final truth. So understood, Arcesilaus expresses his scepticism not by changing the *meaning* of his statements so that they become statements about appearances, but by changing his attitude toward them. A similar attitude pervades modern scientific research, which offers hypotheses as a provisional basis for research without claiming they are true.

Arcesilaus' scepticism is, by this account, a working hypothesis that appears true, but not a view he claims to be true in the realist sense. This explains how he can reject the truth of all claims and still endorse scepticism. In answer to the argument that he inconsistently asserts certain claims (D.L. 4.36, *Ac* 2.77 and Num. in Eus. 737c–d), he may answer that he is committed to them only as hypotheses. He expresses his attitude when asked to discuss philosophy at Hieronymous' birthday celebration. This being a circumstance in which he makes it a practice to shun philosophical discussion, he answers that "the peculiar province of philosophy is just this, to know that there is a time for all things" (D.L. 4.42). Here the use of the verb "to know" (*epistasthai*) and Arcesilaus' implicit point that he knows this is not a time to talk philosophy might seem to contravene his scepticism, but not if he is stating what seems reasonable to him and is willing to admit that his suggestion can, as much as any other claim, be made the subject of equal yet opposing arguments. As we shall see, Carneades adopts a similar position.

ARCESILAUS AND SEXTUS

Though many commentators take issue with his remarks, the proposed account of Arcesilaus vindicates Sextus' claims about the founder of academic scepticism. The only serious difference he notes when he discusses Arcesilaus and the Pyrrhoneans is the formers's failure to change the meaning of his statements so that they refer to appearances, though we have already seen that he adopts an attitude that reserves his judgment.[34] As Sextus himself concludes, Pyrrho's and Arcesilaus' views are "almost identical" (*PH* 1.232). In both men one finds as appeal to opposition, a critique of realism, and a positive philosophy that replaces realism with more subjective declarations that reflect what appears to be the case or (the same thing) that which it is natural or reasonable to accept. For both philosophers the result of scepticism is a rejection of dogmatism in favour of ordinary life. Though most modern commentators have thought otherwise, early Pyrrhonean and academic scepticism are consistent, plausible philosophies.

CARNEADES AND PLAUSIBILITY

Like Pyrrho and Arcesilaus, Carneades proposes a mitigated scepticism intended as a model for everyday life. His many telling arguments against the theology of the day are not, for example, meant to eschew religious practice and belief. "These arguments were advanced by Carneades, *not* with the object of establishing atheism, . . . but in order to prove the Stoic theology worthless" (*DND* 3.44, my emphasis). Carneades adopts a similar attitude to belief in general, attacking philosophical assertions by accepting ordinary views. This accounts for Numenius' remark that "although from his jealousy of the Stoics he [Carneades] stirred up confusion in public, he would himself in secret with his own friends agree, and speak candidly, and affirm as much as any other ordinary person" (Num. in Eus. 738d Gifford). We need only add that he stirred up "confusion" with telling arguments against Stoic epistemology, and that there would be no reason for Carneades to hide his approval of commonplace belief.

The foundation of Carneades' positive philosophy is an adoption of "the plausible" (the *pithanon*) as a guide to "the conduct of life and . . . the attainment of happiness (*eudaimonia*)" (*AM* 7.166). Sometimes *pithanon* is translated as "the probable," but this does not sufficiently

---

34. Sextus does report a wild story about Arcesilaus appearing to be a sceptic while in reality being a dogmatist who uses sceptical arguments to test his companions, passing on knowledge of Plato to the gifted (*PH* 1.234). There is no reason to take this story seriously, especially as it is told of Diocles of Cnidos by Numenius (Eus. 731b). Numenius rejects it.

emphasize the word's connotation of subjectivity.[35] The notion serves as an alternative to the realist truth rejected by the academics, and is founded on the observation that we can judge an impression (*phantasia*) as it relates to *the subject experiencing it* (rather than "the externally existent object"). We thus judge its plausibility—its apparent rather than its actual truth or falsity (*AM* 7.169). Things appear true and false to different degrees, however, and so Carneades distinguishes different kinds of plausibility. An implausible impression appears false; a plausible impression seems true "to an intense degree." Further,

since no impression is ever simple in form, but like links in a chain, one hangs from another, we have to add ... the impression which is at once both plausible and "irreversible" ... And just as some doctors do not deduce that it is a true case of fever from one symptom only—such as too quick a pulse or a very high temperature—but from a concurrence, such as that of a high temperature with a rapid pulse and soreness to the touch and flushing and thirst and analogous symptoms; so also the Academic forms his judgment ... by the concurrence of impressions ... (*AM* 7.176–79)

Impressions are even more plausible when they are irreversible and "tested" by a scrutiny that considers whether they are trustworthy in view of "distance and interval, place, time, mood, disposition" and activity. One asks, "Is the lighting good?" "Are my perceptions possibly distorted?" "Do my impressions stand up to prolonged examination?" and the like.[36]

Sextus illustrates the testing process implied by Carneades' levels of plausiblity with an example:

On seeing a coil of rope in an unlighted room a man jumps over it, conceiving it for the moment to be a snake, but turning back afterwards he inquires into the truth, and on finding it motionless he is already inclined to think that it is not a snake, but as he reckons, all the same, that snakes too are motionless at times when numbed by winter's frost, he prods at the coiled mass with a stick, and then, after thus testing the impression received, he assents to the fact that it is false to suppose that the body presented to him is a snake. (*AM* 7.187–88)

---

35. On this point, see Burnyeat ("Can the Sceptic Live His Scepticism?" p. 123) and the discussion of *isostheneia* above.

36. In the *Outlines* (*PH* 1.227–29), Sextus treats the levels of plausibility in a slightly different order.

Carneades further regulates the use of the plausible with principles dictating different levels of plausibility in different kinds of circumstances (*AM* 7.184–89). Merely plausible impressions are an appropriate guide to action when the matter in question is trivial or when we lack sufficient time to investigate fully (when we are worried about an ambush). Irreversible impressions are to be preferred when we have the time to make them possible, and when we deal with more important matters. Tested impressions are to guide our deliberations in the most important matters (matters contributing to happiness).

Sextus' examples illustrating the plausible are taken from the realm of sense impressions, but other examples are easily imagined. In any situation, we can distinguish apparently true and false impressions and can scrutinize plausible ones to distinguish those which are irreversible. Cicero maintains that this broader application of the plausible provides the ground for a variety of deliberations that take us beyond the senses—whether we should marry, beget a family, accept or not accept scepticism—and for opinions about the future or "about duty or . . . other matters" where practice has made us expert (*Ac* 2.100, 109–10). At the beginning of *De Natura Deorum*, he says the plausible is used to serve and guide the conduct of the academic; his protagonist Cotta is committed to traditional religious views and practices, apparently suggesting that this is another expression of the plausible (*DND* 1.12, 1.61–62, 3.5–6). This makes philosophical sense; our familiarity with the traditions we live with makes them appear more plausible than alternatives. According to Striker, the plausible is only applied to sense impressions and "factual" propositions, but Carneades never said this and a broader application is needed to bring his philosophy in line with life.

CICERO ON THE PLAUSIBLE

Cicero's discussion of Carneades' views is particularly important, both because he considers himself an academic and because he is familiar with the books of Clitomachus, Carneades' heir in the Academy ("a companion of Carneades until quite old age," *Ac* 2.98).[37] In order to ensure that no one suspects him of inventing, Cicero takes his account of plausibility directly from the first of four volumes Clitomachus wrote on suspending judgment. According to Clitomachus' account:

37. Carneades himself wrote nothing, and there is no better source of information on his views.

Carneades holds that there are two ways to classify impressions—as those that can be perceived [to be true] and those that cannot, and as those that are plausible and those that are not; and that . . . the latter division must not be impugned; and that consequently his view is that there is no impression of such a sort to result in perception, but many that result in a judgment of plausibility . . . Thus the wise man will make use of whatever apparently plausible impression he encounters, if nothing presents itself that is contrary to that plausibility, and his whole plan of life will be charted out in this manner. (*Ac* 2.99, cf. 102–3)

Many commentators have not accepted Cicero's or Clitomachus' testimony here, suggesting that they (or at least Cicero) have failed to see that Carneades does not actually accept the plausible. This borders on the incredible, for neither Cicero nor Clitomachus qualify their claims to this effect and it makes no sense to suppose that they could overlook the importance of such a rider (the remarks that are said to contradict the account Cicero gives here are open to other obvious interpretations).[38]

38. Commentators point to Clitomachus' statement that he never understood what Carneades did accept (*Ac* 2.139), concluding that Carneades is not committed to any views. Yet the statement occurs in a long discussion about the appropriate end of life, a discussion in which Cicero wonders whether he "should follow Calliphon, whose opinion indeed Carneades was constantly defending with so much zeal that he seemed to accept it, though Clitomachus used to declare that he had never been able to understand what Carneades did accept." This means only that Clitomachus did not understand what Carneades held *about the proper end of life*, especially as Cicero says elsewhere that Carneades' view of the chief good is "advanced less from a desire to adopt it himself than to use it as a weapon in his battle with the Stoics" (*De Fin* 2.42). Cicero himself wavers on the matter, sometimes writing as though Carneades held the views in question (2.35, 38).

The proposal that Carneades does not accept beliefs based on the plausible is sometimes also founded on the opinion that the academics concealed their opinons (*Ac* 2.60, frag. 21). Yet this itself implies that they have opinions (and accept belief). Cicero does not, moreover, interpret this concealing in a universal way (it does not convince him that he cannot know Carneades' views on scepticism), mentioning exceptions in both cases.

Augustine questions the academic commitment to the *pithanon* (*Con Ac* 3.20.43), but he is a remote source, unsympathetic to academic views, and influenced by the jaundiced claim that academic scepticism is fundamentally insincere and a mere front for Plato's views. In the face of opposing testimony in Clitomachus and Cicero, Augustine's views can count for very little.

More generally commentators have, as with Arcesilaus, made too much of Stoic influence on Carneades. On his innovations, see Stough, *Greek Scepticism*, pp. 50–64. On the views of Couissin and others like him, we will do well to quote Striker ("Sceptical Strategies," p. 73, fn. 49):

Those who ignore Cicero's testimony do so primarily because they think the plausible is incompatible with Carneades' sceptical conclusions. What he rejects is realist truth, however, and this leaves room for plausible beliefs, which are accepted as subjectively convincing and possibly mistaken from a realist point of view. Carneades' commitment to such a view is corroborated by a difficult passage wherein Cicero paraphrases Clitomachus' acccount of the Academics' assertion that the wise man suspends judgment on truth and falsity. Numbering the sentences for reference, we can translate the passage as follows:

(1) . . . there are two ways in which the wise man is said to withhold assent. (2) According to one [the first], he gives assent to nothing at all. (3) According to the other [the second], he holds himself back from responding [*respondendo*) so that he approves of something or disapproves of it, so he neither denies nor affirms anything. (4) This being so, in one way [the first] he assents to nothing at all. (5) Holding to the other [second] way, it is possible to follow plausibility wherever this should be present or absent, responding (*respondere*) "yes" or "no" accordingly. (6) Indeed, since we believe that he who withholds assent from everything is nevertheless moved and does act, there remain impressions of a sort that arouse us to action, and also those to which, when questioned, we would be able to respond (*respondere*) in either way [in the affirmative or negative], following the claim that the impression was like that, without actual assent. (*Ac* 2.104, my translation)

Taken at face value, these remarks are extremely problematic, for sentence (3) contradicts (5) and (6). Taken together, they imply that the wise man withholds assent in the second manner when he refuses to

---

It seems to me that Couissin and, following him, dal Pra underestimate Carneades' originality by stressing only the fact that he took his basic concepts from Chrysippus. If he took over the materials, he did not also take over the arguments, and in fact it seems that he was indeed original, e.g., in pointing out that impressions should not be considered in isolation, and in the attention he paid to the methods we in fact use to ascertain the truth of a given factual statement . . . It will not do to treat Carneades' arguments, even if they were polemically formulated, as reductions ad absurdum of the Stoic doctrines, as dal Pra does: one does not demonstrate inconsistencies in other people's theories by adding inconsistent premises. Carneades did not show that the Stoics were contradicting themselves . . . but that some of their premises were wrong . . . And apart from his criticism of Stoic doctrines, Carneades tried to show that nothing absurd follows if we drop the disputed premises—in fact, as Cicero puts it (Acad. II 146), the sceptic only throws out what is never the case, but leaves everything that is needed. Hence Carneades' philosophy was not entirely negative—though it does not follow that he ever constructed a system for himself.

respond, deny, or affirm, in the process following the plausible so that he can respond, deny, and affirm!

The way around the apparent contradiction is a distinction between two academic methods of responding to questions, impressions, claims, and persons. One is similar to ordinary discourse, where we affirm and deny in keeping with belief. The second occurs in philosophical discourse, where we respond by forwarding antitheses. The latter is the response the Academy emphasizes in its teaching practices. Cicero writes:

It was one of the Sophists, Gorgias of Leontini, who first ventured in an assembly to "invite a question," that is, to ask anyone to state what subject he desired to hear discussed. A bold undertaking, indeed, I should call it a piece of effrontery, had not this custom passed into our own school . . . [first adopted by Socrates and then] revived by Arcesilaus, who made it a rule that those who wished to hear him should not ask him questions but should state their own opinions, and when they had done so he argued against them. But whereas the pupils of Arcesilaus did their best to defend their own position, with the rest of the philosophers, the student who has put the question is then silent; and this still remains the custom in the Academy. The would be learner says, for example, "The Chief Good in my opinion is pleasure," and the contrary is then maintained in formal discourse . . . (*De Fin* 2.2)

This standard way of conducting philosophical discussion is directly associated with Carneades when Cicero reports his arguments against the claim that the wise man will be disturbed by the destruction of his native country (*Tus Dis* 3.54).

Distinguishing these two ways of responding to a claim or question, we can eliminate the problems with Clitomachus' account of the two ways the academic wiseman withholds assent. In philosophical discussion, he withholds assent to any *realist* claim by responding to it with arguments that back an opposing point of view, demonstrating that we cannot establish what is true in the realist sense. In other cases he withholds assent without responding *with opposing arguments*, allowing himself to respond to questions and opinions, and affirming and denying in an *anti-realist* way, so long as he does not give in to realist claims. So understood, Cicero's paraphrase of Clitomachus can be interpreted as follows:

(1) . . . there are two ways in which the wise man is said to withhold assent. (2) According to one, he gives [realist] assent to nothing at all [and responds to

everything with equal yet opposing arguments that produce *epoche*]. (3) According to the other, he holds himself back from responding [with equal yet opposing arguments] so that he approves of something or disapproves of it [in an anti-realist way], so he neither denies nor affirms anything [in philosophical argument]. (4) This being so, in one way [i.e., the realist] he assents to nothing at all. (5) Holding to the other way, it is possible to follow plausibility wherever this should be present or absent, responding [to questions, impressions and opinions] "yes" or "no" accordingly. (6) Indeed, since we believe that he who withholds [realist] assent from everything is nevertheless moved and does act, there remain impressions of a sort that arouse us to action, and also those about which, when questioned, we would be able to respond (*respondere*) in either way [i.e., in the affirmative or negative], following the claim that the impression was like that, without actual assent.

Here as elsewhere, Cicero describes academic anti-realism by saying that the academic follows the claim that some impression "was like that," without actually assenting to its (realist) truth. In describing academic views, both he and Sextus clearly distinguish realist and anti-realist assent when they use the verbs *peithesthai* ("to be persuaded"), *probare* ("to approve," "to accept"), *sequi* ("to follow"), and *videri* ("to appear") to indicate an alternative to assent in the realist sense (see, e.g., *PH* 1.230, *Ac* 2.36, 44, 59, 77, 87, 99, 101, 103, 105, 108, 111, 138, 139 and cf. *AM* 7.166–89). As Cicero typically states the point, the academics accept that something appears or seems a certain way, and they approve and follow the appearance, all the while refusing to commit themselves to its (realist) truth.

THE CONSISTENCY OF CARNEADES' SCEPTICISM

In addition to aligning his scepticism with everday belief, the plausible allows Carneades to accept with consistency the tenets of his scepticism. As Cicero notes in his remarks on Antiochus' attempt to show Carneades inconsistent:

The way in which Antiochus thinks Carneades should preferably have been attacked was this—to make him admit that, since the wise man can have no belief which is not grasped and perceived and known, therefore this particular belief itself, that it is the belief of the wise man that nothing can be perceived, is perceived. Just as if the wise man held no other belief and could conduct his life without beliefs! On the contrary, he holds this particular belief that nothing can be perceived, in just the same way he holds the 'plausible' but not 'perceived' views that have been mentioned; for if he had a mark of knowledge in this case, he would employ the same mark in all other cases, but since he has not got it, he employs plausibilities. (*Ac* 2.109–10)[39]

This seems the logical way to render Carneades' views consistent, though Sextus seems to contradict it with his statement that "the school of Carneades" uses the plausible as a criterion of truth and as a basis for opinions on what is true and false (*AM* 7.173, 179). It is difficult to know what Sextus means by this, especially as his remark may not refer to Carneades himself, but to his followers, his "school".[40] Taken otherwise, it is contradicted by Sextus' remarks elsewhere, which say that Carneades argues for "the nonexistence" of a criterion of truth, elaborates the plausible merely as a criterion for the conduct of life, and stresses its subjective nature (*AM* 7.166–68). More generally, according to Sextus, the academics hold that truth cannot be apprehended (*PH* 1.3, 226).

Alternatively, Sextus' remarks are consistent if his claim about the plausible as a criterion of truth means that Carneades uses the plausible as a basis for statements about that which really is the case (in contrast to statements about what appears to be the case). As we have seen, it is possible to distinguish Arcesilaus and the Pyrrhoneans in this way, and something similar can probably be said of Carneades. Once again, he qualifies his statements, not by reinterpreting them as claims about appearances, but by proposing them as hypotheses that may be ultimately mistaken. From this point of view, he and his followers use the plausible in judging what is true, for the plausible decides which hypotheses about truth they will accept. The important point is that judgments in this sense do not contradict Carneades' scepticism: plausible hypotheses are not claims alleged to be definitely true.

CARNEADES, ARCESILAUS, AND PYRRHO

It should by now be clear that Carneades' views are an amendment of the philosophy Arcesilaus introduces to the Academy. Both philosophers employ similar arguments and both adopt a mitigated scepticism that makes their views compatible with their scepticism by treating these views as subjectively convincing hypotheses rather than true statements.

39. Translating *dicere* as "belief," in keeping with Cicero's decision to use it as a translation of the Greek word *dogma* (see *Ac* 2.27, 29).

40. For some of Carneades' followers do accept such a view.

The main difference is the fine distinction between various kinds of acceptable assertions in Carneades' philosophy. Arcesilaus, like Pyrrho, only distinguishes what appears true and false (hence reasonable), while Carneades' levels of plausibility distinguish impressions that appear true to varying extents.

Despite the continuity of early and later academic scepticism, there is an important way in which Carneades' *pithanon* introduces fundamental changes into the sceptical perspective. We have already seen that the latter is a moral perspective that promotes indifference to external circumstances. This aspect is most prominent in Pyrrho, and retained by Arcesilaus when he introduces scepticism into the debates between the formal schools (debates that the early Pyrrhoneans would probably see as irrelevant to their concerns). In contrast, Carneades' plausible leaves room for more attachments to external circumstances, for it allows as plausible (indeed, very plausible) the notion that it is better to be wealthy than poor, healthy than sick, and admired than despised, in this way weakening the dispassionate attitude toward appearances that characterizes earlier scepticism.Carneades still employs opposition to make difficult circumstances bearable, but his philosophy relaxes this side of scepticism and thus weakens its emphasis on equanimity.

This is what makes Sextus more critical of the third Academy than the second. The problem is that Carneades and his followers "do not describe a thing as good or evil in the way we do; for they do so with the conviction that it is more plausible that what they call good is really good rather than the opposite, and so too in the case of evil, whereas when we describe a thing as good or evil we do not add it as our opinion that what we assert is probable, but simply conform to life undogmatically . . . " (*PH* 1.226). The contrast between Carneades' views and the more dispassionate outlook propounded by the Pyrrhoneans is again invoked by Sextus when he distinguishes academic and Pyrrhonean belief:

Although both the Academics and the Sceptics say that they believe [literally, are persuaded by][41] some things, yet here too the difference between the two philosophies is quite plain. For the word "believe" has different meanings: it means not to resist but simply to follow without any strong impulse or inclination, as the boy is said to believe his teacher; but sometimes it means to

41. Many commentators have criticized Bury's rendering of *peithesthai* as "believe," but this is entirely appropriate, as Sextus considers persuasion in an anti-realist sense and the modern word *belief* encompasses both realist and anti-realist conceptions.

assent to a thing of deliberate choice and with a kind of sympathy due to strong desire, as when the incontinent man believes him who approves of an extravagant mode of life. Since, therefore, the followers of Carneades and Clitomachus declare that . . . they are strongly inclined toward certain things, while we say that our belief is a matter of simple yielding without any consent, here too there must be a difference between us and them. (*PH* 1.230)

It is the additional sympathy, desire, and inclination generated by Carneades' plausible belief that interfere with the Pyrrhonean goal of indifference and *ataraxia* in every circumstance.

Cicero answers such charges, declaring that it is inhuman to be as dispassionate as Pyrrho (see *Ac* 2.32,110). In *De Finibus*, he therefore rejects Pyrrho's account of the good on the grounds that it leaves us with no choice between desirable and undesirable circumstances, teaching as it does that we should accept them all (2.35, 43; 3.11–12; 4.43). Pyrrho might easily answer that we must still choose whether we will adopt this attitude, though the issue is not important here. For our purposes, we need only note that he, the later Pyrrhoneans, and even the earlier academic sceptics adopt a moral stance that is weakened by Carneades' views. They are, in this regard, closer to the Stoics and other philosophers who promote a stronger notion of indifference.

PHILO, METRODORUS, AND CICERO

Carneades' less stringent scepticism is taken even further by Philo and Metrodorus. Carneades himself, they maintain, held "that nothing can be perceived, but . . . that the wise man will assent to something not perceived, that is, will hold an opinion, with the qualification that he will understand that it is an opinion and know that there is nothing that can be comprehended and perceived" (*Ac* 2.148, cf. 35, 59, 67, 78, 112–13). Cicero does not ascribe to this account of Carneades, but adopts a similar view in his personal outlook, remarking that "when the [allegedly cognitive] impressions you talk of have struck my mind or my sense sharply I accept them, and sometimes I actually give assent to them, though nevertheless I do not perceive them, for I hold that nothing can be perceived" (*Ac* 2.65–66).

Carneades probably does not hold the view in question (see *Ac* 2.78, 104). He is said, however, not to "vehemently" deny it (*Ac* 2.112, cf. 2.67), and it is a plausible response to academic reasoning. Its arguments show that truth cannot be established, and one may consistently come to this conclusion while accepting some claims as true, admitting they cannot be justified by argument. Hume accepts ordinary beliefs without a philosophical defense. In both cases, the end result is a mitigated scepticsm that accepts realist claims.

In the hands of thinkers such as Philo and Cicero, later academic scepticism becomes an attack on certainty (which it rejects) rather than realist claims (which it now approves). This explains why Cicero spends so much time delving into "the confined spaces and . . . the briary thickets" of the Stoics and like-minded philosophers:

If I were dealing with a Peripatetic, who would say that we can perceive "an impression formed from a true object," without adding the important qualification "in a manner in which it could not be formed from a false one, " I would meet his frankness with frankness, and would not labour to join issue with him, and if, when I said that nothing can be grasped, he said that the wise man sometimes forms an opinion, I would even refrain from combating him . . . [B]ut as it is what can I do? For I put the question what there is that can be grasped; I receive the answer not from Aristotle or Theophrastus, not even from Xenocrates or Polemo, but from a lesser person [Antiochus]. "A true impression of such a sort that there cannot be a false one of the same sort." I do not encounter any such impression; and accordingly I shall no doubt assent to something not really known, that is, I shall hold an opinion. (*Ac* 2.112–13, cf *Ac* 2.34, 36, 44, 57, 78, 103, 113)

Asked how such belief is possible, Cicero answers that he "may make a positive statement about a thing without there being some defnite and peculiar mark [of certainty and truth] attached to it" (*Ac* 2.35), and can use plausibility in deciding what he will accept. The Stoics themselves must admit that they cannot rely on certainty in all cases (when they are going on a voyage, planning their future, etc.) and that this is possible.

In proposing such an outlook, and in granting realist claims without a philosophical foundation, Philo, Metrodorus, and Cicero add yet another sceptical perspective to ancient discussion and debate.

VI

Later Pyrrhonism

The Academy's drift away from scepticism begins with Clitomachus' successor, Philo of Larissa. He still attacks Stoic epistemology (*PH* 1.235), but attempts to construe the New Academy as a continuation of the Old (*Ac* 1.13, cf. *Ac* 2.13–18), apparently holding that knowledge is at least in theory possible (cf. *PH* 1.35, Stob. 2.7.2). The drift to dogmatism becomes a *fait accompli* when Philo's own successor, Antiochus, renounces the New Academy, adopting many Stoic views.[1]

One result of these developments is Aenesidemus' defection from the Academy in the early years of the first century B.C. "The Academics," he says, "especially the ones now, sometimes agree with Stoic opinions and, to tell the truth, appear to be just Stoics in conflict with Stoics" (*Bibl* 170a, Inwood and Gerson). In answer to such lapses, Aenesidemus reestablishes Pyrrhonism as a more radical alternative, compiling its traditional ten tropes and adding eight modes against causal explanation. His positive philosophy is founded on the use of appearances as a guide to life.

The Pyrrhonism propounded by Aenesidemus and later sceptics is the culmination of all the sceptical trends in Greek philosophy. Borrowing freely from earlier sceptics, these Pyrrhoneans revitalize old themes, develop new arguments, and systematize the various grounds for doubt. As time progresses, they set out more clearly the basic principles that give rise to scepticism—principles formalized in "the problem of the criterion." In response to sceptical conclusions,

---

1. On the history of the Academy after Carneades, see *Ac* 1.26–30, 2.16–39, and Long, *Hellenistic Philosophy*; Tarrant, *Scepticism or Platonism?*, and Dillon, *The Middle Platonists*.

they develop the "practical criterion" as a basis for daily affairs, refining Pyrrho and Timon's acceptance of appearances, providing a more detailed guide to life.

Later Pyrrhonism's belief in equal yet opposing views is emphasized in Sextus and in Diogenes Laertius. It is also implied by the title of Zeuxis' work *On Two-Sided Arguments* (D.L. 9.106) and by the *Sale of the Philosophies*, where Lucian depicts a Pyrrhonean carrying a set of scales to weigh opposing arguments (once the scales balance, the Pyrrhonean can't decide between them). According to Sextus' definition, scepticism

is the ability to place in opposition, in any manner whatsoever, appearances and ideas and thus—owing to the equal force of the opposing objects and arguments—to come firstly to a suspension of judgement (*epoche*), and next to a state of "unperturbedness." . . . [W]e set these in opposition in a variety of ways—appearances to appearances, ideas to ideas, or ideas to appearances and appearances to ideas . . . By "equal force" (*isostheneia*) we mean equality in persuasiveness and lack of persuasiveness, since we do not admit that any of the conflicting arguments takes precedence over any other as being more persuasive . . . The main basic principle of the Sceptic system is that of opposing to every proposition an equal proposition . . . (*PH* 1.8–14)

Confronted by equal opposition, the Pyrrhoneans suspend judgment on the ultimate truth of any claim, invoking the standard formulas "All things are undetermined," "I suspend judgment," "It is no more this than that," "Perhaps it is, perhaps not," and "To every argument an equal argument is opposed."

Within the context of this general strategy, later Pyrrhonism collects an enormous and sometimes clumsy catalogue of arguments that can be used to oppose any view or assertion. Typically, they are presented as critiques of specific notions (induction, syllogisms, proof, definitions, becoming, space, time, number, etc.) or as extremely general modes of reasoning that can be adapted to more specific uses. We have already noted the ten modes Aenesidemus attributes to the earlier Pyrrhoneans.

In some cases, the force of Pyrrhonean conclusions is a function of the enormous number of conflicting views they depend on. One must read Sextus to appreciate this side of Pyrrhonism, though it can be illustrated with his account of moral and aesthetic values. This discussion contrasts different attitudes to sex, beauty, sacrifice, food, adultery, children, the aged, death,[2] violence, bigamy, piracy, thievery, cannibalism, cowardice, manliness, and "all matters of religion or theology." Consider, for example, Sextus' almost endless catalogue of conflicting attitudes to sex. Among the Greeks, sodomy is said to be shameful ("or rather, illegal"), but the Germani see it as a seemly and customary practice. In Thebes, it is said to have been acceptable. The Cynics, Cleanthes, and Chrysippus maintain that it is neither good nor bad.

Having intercourse with a woman, too, in public, although deemed by us to be shameful, is not thought to be shameful by some of the Indians; at any rate they couple publicly with indifference, like the philosopher Crates, as the story goes. Moreover, prostitution is with us a shameful and disgraceful thing, but with many of the Egyptians it is highly esteemed; at least, they say that those women who have the greatest number of lovers wear an ornamental ankle-ring as a token of their proud position. And . . . some . . . girls marry after collecting a dowry before marriage by means of prostitution. We see the Stoics also declaring that it is not amiss to keep company with a prostitute or to live on the profits of prostitution . . . Masturbation, too, which we count loathsome, is not disapproved by Zeno; and we are informed that others, too, practise this evil as though it were a good thing. (*PH* 3.200–206)

Sextus' list continues with many more examples. The Persian Magi are reputed to marry their mothers; some Egyptians marry their sisters. Zeno of Citium, the founder of Stoicism, says it is permissible for a man to rub his mother's private parts with his own, "just as no one would say it is bad for him to rub any other part of her body with his hand."

2. While it seems only human to assume that death is bad, Euripides and others declare otherwise, writing that:

Rather should we bewail
The babe newborn, such ills has he to face
Whereas the dead, who has surcease from woe
With joy and gladness we should bear from home

and, even more bluntly:

Never to be born is the best thing for mortals
Never to have seen the sun
Or if born, to hasten to the gates of Hades
And lie, unmoved, beneath the earth. (*PH* 3.230–31)

Chrysippus' book *The State* approves of a father having children by his daughter, a mother by her son, and a brother by his sister. Even Plato rejects common practice when he suggests that wives be held in common. How then can we be sure of the truth of our opinions on these matters?

The relevance of Pyrrhonean arguments to modern epistemology is most clearly seen in Sextus' discussions of cause, induction, and the external world.[3] In reference to the Pyrrhonean account of cause, Barnes claims that "Sextus did not anticipate Hume" and that "his attempt to show the inconceivability of cause is a simple failure,"[4] but he is mistaken on both counts (indeed, one might go further and say that Hume's arguments are ultimately derived from the Pyrrhoneans).[5] According to Hume, the basis of our belief in cause is our observation of the "constant conjunction" of causes and effects in the past. This conjunction cannot, however, justify our belief in cause, for there seems no way to deduce from it the conclusion that a cause has the power to produce (and must be followed by) its effect. We can, without contradiction, imagine a cause without its effect, for they are distinct objects or events, and it follows that causal necessity cannot be reduced to logical necessity. We might instead maintain that it is probable that causes and effects are necessarily conjoined, but this begs the question, since probability "is founded on the presumption of a resemblance betwixt those objects, of which we have had experience, [those objects we have observed as constantly conjoined], and of those, of which we have had none" (*Tr* 90).

The Pyrrhonean version of this argument appears in Sextus' account

3. It seems to me that moral and cultural relativism cannot be dismissed as easily as modern philosophers have imagined, but that is an issue I must leave for elsewhere. In the present context, we might note that the Pyrrhoneans are unlikely to be cowed even when their oppositions are shown to be passé. As Sextus writes, " . . . we oppose things present sometimes to things present . . . and sometimes to things past or future, as for instance, when someone propounds to us a theory which we are unable to refute, we reply, 'Just as, before the birth of the founder of the School to which you belong, the theory it holds was not yet apparent as a sound theory, . . . so likewise it is possible that the opposing theory is not yet apparent to us, so that we ought not to yield assent to the theory which at the moment seems valid'" (*PH* 1.168, cf. 2.40).

4. Barnes, "Ancient Scepticism and Causation," p. 178.

5. The path of the argument seems to be: the Pyrrhoneans, al-Ghazali, Suarez, Malebranche, Hume. On Malebranche's and Ghazali's influence on Hume, see Naify, *Arabic and European Occasionalism.* He fails to find a connection between Ghazali and Hume, but Lennon provides Suarez as a likely link.

of signs.[6] He defines signs in a broad way, to include anything indicating, or "pointing to" something else. Proofs are signs of their conclusions, bodily motions are signs of the state of the soul, and causes and effects are signs of one another. An "indicative" sign is founded on a necessary connection between the sign and the signified, and informs us of something that must, therefore, exist. A "commemorative" sign (literally, a sign that "reminds one") informs us of something that has been associated with the sign in the past, though the two may not be necessarily conjoined. Commemorative signs are produced by (but not only by) the constant conjunction of cause and effect.

Thus the commemorative sign . . . brings us . . . a recollection of the thing observed along with it and now no longer clearly perceived—as in the case of smoke and fire; for as we have often observed these to be connected with each other, as soon as we see the one—that is to say, smoke—we recall the other—that is to say, the unseen fire. The same account applies to the scar which follows the wound and to the puncture of the heart which precedes death; for on seeing the scar we recall the wound which preceded it, and on viewing the puncture of the heart we foretell the imminence of death. (*AM* 8.151–53)

Commemorative signs do not necessarily indicate that which really is the case, and by arguing that they cannot be shown to do so, the Pyrrhoneans expound an ancient analogue of Hume's critique of cause (applying the critique of signs to physical states taken as signs of the state of the soul produces a variant of the mind-body problem).

Like Hume, Sextus argues that the claim that causes and effects are necessarily conjoined cannot be defended as a truth of logic. For this to be the case, cause and effect would have to be "relative" (*pros ti*) to one another and incapable of being separately conceived (ibid., 154, 161–62).[7] But then they would not be distinct, and it would be impossible for causes to precede effects (see *PH* 3.26–28, *AM* 8.163–70, 9.234–36 and *PH* 2.118–19). As Sextus puts it, "if Cause as

6. As Ken Dorter has pointed out to me, there is an earlier anticipation of Hume's argument in Plato's analogy of the cave, where he portrays his cave dwellers as mistakenly believing that the shadows they see are the cause of the sights and sounds they experience (*Rep* 7.515b–16d). Their mistake is founded on the constant conjunction of particular sounds and sights; it is only when one of them leaves the cave that he comes to see that this is the case.

7. Other relatives include the notions whiter and blacker, sweet and bitter, left and right, and whole and part (see ibid. 9.340).

a relative notion cannot be conceived before its effect, and yet, if it is to be conceived as causative of its effect, it must be conceived before its effect . . . It is impossible for the Cause to be conceived" (*PH* 3.28).

Unlike Hume, Sextus does not discuss the possibility that signs are probably indicative, but the Pyrrhonean critique of inductive inference provides an analogue of Hume's ideas in this regard. Like the Pyrrhonean critique of signs, it is far more comprehensive, especially as Hume overlooks inductive generalizations not founded on causal reasoning. In contrast, the Pyrrhoneans generalize their argument so that it encompasses all cases of induction.

> It is . . . easy, I consider, to set aside the method of induction. For when they propose to establish the universal from the particulars by means of induction, they will effect this by a review either of all or some of the relevant instances. But if they review some, the induction will be insecure, since some of the particulars omitted in the induction may contravene the universal; while if they are to review all, they will be toiling the impossible, since the particulars are infinite and indefinite. Thus on both grounds, as I think, the consequence is that induction is invalidated. (*PH* 2.204, cf. 2.195–97)

It follows, Sextus says elsewhere, that generalizations such as "Every animal moves its lower jaw," "Every man is an animal," and "No man is four-footed" are unfounded (*PH* 2.195–97). Problems with inductive causal inferences are a more specific instance of the problem. Especially as we are unable to observe the future, it is impossible to observe all conjunctions of events; nor can we assume that the events we have not examined are similar to those we have observed.

The Pyrrhonean claim that we cannot know the existence of the external world depends on the kinds of arguments we have already noted in the views of earlier sceptics, in particular, the Cyrenaics. The Pyrrhoneans do not emphasize the problem to the same extent as modern philosophers, though not because it encompasses "a doubt more radical than the traditional sceptic had dared suppose."[8] Indeed, it is just the opposite: the Pyrrhoneans pay less attention to the external world because they focus on more fundamental problems, and because doubts about it are not particularly radical from their point of view (thinkers such as Xeniades, Gorgias, and even Parmenides propose conclusions that are more at odds with ordinary belief). The basic problem giving rise to scepticism about the external world is already

8. Burnyeat, "Idealism in Greek Philosophy," p. 47.

evident in the traditional ten modes, which show that our beliefs are relative to our subjective circumstances and that we cannot, therefore, know the real nature of external objects (see, e.g., *PH* 1.78, 87, 117, 123, 128, 134, 140, 144, 163). Sextus states the general problem thus:

[S]ense does not furnish the intellect with the external objects, but each sense reports its own peculiar affection (*pathos*)—touch, for instance, when warmed by fire, does not supply to the intellect the external and burning fire but the warmth therefrom, that is to say, its own peculiar affection . . . For external objects are unlike our affections, and the impression (*phantasia*) is far different from the thing presented—that of fire, for instance, from the fire, for the latter burns whereas the former is not capable of burning . . . And just as he who does not know Socrates but is looking at the likeness of Socrates does not know whether Socrates resembles the apparent likeness, so the intellect, when it perceives the affections without having discerned the external objects, will not know either the nature of these objects or whether they resemble the affections.

. . . Since, then, that which is perceptible through another is by universal agreement non-evident, and all things are perceived through our affections, than which they are other, all external objects are non-evident and on this account unknowable by us . . . (*AM* 7.354–66, cf. *PH* 2.74–75, *AM* 7.352–53, 385–87)

Stated in this way, it might seem that the Pyrrhoneans raise doubts about the *nature* rather than the *existence* of external objects (a suggestion one finds in Burnyeat), but this would be to misread the texts. From the ancient point of view, the idea that we cannot know the nature of an object encompasses the idea that we cannot know that it exists, for questions about its existence are stated as, "Does the object have a real or nonreal nature?" Questions about existence are thus presented as questions about an object's nature, the Pyrrhoneans emphasizing that "impressions are produced by non-real objects just as by real ones" (*AM* 7.402, cf. 194–95, 427, *PH* 1.104, 113).[9] Sextus implies doubts about the existence of the external world when he says that the Pyrrhoneans do not admit even that external objects possess a real nature (*PH* 1.215), holding that there is no way to refute Gorgias, Xeniades, and others who argue that we have "empty" impressions, and that "none of the objects they [the senses] seem to apprehend have any real existence" (2.49).

9. The matter is put similarly in *Academica* (2.47–48), where Lucullus tells us that the mind may be set in motion by nonexistent objects.

Burnyeat has said that there is not "a single text in Sextus which treats the sceptic's own body as something external in the now familiar sense,"[10] but the argument we have already noted is used to call the body into question in an important passage where Sextus argues that we cannot know the nature of man. Distinguishing the body, intellect, and senses, he comments in a subconclusion "that the senses do not apprehend the body": "Each of the senses is only aware of the perception proper to itself, and this will not be the body's substance. For hearing is perceptive of sound and sound is not the substance. And smell is a judge only of the odorous or mal-odorous [scent]; but no one would be so witless as to class the substance of the body among things [which are] odorous or mal-odorous [scents]. And—not to make a long story of it—the same may be said regarding the rest of the senses. So that the senses do not apprehend the body's substance" (*AM* 7.300).[11]

In other contexts, Sextus takes his critique of our ability to perceive ourselves even further, arguing that we are compounded of body and soul, and that we cannot know that either of them or the senses actually exist (*PH* 2.29–33, *AM* 6.55). In the third book of the *Outlines*, he establishes the universal conclusion that no material objects can be apprehended in a different way, attacking the existence of solidity and dimensions (38–55).

THE PROBLEM OF THE CRITERION

As important as it is, the Pyrrhonean anticipation of modern dilemmas such as the problem of the external world is not the best indication of the depth of Pyrrhonean scepticism. Its significance is revealed in the new modes it adds when systematizing the eclectic arguments of the earlier Pyrrhoneans and presenting the problem of the criterion as the basis of scepticism.[12] According to the usual account of the problem,

10. Burnyeat, "Idealism in Greek Philosophy," p. 41

11. The distinction between sense impressions and the body is further backed by the suggestion that they have a different nature. For example, the sense impressions are incorporeal and the body is corporeal (see *AM* 7.293–300).

12. Even in presenting more specific arguments, the Pyrrhoneans attempt to focus on fundamental principles that have broader consequences for belief. Sextus explains:

[W]e shall attack the most comprehensive dogmas, as in the doubts cast on these we shall find the rest also included. For just as, in a seige, those who have undermined the foundation of a wall find that the towers tumble down along with it, so too in philosophical investigations those who have routed the primary assumptions on which the theories are based have potentially abolished the apprehension of every particular

one cannot justify any criterion of truth because no criterion can be assumed true. A criterion must therefore be justified by deducing it from another criterion of truth, but this entails infinite regress, every new criterion being in need of justification. As Sextus puts the matter:

> In order to decide the dispute which has arisen about the criterion, we must possess an accepted criterion by which we shall be able to judge the dispute; and in order to possess an accepted criterion, the dispute about the criterion must first be decided. And when the argument thus reduces itself to a form of circular reasoning the discovery of the criterion becomes impracticable, since we do not allow them to adopt a criterion by assumption [for the existence of a criterion is in question], while if they offer to judge the criterion by a criterion we force them to a regress *ad infinitum*. (*PH* 2.20).

The Pyrrhoneans' last two sets of (five and two) modes are variations on this theme. Invoking differences of opinion and the relative nature of belief, these modes point out the question begging nature of assumptions about what is truth and force the dogmatists into circular reasoning or infinite regress whenever the latter attempt to prove their claims true (*PH* 1.164–77, 1.178–9).

Like earlier sceptical arguments, the problem of the criterion shows that the beliefs we accept are necessarily relative to our subjective commitments. We normally assume that ordinary perceptions, logical principles, and convincing arguments indicate objective truth, but we can only know that we find them convincing; it begs the question to assume they constitute criteria of objective truth. Questions about the external world arise because our sense impressions are the only access we have to that world and there is no independent way to verify them. To say that principles of logic and morality are correct is problematic because we cannot assume the truth of moral and logical intuitions (especially as moral intuitions appear to differ from individual to individual). The problem of induction arises because the only evidence

---

theory. Thus it is not without plausibility that some compare those who join in plunging into inquiries into particulars to hunters who pursue the quarry on foot, or men who fish with a line, or those who catch birds with bird-lime on a cane; whereas those who call in question all the particulars by starting with the most comprehensive postulates, they compare to men who surround [their prey] with lines and stakes and drag-nets. Hence, as it shows much more art to be able to catch a great number with a single onset than to hunt after the game laboriously one by one, so too it is much more artistic to bring one's counter-argument against all in common rather than to develop it against the particular tenets. (*AM* 9.1–3, cf. *PH* 2.84).

we have for the uniformity of nature is necessarily incomplete and cannot be transcended. Scepticism about any claim can be founded on the problem of the criterion, for any claim is ultimately founded on the belief that it appears true, which need not guarantee truth. We cannot assume otherwise, especially as we know that appearances can be misleading.

The various versions of the problem of the criterion, used throughout Sextus' discussion, demonstrate how well the Pyrrhoneans understand the fundamental questions raised by sceptical inquiry. Rather than rest content with the problem of the external world, the critique of cause, and other questions, they probe more deeply, discussing the questions that give rise to them. It is this that accounts for the depth of Pyrrhonean inquiry and for the breadth of its conclusions. A feel for that breadth can be gleaned from the Pyrrhonean conclusions that all proofs are impossible (*AM* 8.300–481), all things are undetermined, and all arguments can be opposed; from the doubts about syllogisms, dialectic and the use of reason (see, e.g., *PH* 2.144–204, *AM* 8.337–481 and *Ac* 2.42, 2.92–97); and from questions about the existence of external objects, space, time, motion, becoming, perishing, substance, and body (see, e.g., *PH* 3.63–150, 3.38–55). Just how far the Pyrrhoneans go in doubting ordinary views is seen in Sextus' willingness to take issue with arithmetic and defend the assumption "that 3 is 4" in order to establish the consequence "that 6 is 8" (*AM* 8.7–373). As important as some of these specific arguments are, it is the problem of the criterion that serves as the basis of later Pyrrhonism and the key to its sceptical conclusions.

PRACTICAL AFFAIRS

Like Pyrrho and Timon, Sextus and the later Pyrrhoneans present their views as an attack on the uselessness of dogmatist philosophy. The dogmatists are, they say, guilty of unfounded speculation on all matters and there is no way to justify their claims. In place of pointless metaphysics, the Pyrrhoneans propose a more modest outlook that "champions life (*bios*)," promoting happiness in practical affairs.

Later Pyrrhonism therefore adopts a goal of equanimity, *ataraxia* (*PH* 1.10, 25–30). In cases where happiness or unhappiness is determined by opinion, scepticism promotes freedom from disturbance. In cases where disturbance is unavoidable (sickness, accident, etc.), scepticism promotes feelings that are moderate (*PH* 1.30, 3.236, *AM* 11.155). In both cases Pyrrhonism is preferable to dogmatism, for the man who opines that anything is by nature good or bad is forever being disquieted: when he is without the things he deems good he believes himself to be tormented by things naturally bad and he pursues the things which he thinks good. When he has obtained them, he falls into still more perturbations because of his irrational and immoderate elation, and in his dread of a change of fortune he uses every endeavour to avoid losing the things which he deems good. On the other hand, the man who determines nothing as to what is naturally good or bad neither shuns nor pursues anything eagerly; and, in consequence, is unperturbed. (*PH* 1.27–28; cf. *AM* 11.110–67)

Perhaps in response to declarations that Pyrrho's philosophy is inhuman, Sextus adds that the Pyrrhonean is not wholly untroubled, "for we grant that he is cold at times and thirsty, and suffers various affections of that kind" (*PH* 1.29). Even in these cases, the sceptic is better off than others because "he does not also opine that what he suffers is evil by nature, [and so] the feeling he suffers is moderate" (*PH* 3.236, cf. *PH* 1.30, *AM* 11.155, 161).

Ataraxia itself does not, however, provide a comprehensive guide to action. The later Pyrrhoneans therefore follow Pyrrho and Timon and accept appearances as a guide to life. According to Diogenes Laertius, Zeuxis, Antiochus of Laodicea, and Appellas all hold that "the apparent is the Sceptic's criterion, as . . . Aenesidemus says, and so does Epicurus . . . " (D.L. 9.106). Within daily life, it follows that the Pyrrhonean accepts psychological constraints, apparent facts, and custom and convention:

For things which . . . happen of necessity, such as hunger, thirst, and pain, we cannot escape, for they are not to be removed by the force of reason. And when the dogmatists argue that he [the Pyrrhonean] may thus live in such a state of mind that he would not shrink from killing and eating his own father if ordered to do so, the Sceptic replies that he will be able to live so as to suspend judgement in cases where it is a question of arriving at truth, but not in matters of life and the taking of precautions. Accordingly, we may choose a thing or shrink from a thing by habit and may observe rules and customs. (D.L. 9.108, cf. 103)

Pyrrhonean appearances are ultimately formalized in the practical criterion, which guides the subscriber in the conduct of life, serving as a substitute for a criterion of truth. The Pyrrhonean criterion distinguishes four aspects of the sceptical way of life, applying appearances in each case.

Adhering, then, to appearances we live in accordance with the normal rules of life, undogmatically, seeing that we cannot remain wholly inactive. And it would seem that this regulation of life is fourfold, and that one part of it lies in the guidance of Nature, another in the constraint of the affections, another in the tradition of laws and customs, another in the teaching of the crafts. Nature's guidance is that by which we are naturally capable of sensation and thought. Constraint of the affections is that whereby hunger drives us to food and thirst to drink. Tradition of customs and laws is that whereby we regard piety in the conduct of life as good, but impiety as evil. Teaching of the crafts is that whereby we are not inactive in such crafts as we adopt. (*PH* 1.23–24, cf. 1.17)

To appreciate the continuity of the Pyrrhonean tradition, it is important to see that this does not introduce a new position into Pyrrhonism, but merely formalizes what was implicit in its earlier accpetance of appearances.

The various aspects of the practical criterion are invoked in different contexts within Sextus' discussion. In introducing arguments against dogmatist theology, he appeals to the Pyrrhonean commitment to custom and convention, "first premising that, following the ordinary view, we affirm undogmatically that Gods exist and that we reverence Gods and ascribe them foreknowledge" (*PH* 3.2, cf. *AM* 9.49, and the report that Pyrrho was a high priest at Elis). On the topic of medicine, Sextus speaks of affections and the constraints of nature.[13]

So then, just as the Sceptic, in virtue of the compulsion of the affections, is guided by thirst to drink and by hunger to food, and in like manner to other such objects, in the same way the Methodical[14] physician is guided by the pathological affections to the corresponding remedies—by contraction to dilatation, as when one seeks refuge in heat from the contraction due to the application of cold, or by fluxion to the stoppage of it, as when persons in a hot bath, dripping with perspiration and in a relaxed condition, seek to put a stop to it and for this reason rush off into the cool air. It is plain, too, that conditions which are naturally alien compel us to take measures for their removal, seeing that even the dog when it is pricked by a thorn proceeds to remove it. And in short—to avoid exceeding the limits proper to an outline of this kind by a detailed enumeration—I suppose that all the facts described . . . can be classed

13. The practical aspects of later Pyrrhonism are brought out in its association with a group of doctors including Menodotus, Herodotus, and Sextus himself.

14. According to Sextus, some allege that scepticism and medical empiricism are the same, but they are mistaken and the sceptic can more easily endorse the Methodic school, which rejects hypotheses about nonevident causes.

as instances of the compulsion of the affections, whether natural or against nature. (*PH* 1.238–39)

In discussing ambiguity, Sextus invokes the Pyrrhonean commitment to crafts, suggesting that training in them, not in dialectic, is the best way to resolve practical ambiguities:

For if the Ambiguity is a word or phrase having two or more meanings, and it is by convention that words have meaning, then all such ambiguities as can be usefully cleared up—such, that is, as occur in the course of some practical affair—will be cleared up, not by the dialectician, but by the craftsmen trained in each several art, as they have personal experience of the conventional way adopted by themselves . . . And in the ordinary affairs of life we see already how people—ay, even slave boys—distinguish ambiguities when they think such distinctions are of use. Certainly, if a master who had servants with the same name were to bid a boy called, say, "Manes" . . . to be summoned, the slave-boy will ask "Which one?" (*PH* 2.256–57)

In contrast, the ambiguities of the dogmatists "are no doubt useless for a life devoid of dogmatism" (ibid. 258).

The Pyrrhoneans emphasize utility in their response to the critique of cause. Hume condemns them for inhumanly rejecting all belief, but they adopt a position similar to his own, proposing that we accept the causes and effects we depend on in everyday affairs, granting that we cannot prove that they indicate the way things really are. As Sextus puts it, commemorative signs are good because they are "relied upon in living experience; when a man sees smoke, fire is signified, and when he beholds a scar he says that there has been a wound. Hence not only do we not fight against living experiences, but we even lend it our support by assenting undogmatically to what it relies on . . . " (*PH* 2.102, cf. *AM* 8.152–58).[15] The only difference between this and Hume's own account of cause is the Pyrrhonean anti-realist ("undogmatic") conception of belief.

THE CONSISTENCY OF LATER PYRRHONISM

The consistency of later Pyrrhonism lies, from an ancient point of view, in its distinction between appearances, impressions, and affections,

15. Cf. the examples in Barnes, "Ancient Scepticism and Causation," pp. 154–55. As Barnes puts it, "Sextus' attitude to causal propositions is by no means uniformly hostile."

which are evident, and the nonevident world beyond them (appearances and the nonevident are opposites—see, e.g., *PH* 2.88–94). Nonevident things "never appear of themselves but may be thought to be apprehended, if at all, owing to other things" (*PH* 2.98). The external world is, for example, nonevident; "since . . . that which is perceptible through another is by universal agreement non-evident, and all things are perceived through our affections, which are other than they, all external objects are nonevident and on this account unknowable by us" (*AM* 7.366, cf. 358). Statements about the nonevident are "dogmatic" and cannot be justified.

Given the distinction between appearances and the nonevident, Sextus describes scepticism as the rejection of belief (*dogma*) when it is understood as "assent to any of the non-evident things investigated by inquiry" (*PH* 1.13, and see 1.16, 20). This leaves room for Pyrrhonean beliefs, which refer to appearances and impressions rather than to the nonevident things that lie beyond them. In this sense, Pyrrhonean beliefs are undogmatic. As Sextus reminds us, that which "we neither posit nor deny is some one of the dogmatic statements made about the non-apparent . . . " (*PH* 1.193).

When we say "To every argument an equal argument is opposed," . . . the word "argument" we use not in its simple sense, but [in a sense], which establishes a point dogmatically (that is to say with reference to the non-evident) . . . So whenever I say "To every argument an equal argument is opposed," what I am virtually saying is "To every argument investigated by me which establishes a point dogmatically, it seems to me that there is opposed another argument, establishing a point dogmatically, which is equal to the first in respect of credibility and incredibility. (*PH* 1.202, cf. 1.193, 203, 208)

This leaves room for accepting each situation "as it appears to us at the moment" (*PH* 1.4), however, and this is the nature of Pyrrhonean belief (see, e.g., *PH* 1.14–15, 17, 19, 21–24, 35, 87, 123, 127, 135, 140, 198, 200, 223, *AM* 11.18 and cf. D.L. 9.74, 104–5). It follows that the Pyrrhonean does not attack belief (*dogma*) in the broad sense of the "approval of a thing" (a sense that encompasses the approval of appearances, affections, and impressions), but leaves room for "assent to the states which are the necessary result of impressions" (*PH* 1.13, 1.193, 203, 208, 2.102, *AM* 7.391).

Sextus answers the charge of inconsistency by appealing to these distinctions when he discusses the Pyrrhoneans' usual conclusions:

"no more this than that," "I determine nothing," "perhaps," and so on. As he repeats time and time again, Pyrrhonean claims undermine themselves if they are understood as true from a dogmatic point of view. Pyrrhonism thus purges itself, refusing to hold that it is true in the dogmatic sense (*PH* 1.206) and propounding sceptical conclusions as statements that undogmatically "announce" appearances (*PH* 1.14–15, 191, 193, 195, 196, 197, 198, 199, 200, 201, 202, 203). "For in . . . [the dogmatic] sense, no doubt, it will be found that the Sceptic determines nothing, not even the very proposition 'I determine nothing'; for this is not a dogmatic assumption, that is to say assent to something non-evident, but an expression indicative of our own mental condition. So whenever the Sceptic says: 'I determine nothing,' what he means is 'I am now in such a state of mind as neither to affirm dogmatically nor deny any of the matters now in question'" (*PH* 1.197). Sextus comes to the following conclusion at the end of his lengthy discussion of Pyrrhonean expressions:

[I]n regard to all the Sceptic expressions, we must grasp first the fact that we make no positive assertion respecting their absolute truth, since we say that they may possibly be confuted by themselves, seeing that they themselves are included in the things to which their doubt applies . . . And we also say that we employ them . . . without precision and, if you like, loosely; for it does not become the Sceptic to wrangle over expressions, and . . . it is to our advantage that even to these expressions no absolute significance should be ascribed, but one that is relative and relative to the Sceptics. Besides this we must also remember that we do not employ them universally about all things, but about those things which are non-evident and are objects of dogmatic inquiry, and that we state what appears to us and do not make any positive declarations as to the real nature of external objects; for I think that, as a result of this, every sophism directed against a Sceptic expression can be refuted. (*PH* 1.206–9)

Sextus' last remark is particularly apropos in light of the almost universal failure to appreciate the details of Pyrrhonean assent. The standard view confuses dogmatic and undogmatic claims, and appearances and the non-evident, and concludes that the Pyrrhoneans, "allowing of no criterion and regarding every argument as equally true and equally false, arrived at results as fatal to themselves as the dogmatists."[16] Given the great care the Pyrrhoneans take in

16. Maccoll, *The Greek Sceptics*, p. 105.

distinguishing the claims they make and those they take issue with (in the opening paragraph of the *Outlines*, Sextus warns the reader that "we simply record each situation, like a chronicler, as it appears to us at the moment," and do not "positively affirm that the situation is exactly as we state it"), it is the standard view, not Pyrrhonism, which is puzzling.

PYRRHONEAN ANTI-REALISM

The Pyrrhonean distinction between appearances and the nonevident confirms our earlier proposition that Pyrrhonism is an ancient form of anti-realism. According to realism, we can transcend our subjective point of view and know the nature of the external world. Sceptical arguments, the Pyrrhoneans answer, make this seem impossible; so they restrict themselves to beliefs and statements interpreted in terms of sense impressions and other subjective appearances.[17] Like their idealist counterparts, Pyrrhonean claims are thus "the announcement of a human state of mind" (*PH* 1.203), though the Pyrrhoneans leave no room for an incorrigible knowledge of sense impressions, and they do not say their claims are necessarily true. On the contrary, Pyrrhonean modes are as applicable to idealist claims as any others, and the Pyrrhonean rejection of our ability to establish the nature of our impressions is reflected in the treatment of the Cyrenaic claim that they are infallibly apprehended and thus a criterion of truth (*AM* 7.190–98). Rather that advocate such a view, the Pyrrhoneans treat it as yet another dogmatist account of truth which is opposed by (and is as unacceptable as) the alternatives in Plato, Democritus, Gorgias, Epicurus, Aristotle, and so on.[18] Unlike all these thinkers, the Pyrrhoneans accept no criterion of truth.

The Pyrrhonean proposes impressions as a subjective, and possibly mistaken, basis for practical affairs. As we have already noted, Sextus carefully avoids the claim that we know appearances, saying only that the Pyrrhoneans grant that appearances appear. One finds the same

17. Sextus defends the possibility of such belief: "The Sceptic is not, I suppose, prohibited from the mental conception which arises through the reason itself as a result of passive impressions and clear appearances and does not at all involve the reality of the objects conceived; for we conceive, as they say, not only of real things but also of unreal. Hence both while inquiring and while conceiving the Suspensive person continues in the Sceptical state of mind" (*PH* 2.10).

18. On this point, cf. Burnyeat, "Idealism in Greek Philosophy," pp. 38–39, and Galen, 8.711.

attitude in the claim that the Pyrrhoneans do not overthrow sense impressions and do not doubt appearances themselves. "No one, I suppose, disputes that the underlying object has this or that appearance" (*PH* 1.19–22). This means only that the Pyrrhonean refrains from disputing appearances, and that "even if we do argue against the appearances, we do not propound such arguments with the intention of abolishing them, but by way of pointing out the rashness of the Dogmatists; for if reason is such a trickster as to all but snatch away the appearances from under our very eyes, surely we should view it with suspicion in the case of things non-evident so as not to be rash in following it" (*PH* 1.20). According to this account, appearances are to be accepted and adhered to, not because we can establish their true nature, but because we need a foundation for the conduct of practical affairs. The Pyrrhonean notion of appearances thus represents a move to mitigated scepticism rather than to idealism, though the Pyrrhoneans interpret appearances as subjective determinants of belief, thus propounding them in an anti-realist way.

Later Pyrrhonism is in this regard like those forms of anti-realism that go beyond idealism and completely do away with realist truth. The suggestion (by Kant, Poincaré, Wittgenstein, Putnam, and others) that truth is relative to the structure of the human mind, social and linguistic conventions, or modes of life is, for example, an analogue of the Pyrrhonean's explicitly subjective notion of belief. The difference is that the Pyrrhoneans continue to define truth as realist truth, and do not redefine it to say their claims are true. In the moral sphere, Pyrrhonism is similar to emotivism, for it suggests that moral preferences are subjective and eliminates all professions of moral truth.

THE STANDARD INTERPRETATIONS

Modern interpretations of later Pyrrhonism can be distinguished by their emphasis on the practical side of Pyrrhonism or by their attempts to make it logically consistent. On the one hand, Zeller, Maccoll, Burnyeat, and others try to make the Pyrrhonean outlook compatible with universal *epoche* by holding that the Pyrrhoneans reject all belief. The problem is that this severs Pyrrhonism from ordinary life and that the endorsement of Pyrrhonism as a philosophical perspective, contradicting many of the texts we have already noted. In answer to such concerns, Hallie, Frede, Barnes, and others have allowed for Pyrrhonean belief by arguing that *epoche* does not encompass all belief. But this contravenes Pyrrhonean assertions about suspending judgment on all claims.

One of the standard interpretations preserves the logical consistency of Pyrrhonism, the other its commitment to practical affairs. Different commentators choose different sides of a dilemma that is actually a false dilemma. Resolving the problems with both interpretations is not difficult: the Pyrrhoneans attack a specifically realist account of truth, reject *all* claims to realist truth, and construct their positive philosophy on *anti-realist* statements about appearances and impressions. Ironically, it is Burnyeat who most clearly recognizes the realist nature of the truth the Pyrrhoneans attack; still insisting that they reject all claims, he fails to see that their attack achieves consistency with an anti-realist notion of belief.

In the controversy between the sceptic and the dogmatists over whether any truth exists at all, the issue is whether any proposition of a class of propositions can be accepted as true of a real objective world as distinct from mere appearance. For "true" in these discussions means "true of a real objective world"; the true, if there is such a thing, is what conforms with the real, an association traditional to the word *alethes* since the earliest period of Greek philosophy (cf. M XI 221).

Now clearly, if truth is restricted to matters pertaining to real existence, as contrasted with appearance, the same will apply [to related sceptical conceptions] . . . The notions involved, consistency and conflict, undecidability, *isostheneia, epoche, ataraxia*, since they are defined in terms of truth, will all relate, via truth, to real existence rather than appearance. In particular, if *epoche* is suspending belief about real existence as contrasted with appearance, that will amount to suspending all belief, *since belief is accepting something as true.* (my emphasis)[19]

The problem is that the Pyrrhoneans can accept belief without interpreting it as true *in the realist way*, endorsing it in an anti-realist sense (as subjective, and not necessarily indicative of the realist's external, objective world). Thus we can make room for their claim that Pyrrhonism is not opposed to life, belief, and practical affairs. Unlike the dogmatists' metaphysical speculation, the Pyrrhonean anti-realist notion of belief confirms rather than obstructs quotidian affairs. With

19. Burnyeat, "Can the Sceptic Live His Scepticism," p. 121.

the use of antithesis to dispel disturbing thoughts, it provides a ground for happiness. In contrast, the universal refusal of belief usually associated with the Pyrrhoneans would destroy rather than create tranquillity. As Burnyeat puts it at one point, "The problem is to see why this should produce tranquillity rather than anxiety."[20] It is indeed the problem, but one that undermines Burnyeat's own interpretation of the Pyrrhoneans and not their actual views.

20. Ibid., 139.

VII

Ancient Scepticism and Modern Epistemology

Our account of later Pyrrhonism completes the present history of the sceptics. From a general point of view, it suggests that the uniqueness of modern and contemporary epistemology has been exaggerated, that ancient philosophers had a long and involved debate on the possibility of realist epistemology, and that ancient scepticism and the views of some of its predecessors are a precursor to modern anti-realism. In this chapter, we briefly look at ancient scepticism in the context of modern, and especially contemporary, thought. Scepticism, we shall see, is a plausible alternative to modern and contemporary epistemology.

The connection between scepticism and anti-realism shows how misleading discussions of the latter are. For though anti-realism is presented (and often trumpeted) as an answer to scepticism's attack on truth, the truth it defends is not the truth rejected by the sceptics. It can best be said that sceptics and anti-realists both attack and reject realism, offering anti-realist beliefs and statements as an alternative, and that the common claim that tendencies in this direction originate with Berkeley and with Kant is a modern misconception.

Scepticism's similarity to modern anti-realism is enough to make the sceptics worthy of attention, though there remain two differences that warrant special comment. The first is the sceptics' refusal to grant our ability to know our mental states, a refusal that drives a wedge between scepticism and idealism. The second is the sceptics' definition of truth in a realist sense, which distinguishes the sceptics from modern anti-realists.[1] To assess the plausibility of scepticism as a philisophical

1. Another important difference is the ancient focus on distinctions between the views and outlooks of different individuals (on this point, see the discussion of the Cyrenaics in chapter 3).

perspective within the context of modern thought, we need to discuss these differences in turn.

MENTAL STATES

We have already seen that the sceptic accepts sense impressions as a subjective basis for belief. Idealists also accept them, though they do so to establish a remnant of realist truth. According to their arguments, external objects are unknowable because they are apprehended through sense impressions (being, in Pyrrhonean terms, "non-evident"), though perceptions and other mental states are directly experienced and can, therefore, be known to exist. According to the idealists, it follows that we can preserve the truth of ordinary claims if we interpret them in terms of mental states.

Descartes anticipates this idealist answer to the sceptics in his famous dictum, "I think, therefore I am," though he himself does not employ it as grounds for an idealist epistemology, arguing instead that its self-evident nature provides clearness and distinctness as a mark of truth.[2] According to Burnyeat:

2. I know of no exact account of the *cogito* in ancient thought, though the notion that we can know the nature of our mental states is the core of Cyrenaicism and there is a neglected anticipation of Descartes' argument in a long fragment of Oenomaus (second century A.D.) reported by Eusebius. It argues against a soothsayer by maintaining that our self-consciousness proves that we exist, and that once we have accepted this conclusion, it is arbitrary not to rely on our impressions in other kinds of circumstances.

Are we, I and thou, anything? You will say, Yes. But whence do we know this? Whereby did we determine that we do know it? Is it not the fact that nothing else is so satisfactory a proof (of our existence) as our conscious sensation and apprehension of ourselves?

... 'For if this is not to be so ... thou [and Chrysippus] knowest not ... what Arcesilaus [his adversary] is, and what Epicurus, or what the Porch is, or what the young men, or what the Nobody [Chrysippus] is, he neither knows nor can know; for he knows not even what comes far earlier, whether he himself is anything.

... there is no more trustworthy criterion than that of which I speak; nor if there seem to be any others, could they be made equal to this, if equal, could not surpass it.

'So then, someone may say, since thou ... are indignant if anyone should wish to deny your consciousness of yourselves—for of those many books of yours it is no longer possible to deny the existence—come, let us be indignant on the other side.

How, pray? Is this self-consciousness to be the most trustworthy and primary evidence wherever it pleases you? But where it pleases you not, is there some occult power, Fate, or Destiny, to tyrannize over it? (Eus. 256c–7d)

The beauty of the procedure is that it is a truth he has reached without applying a criterion . . . The Pyrrhonists argued that you cannot determine what is true and what is false without first settling on a criterion of truth. And they make sure that no proposed criterion would hold good under examination. But Descartes can go the other way round. He has got a truth without applying a criterion, and he can use this unassailable truth to fix the criterion of truth. The criterion is the clear and distinct perception which is what has assured him that he is a thing which thinks . . . Once again the move is proof against all the resources of the ancient tradition.[3]

Such remarks vastly underestimate the sceptic, who may answer that the attempt to establish a criterion by appealing to particular instances of truth simply begs the question, and that it is impossible to know these instances are true unless one assumes a criterion of truth. Sextus notes, in his discussion of a similar move in ancient times:

Demetrius the Laconian, one of the notables of the Epicurean School, used to declare that . . . "when we have established one of the particular proofs (for example, that which deduces that indivisible elements exist, or that void exists) and shown that it is sure, we shall at once have secured, as included in this, the trustworthiness of generic proof; for where there exists the particular of a genus, there we certainly find also the genus of which it is the particular" . . . But this, though it seems to be plausible, is in fact impossible. For, in the first place, no one will allow the Laconian to establish his particular proof when his generic proof does not pre-exist; and just as he himself claims that, if he possesses the particular proof, he at once possesses also the generic, so too the Sceptics will claim that, to gain credence for the particular, its genus must first be proved. (*AM* 8.348–50)

In the case of Descartes, the Pyrrhonean will answer that one cannot accept, "I think, therefore I am," since this assumes what needs to be proved—that what is clear and distinct is true. If, in contrast, this is questioned, there is no reason to accept the premise or the conclusion of the *cogito*.

One might answer that this does not account for the force of Descartes' claims: we are immediately aware of our thinking, so it cannot be doubted. Here there is a link to the idealists' central thesis: we can know our mental states in a way that refutes sceptical doubts. Granting the historical significance of this thesis, is there a way to defend it in the face of the persistent sceptic? It seems contradictory to

3. Burnyeat, "Idealism in Greek Philosophy," p. 49.

suggest that we might mistakenly think that we are thinking, or that we could think without existing; but this argument will not move the sceptic, who is willing to maintain that even the law of noncontradiction is possibly mistaken. Unintuitive though the suggestion may appear, there is no clear proof of the validity of the principles of logic (to assume that lack of intuitiveness is a mark of falsity is to assume, not prove, that we cannot be mistaken in our fundamental intuitions). On the contrary, the attempt at proof precipitates the problem of the criterion and leads (as the tortoise points out to Achilles in Lewis Carroll's famous tale) to circularity or regress. The sceptics use the law of noncontradiction and our awareness of our mental states in philosophy and practical affairs, but still deny they can be shown true in the realist sense. In modern philosophy, Nietzsche adopts a similar attitude in *The Will to Power*, remarking that "the subjective constraint that prevents one from contradicting here is a biological constraint: the instinct . . . is in our blood, we *are* almost this instinct . . . But what simplicity it is to attempt to derive from this fact that we possess an absolute truth! . . . We are not able to affirm and deny one and the same thing: This is a principle of subjective experience . . . "[4]

CONTEMPORARY ANTI-REALISM

The second major difference between scepticism and modern anti-realism is the septics' view of language. Unlike their modern counter-parts, they grant that realist claims are meaningful, assume a realist account of truth,[5] and always reject realism on philosophical rather than linguistic grounds. The sceptics view their philosophy, in consequence, as a means of undermining truth, and not as a struggle to establish (an alternative account of) "true" belief. The practical consequences of this aspect of scepticism are embedded in its moral views, for disposing of truth allows its practitioners to suspend judgment on the question whether any circumstances are fortunate or unfortunate, thus promoting the psychological goals of equanimity and indifference. In contrast, modern anti-realists replace realist truth with a more subjective account of truth and knowledge that grants human "knowledge" of fortunate and unfortunate circumstances, thereby undermining the notion that we cannot know misfortune.

4. Nietzsche, *The Will to Power*, pp. 31–32 (translated by Kaufman).
5. And take, in this regard, issue with the adoption of an antirealist account of truth proposed by Protagoras and some minor sophists.

Especially within contemporary philosophy, the different views of language that characterize scepticism and modern anti-realism are significant, for those who attack realism attach great importance to the claim that realist interpretations of truth and ordinary claims are mistaken; they argue that the very question whether our claims are true or certain is founded on a misunderstanding of terms such as *true, false, known, certain,* and so on.[6] In this way they undermine (or, as it is often put, "dissolve") the sceptical proposal that our beliefs may not be true (for that proposal assumes that it makes sense to talk of realist truth).

The most important philosopher to approach scepticism from this perspective is Wittgenstein.[7] In his *Tractatus*, he reduces all meaningful statements to atomic propositions composed of names that refer to simple objects, concluding that meaningful statements can discuss only the possible arrangement of the basic objects of the world, and cannot question their existence (4.172–74, 5.62, cf. 5.564 and *Notebooks* 85). Sceptical questions therefore lie beyond the limits of language; "scepticism is *not* irrefutable, but palpably senseless, if it would doubt where a question cannot be asked. For doubt can only exist where there is a question; a question only where there is an answer, and this only where something *can be said*" (6.51).

Wittgenstein himself rejects his earlier account of language in later work, but still holds that sceptical claims are meaningless. According to his new account, language assumes a form of life and must be understood in terms of its role within that form. "What has to be accepted, the given is—so one could say—forms of life" (*PI* 226, cf. 240–41, *OC* 87–88, 94–95, 144, 225, 345, 411, 670). Specific claims must therefore be understood within the context of the activities (and the "language games") that characterize our mode of life. From the point of view of scepticism, the important point is that words such as

6. Berkeley anticipates contemporary moves when he attempts to elude scepticism by appealing to an analysis of language. He declares that we must interpret ordinary statements as statements about sense impressions: "So long as we attribute a real existence to unthinking things, distinct from their being perceived, it is not only impossible to know with evidence the nature of any unthinking being, but even that it exists . . . But all this doubtfulness . . . vanishes if we annex a meaning to our words . . . since the very existence of an unthinking being consists in being perceived" (*PHK* 87–88).

7. In the present context I cannot, of course, discuss the secondary literature on Wittgenstein's philosophy or the details of contemporary anti-realism. Here I can only try to capture its spirit and refer to some general problems with its critique of scepticism.

truth, *mistake*, *certainty*, and *justification* must be understood in terms of
their ordinary use, and sceptical questions are, therefore, allegedly
nonsensical, referring as they do to an objective world that transcends
it. "To be sure, there is justification, but this justification comes to an
end" when we attempt to transcend our form of life and ask more
fundamental questions. In answer to such questions, we can only say
that we act in certain ways, and that this determines the proper use of
terms within our language (*OC* 192, cf. 166, 188–89, 253 and *PI* 217).

Is it wrong for me to be guided in my actions by the propositions of physics? Am
I to say I have no good ground for doing so? Isn't this precisely what we call a
"good ground"? (*OC* 608)

Sure evidence is what we *accept* as sure, it is evidence that we go by in *acting*
surely, action without any doubt.

What we call "a mistake" plays a quite special part in our language-games,
and so too does what we regard as certain evidence. (*OC* 196–97, cf. 507, 643,
648, 659–62)

Was I justified in drawing consequences? What is *called* justification here?
How is the word "Justification" used? Describe language games. (*PI* 486)

There are e.g. historical investigations and investigations into the shape and
also the age of the earth, but not into whether the earth has existed during the
last hundred years. Of course, many of us have information about this period
from our parents and grandparents; but mayn't this be wrong?—"Nonsense!"
one will say. "How should all these people be wrong?"—But is that an
argument? Is it not simply the rejection of an idea? And perhaps the
determination of a concept? For if I speak of a possible mistake here, this
changes the role of "mistake" and "truth" in our lives. (*OC* 138)

According to this account, sceptical doubts are undermined once we
see that the words the sceptic uses have meaning only within the
context of specific language games that dictate that we have "knowledge," "truth," and "certainty." In answer to the sceptic, we can say
that we are "sure" of our claims if "a language game exists in which this
assurance is employed. If anatomy were under discussion I should say:
'I know that twelve pairs of nerves lead from the brain.' I have never
seen these nerves, and even a specialist will only have observed them in
a few specimens. This is just how the word 'know' is correctly used here"
(*OC* 620–21, cf. 268). To question an inference that obeys the laws of
logic is similarly misguided, for "it is just this that is called 'thinking',
'speaking', 'inferring', 'arguing'" (*RFM* 1:155). More generally,
our inability to transcend ordinary usage shows that it cannot be

questioned, and that an expression such as "I know" is properly applied only in those "cases in which it is used in normal linguistic exchange" (*OC* 260, cf. *Philosophical Remarks*, 57).

In more recent philosophy, Putnam proposes similar arguments in answer to a science fiction version of the problem of the external world. He imagines a scenario in which an evil scientist removes a person's brain and places it in a vat of nutrients to keep it alive. The nerve endings are attached to a computer that monitors mental activity and sends the brain a variety of inputs. The brain perceives physical objects, events, and other people, mistakenly imagining that it is still attached to a body which walks, talks, and participates in everyday affairs. Any of our impressions could, in principle, be thus produced by computer simulation, and therefore Putnam asks how we can know that we are not a brain in such a vat. As the Pyrrhoneans might put it, the world beyond our immediate impressions is nonevident, and there seems to be no way to know what causes these impressions.

In discussing his scenario, Putnam argues that a person who was a brain in a vat could not meaningfully formulate the hypothesis that this is so. Like Wittgenstein, he reasons that the meanings of our words are "ultimately connected" with our interactions in the world and concludes that it is impossible to refer beyond them:

. . . when the brain in a vat . . . thinks "There is a tree in front of me", his thought does not refer to actual trees. On some of the theories we shall discuss it might refer to trees in the image, or to the electronic impulses that cause tree experiences, or to the features of the program that are responsible for those electronic impulses . . .These theories are not ruled out by what was just said, for there is a close causal connection between the use of the word "tree" in vat-English and the presence of [these phenomena] . . . On these theories the brain is *right*, not *wrong*, in thinking "There is a tree in front of me." Given what "tree" refers to in vat-English and what "in front of" refers to . . . the truth conditions for "There is a tree in front of me" . . . are simply that the tree in the image be "in front of" the "me" in question—in the image—or perhaps, that the kind of electronic impulse that normally produces this experience be coming from the automatic machinery . . . These truth conditions are certainly fulfilled.[8]

Putnam thus rejects the realist notion that truth amounts to some kind of correspondence between claims and objects existing in an

8. Putnam, *Reason, Truth and History*, p. 14. Cf. Harrison, "A Philosopher's Nightmare."

external world that transcends our experiences. Rather, he adopts an "internalist" perspective, maintaining that truth is "some sort of ideal coherence of our beliefs with each other and with our experiences . . . [rather than] correspondence with mind-independent or discourse-independent 'states of affairs.' There is no God's eye point of view that we can know or usefully imagine; there are only the various points of view of actual persons reflecting various interests and purposes that their descriptions and theories subserve."[9]

Before we turn to problems with the views of philosophers such as Wittgenstein and Putnam, the reader is reminded that we should not exaggerate the significance of their attempts to reject sceptical conclusions. All that distinguishes them from the sceptics is their account of the word *true*, and this should not be construed as though it were a more substantive issue. Philosophically, the important point is that realism, in both cases, is supplanted by a more subjective notion of belief (a point that at least Wittgenstein has appreciated).[10] Indeed, this subjectivity lies behind the linguistic attempt to reject scepticism, for the anti-realists claim that language is itself subjectively defined and that is why it cannot transcend subjective points of view. According to the *Tractatus*, it cannot transcend the basic objects that make up the ("my") world. According to the later Wittgenstein, it cannot transcend our form of life. According to Putnam, it cannot transcend our interactions with the world around us.

It is impossible to discuss anti-realist accounts of language in detail here. There are, however, reasons for suspecting them. To begin with, they often beg the questions that concern us, motivated as they are, by a desire to defeat the sceptics (see e.g., Bouwsma's critique of Descartes' argument for scepticism). In answer to this goal, it can be said that there is no need to defeat the sceptics, especially as they offer a plausible philosophy in keeping with our ordinary view of language. In contrast, contemporary anti-realists offer an account of language that is at least extremely unintuitive. In the case of scepticism, it undermines claims that are *prima facie* meaningful and apparently understood with little difficulty by most philosophers within the Western

9. Ibid., pp. 49–50.
10. Thus Wittgenstein fully realizes the radical relativism that is the final outcome of his views. See, for example, *OC* 238, the *Lectures and Conversations*, "Remarks on Fraser's *Golden Bough*," and his "Lecture on Ethics" (and cf. Bambrough, *Moral Scepticism*; Winch, *The Idea of a Social Science*; Bouwsma, "Descartes' Evil Genius"; and Black, "Necessary Statements and Rules").

philosophical tradition (the conclusion that such claims are meaning-less might actually be proposed as a reductio ad absurdum of the anti-realist view). As Gellner writes in a critique of contemporary philosophy's preoccupation with questions of meaning:

The notion of what cannot be said, of the difficulty of saying things, of the traps which beset the attempts, is already conspicuously present with the Idealists . . . By the time we reach positivism and then the linguistic philosophers, this is no longer a preoccupation, but an obsession. The identification of the stigmata of nonsense becomes the central theme of thought, and one which underlies and pervades all else . . . It is not perhaps an unworthy occupation: but why is it so intense . . . , why is it so persistent? Why—and this is the crucial question—do they feel the danger of falling into nonsense to be so pervasive, so close, so haunting, and the goal of speaking sense to be so . . . difficult to achieve? Why do they not, like earlier generations, treat talking sense as the natural and secure birthright of sane men of good faith and sound training, and the talking of nonsense as a real but not very significant danger, like slipping on a banana skin?[11]

One can, of course, *make* scepticism nonsensical by defining language appropriately, but that would be arbitrary and *ad hoc* unless it were justified independently.

A further problem with modern anti-realism is its apparent failure to appreciate the extent to which ordinary language can transcend our ordinary point of view. Indeed, it regularly transcends the everyday experience that gives it its initial meaning when it is used in history, science, fiction, novels, myth, and discussions of other cultures and the future (in talk of giants, cyclopes, major nuclear destruction, Stone-Age humans, dinosaurs, and so on). In such applications, we extend language beyond mundane concepts by extrapolating from ordinary life (we have never seen major nuclear destruction or a twenty-foot giant, but we have seen or heard of wars and tall people). The sceptics do something similar when they discuss the limits of knowledge. Thus, we may not know visions as complex as daily perception, but we know of dreams, hallucinations, and illusions and can by analogy expand our understanding to encompass the sceptical suggestion that ordinary life may be illusory. We already understand the claim that beliefs were mistaken in the past, and in view of this can understand the notion that our fundamental convictions may prove mistaken in the future. It

11. Gellner, "The Crisis in the Humanities and the Mainstream of Philosophy, p. 59.

is precisely because we understand justification in ordinary contexts that we can ask whether it is possible to extend it and justify and prove basic beliefs. The ordinary contrasts between better and worse, true and false, consistent and inconsistent, useful and useless similarly allow us to grasp the sceptical hypothesis that there may be some perspective that is better, truer, more consistent, or more useful than the one we now have. In these and other ways, sceptical ideas *are* rooted in ordinary experience. The sceptic is able, therefore, to accept the anti-realist view that language is rooted in ordinary experience, pointing out that the two are not so tightly bound that we cannot extend our thought and language further. Not just scepticism but any attempt to change our outlook on the world requires that we move beyond ordinary language (cf., e.g., Nietzsche's genealogy of morals and his at least understandable suggestion that we transcend and reject our accepted notion of good.) Putnam illustrates how easily we can extend language beyond its ordinary context with his own brain-in-the-vat scenario.[12]

THE SCEPTICAL PERSPECTIVE

A definitive rejection of anti-realist accounts of language would require much more comment, but by now it should be clear that ancient scepticism offers a plausible alternative to modern and contemporary outlooks. Contrary to popular misconceptions, it does not dismiss practical affairs, daily belief, or intellectual inquiry, but offers instead a sophisticated view that includes a critique of realism, a more subjective notion of belief, and a recognition of the limits of the human ability to know. Rather than being inconsistent, it clearly distinguishes realist and anti-realist claims, disposing of the former and accepting sceptical conclusions and ordinary life in a way that is in keeping with the latter. Also mistaken is the notion that ancient scepticism overlooks the incorrigible nature of the individual's knowledge of mental states and

---

12 Anti-realist accounts of language often have more in common with Orwell's newspeak in *Nineteen Eighty-Four* than with ordinary language. Newspeak aims to narrow the range of human speech so that it becomes impossible to raise questions about basic ideological commitments. Anti-realist accounts of language argue that its limits are so narrow that we cannot raise questions about the correctness of our accounts of truth. Though it is more subtle, this too is an ideological commitment. In answer to both perspectives, it must be said that ordinary language is more flexible than newspeak, and that it has no difficulty "bootstrapping" itself beyond ordinary notions and assumptions.

the possibility of idealism (or, in the ancient world, Cyrenaicism). Rather, the sceptic sees that claims about mental states are susceptible to sceptical conclusions. Finally, scepticism does not, as many believe, attempt to move beyond the limits of language; it constructs its arguments by appealing to language and experience firmly rooted in ordinary life.

Given the plausibility of scepticism, one must wonder why it has been so drastically misrepresented, misunderstood, and underestimated, and why the notion that we must defeat the sceptic has become such a central feature of philosophical inquiry. The answer has more to do with the social forces that shape philosophical inquiry than with the logic of sceptical views. Scepticism is dismissed, not because it has been studied carefully and found wanting, but because it goes against the spirit of Western thought as modern philosophy has portrayed it. That account glorifies the use of reason, the possibility of science, and the human ability to establish truth, and has no patience with sceptics who attack these ideals. Instead of trying dispassionately to understand the sceptics or the subtleties of their views (cf. the quotes in chapter 1), philosophers treat them the way most heretics are treated—with little emphasis on the details of their views, with little or no reserve in exploiting the misunderstanding this encourages, and with rhetorical appeals to the notion that truth and reason must be saved. Even when philosophers argue for positions that resemble scepticism, they present their views as an attack on it. Not surprisingly, the resulting picture of the sceptic is an easy target and a focus for bad feeling. "Truth" and reason are always vindicated, though the truth and objectivity that the sceptics attack are relinquished in the process, replaced with a subjective notion of belief and a new definition of the word *true*. The modern attempt to vindicate truth and reason against sceptics promoting its demise is little more than a linguistic sleight of hand.

The fundamental difference between the sceptics and most modern philosophers is the latter's positive conclusions. Modern thinkers offer and defend subjective notions of belief in order to *undermine* the conclusion that human perception of the world may in the final analysis be mistaken. Scepticism, therefore, offers an outlook more modest than that of most modern philosophers. Allowing us to retain ordinary standards for belief, the sceptic forces us to admit that they may be mistaken and that we cannot know ultimate reality. As Sextus says repeatedly, scepticism shows that the basis of our belief in objective truth is overconfidence in human abilities, which is founded on "the dogmatists' ailment, self-conceit." Like Sextus, Montaigne stresses humility when he revives Pyrrhonean thinking, declaring that presumption is "our original malady" and that it is vain and presumptuous to think humans, philosophy, or reason can penetrate ultimate reality. According to the sceptics, the best that we can hope for is an outlook respecting our desire to lead a satisfying life but admitting that human reason has stringent limits which cannot be transcended. Ultimate truth cannot be established. "The important thing," as Abbé Giliani said to Mme d'Epinay, "is not to be cured, but to live with one's ailments."[13]

13. Camus, *The Myth of Sisyphus*, p. 29.

APPENDIX

Flourishing Dates of Ancient Thinkers*

600–500 B.C. Thales, Anaximander (610–546), Xenophanes (570–478), Anaximenes, Themistoclea, Pythagoras, Theano of Crotona, Myia, Heracleitus

500–400 B.C. Parmenides, Epicharmus, Anaxagoras (534–462), Empedocles (521–461), Zeno, Leucippus, Archelaus, Democritus (494–404), Protagoras (490–420), Melissus, Gorgias (480–380), Socrates (470–399), Diotima, Euclides of Megara (430–360), Speusippus

400–300 B.C. Aristippus (435–350), Antisthenes (446–366), Pheado, Metrodorus of Chios, Plato (428–347), Diogenes of Sinope (410–320), Anaxarchus, Arete of Cyrene, Stilpo (380–300), Monimus, Aristotle (384–322), Pyrrho (365–275), Nausiphanes, Zeno of Citium (360–260),Epicurus (341–270), Colotes, Xenocrates, Polemo, Theophrastus, Crates of Thebes (365–285)

300–200 B.C. Phintys, Diodorus Cronus (d. 284), Hopparchia, Strato of Lampsacus, Timon (325–235), Crantor (335–275), Crates of Athens, Hermarchus, Arcesilaus (315–241), Cleanthes (331–232), Polystratus, Hieronymus (290–230), Ariston of Chios, Chrysippus (280–206), Perictione (?), Lacydes, Praylus of the Troad, Chrysippus (280–207), Philo the Dialectician, Zeno of Tarsus

---

* Names are listed in rough chronological order, though many of the details are open to dispute. In addition to well-known philosophers, I have included the names of a number of obscure thinkers either because they are relevant to the sceptical tradition, or because they provide a more accurate impression of the extent of philosophical activity in antiquity. For the dates of Anaxagoras, Empedocles, and Democritus, see Owens, *The History of Ancient Western Philosophy*, appendix, "The Chronology of Empedocles." For the dates of women philosophers I have listed, see Waithe.

200–100 B.C.	Diogenes of Babylon (240–152), Antipater of Tarsus, Telecles, Evander, Hegesinus, Carneades (214–129), Charmidas, Panaetius (185–110), Clitomachus (187–110), Mnesarchus, Metrodorus the Academic, Philo of Larissa, Appolodorus of Seleucia
100–0 B.C.	Theano II, Aesara of Lucania (?), Posidonius, Aenesidemus, Antiochus, Zeuxippus, Zeuxis the Pyrrhonean, Lucretius (99–55), Athenaeus of Attaleia, Archedemus, Philodemus, Antipater of Tyre, Arius Didymus, Cicero (106–43)
A.D. 0–100	Philo of Alexandria (30 B.C.–A.D. 45), Agrippa (?), Seneca (55 B.C.–A.D. 39), Aristocles, Antiochus of Laodicea on the Lycus, Favorinus, Epictetus (50–130), Plutarch (46–120), Dio Chrysostom, Aetius
A.D. 100–200	Hierocles, Menodotus of Nicomedia, Diogenes of Oenoanda, Numenius, Aulus Gellius, Lucian (115–200), Apuleius, Marcus Aurelius, Justin Martyr (110–65), Galen, Hippolytus, Clement of Alexandria
A.D. 200–300	Sextus Empiricus, Minucius Felix, Tertullian (160–230), Athenaeus, Origen (185–254), Porphyry, Alexander of Aphrodisias, Ammonius Saccas, Plotinus (205–70), the Greek author of the *Asclepius* (?), Lactantius (240–320), Iamblichus
A.D. 300–400	The Latin adaptor of the *Asclepius* (?), Eusebius (260–340), Diogenes Laertius, Alexander Lycopolis, Augustine (354–430), Themistius, Nemesius, Syrianus, Stobaeus (?), Plutarch of Athens, Calcidius (?), Hypatia of Alexandria, Asclepigenia of Athens

Bibliography

A NOTE ON ANCIENT THINKERS*

Most of the relevant ancient texts on the sceptics are available with a translation in A. A. Long and D. N. Sedley, *The Hellenistic Philosophers* (New York: Cambridge University Press, 1987, 2 vols.). A useful translation of the basic texts is also found in Brad Inwood and L. P. Gerson, *Hellenistic Philosophy: Introductory Readings* (Indianapolis: Hackett Publishing, 1988). Discussions of the sceptics' modes in Sextus, Philo, and Diogenes Laertius are examined and translated by Julia Annas and Jonathan Barnes in *The Modes of Scepticism: Ancient Texts and Modern Interpretations* (New York: Cambridge University Press, 1985). A very readable introduction to Sextus Empiricus is found in *Selections from the Major Writings of Sextus Empiricus on Scepticism, Man, and God*, ed. by Philip P. Hallie, trans. by Sanford G. Etheridge (Indianapolis: Hackett Publishing, 1985).

Readily available editions of the most important extant works that shed light on scepticism are *Sextus Empiricus*, with a translation by R. G. Bury (Cambridge: Harvard University Press, 1933–49, 4 vols.); Sextus Empiricus, *Against the Musicians*, with a translation by Denise Davidson Greaves (Lincoln: University of Nebraska Press, 1986); Marcus Tullius Cicero, *Academica* and *De Natura Deorum*, with a translation by H. Rackham (Cambridge: Harvard University Press, 1979); Diogenes Laertius, *Lives of Eminent Philosophers*, with a translation by R. D. Hicks (Cambridge: Harvard University Press, 1925, 2 vols.); Pamphili Eusebius, *Preparatio Evangelica*, translated by Edwin Hamilton Gifford (Oxford: Clarendon Press, 1903, 2 vols.); and Plutarch, *Moralia* (esp. "Adversus Colotum"), with a translation by Frank Cole Babbit et al. (Cambridge: Harvard University Press, 1928–69).

*Authors and works referred to sparingly are not listed in the bibliography, though they do appear in the index locorum. In most cases, the relevant passages can be found in one of the collections listed here.

The most important texts on the sceptics' predecessors are available in H. Diels and W. Kranz, *Die Fragmente der Vorsokratiker* (Zürich: Weidmann, 1964, 11th ed.) and, with a translation, in G. S. Kirk, J. E. Raven, and M. Schofield, *The Presocratic Philosophers* (New York: Cambridge University Press, 1983, 2d ed.). Other useful translations are found in Kathleen Freeman, *Ancilla to the Presocratic Philosophers* (Oxford: Basil Blackwell, 1952) and Rosamond Kent Sprague, ed., *The Older Sophists* (Columbia: University of South Carolina Press, 1972). For collections of the fragments of specific pre-Socratics with translations and commentary, see T. M. Robinson's *Heraclitus: Fragments* (Toronto: University of Toronto Press, 1987); David Gallop's *Parmenides of Elea: Fragments* (Toronto: University of Toronto Press, 1984); and H. D. P. Lee's *Zeno of Elea* (Amsterdam: Adolf M. Hakkert, 1967).

Other available editions of works that are helpful in understanding the sceptics, their predecessors, and their contemporaries are *The Collected Dialogues of Plato* (esp. the Socratic dialogues), edited by Edith Hamilton and Huntington Cairns, translated by many hands (Princeton: Princeton University Press, 1973); Augustine, *Against the Academicians,* translated by Sister Mary Patricia Garvey (Milwaukee: Marquette University Press, 1957); Lucian, *Selected Works,* translated by Bryan Reardon (Indianapolis: Bobbs-Merrill, 1965); Marcus Tullius Cicero, *De finibus,* with a translation by H. Rackham (Cambridge: Harvard University Press, 1966–67); Marcus Tullius Cicero, *De republica, de legibus,* with a translation by Clinton Walker Keyes (Cambridge: Harvard University Press, 1943); Marcus Tullius Cicero, *Tusculan Disputations,* with a translation by J. E. King (Cambridge: Harvard University Press, 1966); Photius, *Bibliotheque,* with a French translation by René Henry (Paris: Les Belles Lettres, 1959); *The Basic Works of Aristotle* (esp. the *Metaphysics*), edited by Richard McKeon, translated by many hands (New York: Random House, 1970); Lactantius, *The Divine Institutions,* translated by Sr. Mary Francis McDonald (Washington: Catholic University of America Press, 1964); Marcus Aurelius, *Meditations,* with a translation by A. S. L. Farquharson (Oxford: Clarendon Press, 1968); Xenophon, *Memorabilia,* with a translation by E. C. Marchant (New York: G. P. Putnam's Sons, 1923); and *Epictetus,* with a translation by W. A. Oldfather (Cambridge: Harvard University Press, 1966–67).

SECONDARY SOURCES

Arnold, E. Vernon. *Roman Stoicism.* New York: Humanities Press, 1958.

Bambrough, Renford. *Moral Scepticism and Moral Knowledge.* London: Routledge and Kegan Paul, 1979

Barnes, Jonathan. "Ancient Scepticism and Causation." In *The Skeptical Tradition,* edited by M. F. Burnyeat. Berkeley: University of California Press, 1983.

— "The Beliefs of a Pyrrhonist." *Proceedings of the Cambridge Philological Society* 101 (1982): 1–29.

— *The Presocratic Philosophers.* Boston: Routledge and Kegan Paul, 1979.

Bates, Marston. *Gluttons and Libertines: Human Problems of Being Natural.* New York: Vintage (Random House), 1967.

Bayle, Pierre. *Historical and Critical Dictionary.* Translated by Richard H. Popkin. Indianapolis: Bobbs-Merrill, 1965.

Beck, L. J. *The Metaphysics of Descartes.* Oxford: Oxford University Press, 1965.

Bergmann, Gustav. *Meaning and Existence.* Madison: University of Wisconsin Press, 1960.

Berkeley, George. *A Treatise Concerning the Principles of Human Knowledge.* Edited by Colin M. Turbayne. Indianapolis, Bobbs-Merrill, 1957.

Black, Max. "Necessary Statements and Rules." *Philosophical Review* 67 (1958): 313–41.

Boswell, James. *The Life of Samuel Johnson.* New York: The Modern Library, 1931.

Bouwsma, O. K. "Descartes' Evil Genius." *Philosophical Review* 58 (1949): 141–51.

Brochard, V. *Les Sceptiques grecs.* Paris: Librarie philosophique J. Vrin, 1959.

Brumbaugh, Robert S. *The Philosophers of Greece.* Albany: State University of New York Press, 1981.

Burnyeat, Myles. "Protagoras and Self-Refutation in Later Greek Philosophy." *Philological Review* 85 (1976).

— "Can the Sceptic Live His Scepticism?" In Schofield, Burnyeat, and Barnes, eds., *Doubt and Dogmatism: Studies in Hellenistic Epistemology.* Oxford: Oxford University Press, 1980.

— "Idealism in Greek Philosophy: What Descartes Saw and Berkeley Missed." In *Idealism Past and Present,* edited by Godfrey Vesey. New York: Cambridge University Press, 1982.

— ed. *The Skeptical Tradition.* Berkeley: University of California Press, 1983.

— "The Sceptic in His Time and Place." In *Philosophy in History,* edited by Rorty, Schneewind and Skinner. New York: Cambridge University Press, 1984.

Bury, R. G. "Introduction." In *Sextus Empiricus,* vol. 1 (see the primary sources).

Calderon, Don Pedro. *La Vida es sueno.* Edited by Albert E. Sloman. Manchester: Manchester University Press, 1961.

Camus, Albert. *The Myth of Sisyphus.* Translated by Justin O'Brien. New York: Vintage Books, 1955.

Carries, L. S. "Scepticism Made Certain." *Journal of Philosophy* 71 (1974): 140–50.

Carroll, Lewis. "What the Tortoise Said to Archilles." In *Readings on Logic,* edited by Copi and Gould, 2d ed. New York: Macmillan, 1972.

Chisholm, Roderick M. *Theory of Knowledge.* Englewood Cliffs: New Jersey, 1966.

Cornford, Francis Macdonald. *Plato and Parmenides.* London: Routledge and Kegan Paul, 1951.

— *The Unwritten Philosophy and Other Essays.* Cambridge: Cambridge University Press, 1950.

Couissin, Pierre. "The Stoicism of the New Academy." Translated by Jennifer Barnes and M. F. Burnyeat. In *The Skeptical Tradition*, edited by Burnyeat.

Curley, E. M. *Descartes against the Skeptics*. Cambridge: Harvard University Press, 1978.

DeLacy, Philip. "*Ou Mallon* and the Antecedents of Ancient Scepticism." *Pronesis* 3 (1958).

René Descartes. *Conversations with Burnman*. Translated by John Costingham. Oxford: Clarendon Press. 1976.

— *Oeuvres de Descartes*. Edited by C. Adam and P. Tannery. Paris: J. Vrin, 1964.

— *Philosophical Works*. Edited and translated by E. S. Haldane and G. T. R. Ross. 2 vols. New York: Cambridge University Press, 1955.

Dillon, John M. *The Middle Platonists: 80 B.C. to A.D. 220*. Ithaca: Cornell University Press, 1973.

Edwards, Paul, *Encyclopedia of Philosophy*. 8 vols. New York: Macmillan, 1967.

Edwyn. *Stoics and Sceptics*. Oxford: Clarendon Press, 1913.

Ewing, Alfred Cyril. *Idealism: A Critical Survey*. London: Methuen, 1961.

Feyerabend, Paul. *Against Method*. London: Verso, 1976.

Flintoff, Everard. "Pyrrho and India." *Phronesis* 25 (1980): 88–108.

Frankl, Victor E. *The Unheard Cry for Meaning*. New York: Simon and Schuster, 1978.

Frede, Michael. "The Sceptic's Two Kinds of Knowledge and the Question of the Possibility of Knowledge." In *Philosophy in History*, edited by Rorty, Schneewind and Skinner.

Freeman, Kathleen. *Companion to the Presocratic Philosophers*. Oxford: Basil Blackwell, 1959.

Fritz, Kurt von. "Zenon von Elea." *Real Encyclopadie der classischen Altertumswissenschaft*. Edited by August Friedrich von Pauly. Stuttgart: A. Druckenmuller, 1972.

Furley, D. J. *Two Studies in the Greek Atomists*. Princeton: Princeton University Press, 1967.

Gallop, David. "Introduction." In *Parmenides of Elea: Fragments* (see the note on primary sources).

Gellner, Ernest. "The Crisis in the Humanities and the Mainstream of Philosophy." In *Crisis in the Humanities*, edited by J. H. Plumb. Harmondsworth: Penguin, 1964.

— *Words and Things*. Rev. ed. London: Routledge and Kegan Paul, 1979.

Goodman, Nelson. *Ways of Worldmaking*. Indianapolis: Hackett Publishing, 1985.

Gouhier, Henri. *La Pensée metaphysique de Descartes*. Paris: J. Vrin, 1962.

Grayling, A. C. *The Refutation of Scepticism*. La Salle: Open Court Publishing, 1985.

Groarke, Leo. "Descartes' First Meditation: Something Old, Something New, Something Borrowed." *Journal of the History of Philosophy* 22 (1984): 282–301.

— "On Nicholas of Autrecourt and the Law of Non-Contradiction." *Dialogue* 23 (1984): 129–34.

— "Parmenides' Timeless Universe." *Dialogue* 24 (1985): 535–41.

— "Parmenides' Timeless Universe, Again." *Dialogue* 26 (1987): 549–52.

Guthrie, W. K. C. *A History of Greek Philosophy.* 6 vols. Cambridge: University Press, 1962.

Hallie, Philip P. "A Polemical Introduction." In *Selections from the Major Writings of Sextus Empiricus on Scepticism, Man and God* (see the note on primary sources).

Harrison, Jonathan. "A Philosopher's Nightmare: or, The Ghost Not Laid." *Proceedings of the Aristotelian Society* 67 (1967).

Jaeger, Werner. *The Theology of the Early Greek Philosophers.* London: Clarendon Press, 1947.

Johnson, Oliver. *Scepticism and Cognitivism.* Los Angeles: University of California Press, 1978.

Kekes, John. "The Case for Scepticism." *Philosophical Quarterly* 25 (1975): 28–39.

Kerferd, G. B. *The Sophistic Movement.* Melbourne: Cambridge University Press, 1981.

Kirk, G. S. *Heraclitus: The Cosmic Fragments.* Cambridge: Cambridge University Press, 1954.

Kuhn, Thomas S. *The Structure of Scientifiic Revolutions.* Chicago: University of Chicago Press, 1962.

Lehrer, Keith. "Scepticism and Conceptual Change." In *Empirical Knowledge,* edited by Roderick Chisholm and Norman Swartz. Englewood Cliffs: Prentice Hall, 1973.

Lennon, Thomas M. "*Verita Filia Temporis*: Hume on Time and Causation," *History of Philosophy Quarterly* 2 (1985).

Lewis, C. I. "The Given Element in Empirical Knowlege." *The Philosophical Review* 61 (1952): 168–75.

Long, A. A. *Hellenistic Philosophy: Stoics, Epicureans, Sceptics.* Duckworth: London, 1974.

Maccoll, Norman. *The Greek Sceptics, from Pyrrho to Sextus.* London: Macmillan, 1869.

Matson, Wallace. *A New History of Philosophy.* Toronto: Harcourt Brace Jovanovich, 1987.

— "Why Isn't the Mind-Body Problem Ancient?" In *Mind, Matter and Method: Essays in Philosophy and Science in Honor of Herbert Feigl,* edited by Paul Feyerabend and Grover Maxwell. Minneapolis: University of Minresota Press, 1966.

Minton, Arthur J., and Thomas A. Shipka. *Philosophy: Paradox and Discovery.* Toronto: McGraw Hill, 1982.

Montaigne, Michel E. de. "Apologie de Raymond Sebond." In *Les Essais de Michel de Montaigne,* edited by Pierre Villey. Paris: F. Alcan, 1922.

— *The Essays of Michel de Montaigne*. Translated by Jacob Zeitlin. New York: A. A. Knopf, 1935.

Moore, G. E. "A Defence of Common Sense" and "Proof of an External World." In *Classics of Analytic Philosophy*, edited by Robert R. Ammerman. Toronto: McGraw-Hill, 1965.

Mourelatos, Alexander P. D. *The Route of Parmenides*. New Haven: Yale University Press, 1970.

Naess, Arne. *Scepticism*. New York: Humanities Press, 1968.

Naify, James Fredrick. *Arabic and European Occasionalism*. Ph.D. diss., University of California at San Diego, 1975.

Nicholas of Autrecourt. "Letters to Bernard of Arezzo." Translated by Ernest A. Moody. In *Philosophy in the Middle Ages*, edited by Arthur Hyman and James J. Walsh. 2d ed. Indianapolis: Hackett Publishing, 1973.

Nietzsche, Friedrich. *Twilight of the Idols*. Translated by J. Hollingdale. Harmondsworth: Penguin, 1977.

— *The Will to Power*. Translated by Walter Kaufmann. New York: Random House, 1977.

Norton, David Fate. *David Hume: Common-Sense Moralist, Sceptical Metaphysician*. Princeton: Princeton University Press, 1982.

— "The Myth of British Empiricism." *History of European Ideas* 1 (1981).

Orwell, George. *Nineteen Eighty-Four*. Harmondsworth: Penguin, 1949.

Owens, Joesph. *A History of Ancient Western Philosophy*. New York: Appleton-Century-Crofts, 1959.

Patrick, Mary Mills. *The Greek Sceptics*. New York: Columbia University Press, 1929.

Penelhum, Terence. *God and Skepticism: A Study in Scepticism and Fidiesm*. Boston: D. Reidel, 1983.

Poincaré, Henri. *Science and Hypothesis*. New York: Dover, 1952.

Popkin, Richard. *The History of Scepticism from Erasmus to Spinoza*. Berkeley: University of California Press, 1979.

Putnam, Hilary. *Reason, Truth and History*. Cambridge; Cambridge University Press, 1981.

Reichenbach, Hans. *The Rise of Scientific Philosophy*. Berkeley: University of California Press, 1959.

Rescher, Nicholas. *Scepticism: A Critical Reappraisal*. Oxford: Basil Blackwell, 1980.

Robin, Léon. *Pyrrhon et le scepticisme grec*. Paris: Presses Universitaires de France, 1944.

Robinson, John Mansley. *An Introduction to Early Greek Philosophy*. Boston: Houghton Mifflin, 1968.

Rollins, C. D. "Solipsism. In *Encyclopedia of Philosophy*, edited by Paul Edwards.

Rorty, Richard. *Philosophy and the Mirror of Nature*. Princeton: Princeton University Press, 1980.

Rorty, Richard, J. B. Schneewind, and Quentin Skinner. *Philosophy in History:*

Essays on the Historiography of Philosophy. New York: Cambridge University Press, 1984.

Rozeboom, W. "Why I Know So Much More Than You Do." *American Philosophical Quarterly* 4 (1967): 281–90.

Russell, Bertrand. *A History of Western Philosophy*. London: George Allen and Unwin, 1946.

— *Wisdom of the West*. Edited by Paul Folkes. London: Open Court, 1914.

Schmitt, Charles B. *Cicero Scepticus: A Study of the "Academia" in the Renaissance*. The Hague: Martinus Nijhoff, 1972.

— *Gianfrancesco Pico della Mirandola and His Critique of Aristotle*. The Hague: Martinus Nijhoff, 1967.

Schofield, Malcolm, Myles Burnyeat, and Jonathan Barnes. *Doubt and Dogmatism: Studies in Hellenistic Epistemology*. Oxford: Oxford University Press, 1980.

Sedley, David. "The Motivation of Greek Scepticism." In *The Skeptical Tradition*, edited by Burnyeat.

— "The Protagonists." In *Doubt and Dogmatism*, edited by Schofield, Burnyeat, and Barnes.

Sidgwick, Henry. "The Sophists." *Journal of Philology* 4 (1872).

Slote, Michael. *Reason and Scepticism*. London: George Allen and Unwin, 1970.

Smith, Norman Kemp. *Studies in the Cartesian Philosophy*. New York: Russell and Russell, 1962.

Solmsen, Friedrich. "The Tradition about Zeno of Elea Re-examined." *Phronesis* 16 (1971): 116–41.

Stokes, M. C. *One and Many in Presocratic Philosophy*. Washington: Center for Hellenistic Studies, 1971.

Stough, Charlotte. *Greek Scepticism: A Study in Epistemology*. Berkeley: University of California Press, 1969.

— "Sextus Empiricus on Non-Assertion." *Phronesis* 19 1984: 137–64.

Striker, Gisela. "Sceptical Strategies," In *Doubt and Dogmatism*, edited by Schofield, Burnyeat, and Barnes.

— "The Ten Tropes of Aenesidemus." In *The Skeptical Tradition*, edited by Burnyeat.

Stroud, Barry. *The Significance of Philosophical Scepticism*. Oxford: Clarendon Press, 1984.

Tarán, Leonardo. *Parmenides*. Princeton: Princeton University Press, 1965.

Tarrant, Harold. *Scepticism or Platonism? The Philosophy of the Fourth Academy*. Cambridge: Cambridge University Press, 1985.

Thoreau, Henry David. *Walden*. New York: New American Library, 1980.

Tsekourakis, Damianas. *Studies in the Terminology of Early Stoic Ethics*. Wiesbaden: Franz Steiner, 1974.

Verdenius, W. J. *Parmenides: Some Comments on His Poem*. Amsterdam: Adolf M. Hakkert, 1964.

Vlastos, Gregory. "Plato's Testimony Concerning Zeno of Elea." *Journal of Hellenic Studies* 95 (1975).

Waithe, Mary Ellen, ed. *A History of Women Philosophers*. Vol. 1, *600 B.C.–500 A.D.* The Hague: Martinus Nijhoff, 1987.

West, M. L. *Early Greek Philosophy and the Orient*. Oxford: Clarendon Press, 1971.

Wilbur, J. B., and H. J. Allen. *The Worlds of the Greek Philosophers*. Buffalo: Prometheus Books, 1979.

Williams, Bernard, "Philosophy." In *The Legacy of Greece*, edited by M. I. Finley. Oxford: Oxford University Press, 1981.

Winch, Peter. *The Idea of a Social Science*. London: Routledge and Kegan Paul, 1958.

Wittgenstein, Ludwig. *Lectures and Conversations of Aesthetics, Psychology and Religious Belief*. Edited by Cyril Barret. Berkeley: University of California Press, 1972.

— *Notebooks, 1914–1916*. G. H. von Wright and G. E. M. Anscombe, eds. Translated by G. E. M. Anscombe. Oxford: Basil Blackwell, 1961.

— *On Certainty*. G. E. M. Anscombe and G. H. von Wright, eds. Translated by G. E. M. Anscombe. Evanston: Harper and Row, 1969.

— *Philosophical Investigations*. G. E. M. Anscombe and G. H. von Wright, eds. Translated by G. E. M. Anscombe. Oxford: Basil Blackwell, 1953.

— *Philosophical Remarks*. Rush Rhees, ed. Translated by Raymond Hargreaves and Roger White. Oxford: Basil Blackwell, 1975.

— "Remarks on Fraser's *Golden Bough*." In *Wittgenstein: Sources and Perspectives*, C. G. Luckhardt, ed. Hassocks: The Harvester Press, 1979.

— *Remarks on the Foundations of Mathematics*. G. H. von Wright, R. Rhees, and G. E. M. Anscombe, eds. Translated by G. E. M. Anscombe. Cambridge: M. I. T. Press, 1967.

— *Tractatus Logico-Philosophicus*. Translated by C. K. Ogden. London: Routledge and Kegan Paul, 1922.

Zeller, Eduard. *Stoics, Epicureans and Sceptics*. Translated by Oswald J. Reichel. New York: Russell and Russell, 1962.

— *Socrates and the Socratic Schools*. Translated by Oswald J. Reichel. New York: Russell and Russell, 1962.

INDEX LOCORUM

References to ancient authors only are listed in this index. Fragment numbers refer to the B section of DK unless otherwise stated.

Alcmaeon
frag. 1: 37
frag. 1a: 37fn.15
frag. 2: 37fn.16
Anaxarchus
frag. A.15: 65
frag. A.16: 65

Aristotle
De anima
404a29: 55, 76
De generatione et corruptione
A1, 315b6: 54, 55
Metaphysics
A4, 985b9: 53fn.4
A5, 986b18: 38fn.20
B4, 1000b6: 44
G4, 1007b18: 61
G5, 1009b1–30: 44, 46, 53–54
K6, 1062b13: 61
Physics
G4, 203b25: 53fn.4

Athenaeus
The Diepnosophists
337: 93
419d–e: 89
Augustine
Against the Academicians
3.20.43: 116fn.38

Cicero
Academica
frag. 21: 116fn.8

1.13: 124
1.19; 110fn.1
1.26–30: 124fn.
1.45–46: 98, 100, 104, 106, 111
2.7: 99fn.4, 106fn.3
2.8: 100
2.13–18: 106, 124
2.16–39: 124fn.1
2.20: 73
2.27: 120fn.39
2.29: 120fn.39
2.32: 122
2.34: 123
2.35: 122, 123
2.36: 119, 122, 123
2.40–41: 103, 106
2.42: 102fn.14, 133
2.43–44: 105, 106, 111fn.33, 119, 123
2.47–48: 101, 104, 130fn.9
2.51: 76
2.57: 123
2.59: 119, 122
2.60: 116fn.38
2.65–67: 122
2.72–76: 34, 101
2.77–78: 103, 106, 112, 119, 122, 123
2.79–85: 35, 101, 103, 106
2.87: 119
2.89–90: 76
2.92–97: 101fn.9, 133
2.98: 115
2.99: 106, 116, 119
2.100: 115
2.101: 14, 119

2.101–3: 116, 119, 123
2.104: 117–19, 122
2.105: 119
2.108: 119
2.109–10: 115, 119–20, 122
2.111: 119
2.112–13: 122, 123
2.129–34: 74, 101
2.138: 119
2.139: 116fn.38, 119
2.142–44: 74, 101
2.146: 117fn.38
2.148: 122
De finibus
1.20: 35
2.2: 100, 106fn.23, 118
2.35: 116fn.38, 122
2.38: 116fn.38
2.42: 116fn.38
2.43: 122
3.11–12: 122
4.43: 122
4.45: 110fn.31
De natura deorum
1.12: 115
1.57: 106fn.23
1.61–62: 16, 115
1.63: 51
1.76–77: 33
1.81–88: 33, 51
3.5–6: 15, 115
3.38–39: 102fn.17
3.44: 106fn.23, 113
De republica
3.4.8–32: 51
On Old Age
47: 69
Tusculan Disputations
3.54: 108, 118
3.59–60: 108

Democritus
frag. A.8: 53fn.4
frag. A.13: 59
frag. A.20: 58
frag. A.23: 58
frag. A.37: 52
frag. 3: 56
frag. 6: 52
frag. 7: 52–54
frag. 8: 52
frag. 9: 52, 54
frag. 10: 52

frag. 11: 52
frag. 14: 59
frag. 15: 59
frag. 125: 52, 53
frag. 154: 53
frag. 172: 56fn.9
frag. 191: 56
frag. 230: 57
frag. 289: 57

Diogenes Laertius
Lives of Eminent Philosophers
2.21: 70
2.28: 66
2.34–35: 70
2.69: 74fn.27
2.75: 74
2.79: 74n27
2.83–84: 74
2.91: 74
2.92: 72–73, 77
2.93: 72
2.94: 74
2.95: 72
2.107: 87
4.28: 100
4.33: 99fn.3
4.34: 98fn.2
4.36: 112
4.37: 66fn.21, 105fn.22
4.42: 112
4.43: 98fn.2
4.59: 100
4.60: 99
4.62: 99, 105fn.22
4.64–65: 100fn.6, 108fn.27
6.83: 72
7.51: 93fn.23, 102fn.14
7.76: 109fn.28
8.57: 43
9.21–23: 38fn.20
9.25: 43
9.38–40: 54fn.5
9.45: 57
9.51: 58, 59
9.55: 58
9.59–60: 65
9.61: 71, 81fn.1, 85, 87, 93, 95
9.62: 85, 92fn.21
9.63: 81fn.1, 89, 90
9.64: 89
9.65: 87
9.66: 90, 91

9.67: 81, 83, 89
9.68: 89, 90
9.69: 86, 87
9.70: 85
9.71: 105fn.22
9.72: 41
9.73–74: 105fn.22, 137
9.76: 96
9.79–80: 35
9.82: 84fn.6
9.83: 51
9.85–86: 35
9.87–88: 33
9.91: 81fn.1, 86
9.103–5: 92fn.21, 93, 96, 134, 137
9.106: 92, 97, 125, 134
9.107: 107fn.26
9.108: 134
9.111: 86
9.113: 93
9.115–16: 96fn.27
Dissoi Logoi
3: 50
10: 50
13–14: 50
18: 51
section IV: 50
section IX: 50

Empedocles
frag. 105: 44
frag. 106: 44
frag. 108: 44
frag. 109: 44
frag. 134: 44
frag. A86: 44

Epicharmus
frag. 2: 38
frag. 5: 37
frag. 10: 37
frag. 15: 37
frag. 64: 37

Epictetus
Discourses
1.27.18: 76
2.20.28: 76fn.33
7.27: 71
Enchiridion
1: 71

Euripides
frag. 189N: 79

Eusebius
Preparatio Evangelica
256c–257d: 144fn.2
718c: 73
726d: 105
729b: 110fn.31
729c: 99fn.3
730c: 66fn.21
731–33: 105fn.22
731a–b: 99fn.3, 105, 113fn.34
731c: 110fn.31
734–36: 99
736–38: 105fn.22
736d: 100fn.6, 103fn.19
737c–d: 112
737d: 100
738a: 105
738d: 113
758c–d: 85, 89, 95
759c: 96
759d: 93
761a: 90
762a: 93
763: 91
763b: 83fn.2
763c: 37
764a: 74
764c: 72–74
764d–65c: 74fn.26, 76, 81

Gellius
Attic Nights
29.15–21: 71
Gorgias
frag. 3: 51

Heracleitus
frag. A.6: 34fn.5
frag. 3: 34
frag. 9: 35
frag. 12: 34fn.5
frag. 21: 35
frag. 26: 35
frag. 46: 34
frag. 49a: 34
frag. 54: 34
frag. 55: 35fn.9
frag. 56: 34
frag. 58: 34fn.6
frag. 59: 34
frag. 60: 34
frag. 61: 35
frag. 75: 35

frag. 78: 36fn.11
frag. 79: 34fn.6
frag. 82: 35
frag. 83: 35
frag. 86: 36fn.11
frag. 88: 35
frag. 89: 35
frag. 96: 34fn.6
frag. 99: 34fn.6
frag. 103: 34
frag. 107: 34, 36
frag. 117: 35
frag. 123: 34, 36
frag. 124: 34
frag. 136: 35

Hippolytus
Refutatio Omnium Haeresium
123.3:105

Lactantius
The Divine Institutions
5.16.2–4: 51fn.1
5.16.12: 51fn.1
6.6.2–4: 51fn.1
6.6.19: 51fn.1
6.6.23: 51fn.1

Lucretius
De rerum natura
4.483–512: 10

Marcus Aurelius
Meditations
1.15: 72
2.15: 71

Metrodorus
frag. 2: 64

Nausiphanes
frag. 3: 64fn.17
frag. 4: 64fn.17

Parmenides
frag. 1: 41
frag. 6.4–9: 39
frag. 7.5: 41fn.26
frag. 8: 41
frag. 8.21–30: 40
frag. 8.38–41: 40
frag. 8.44–49: 40
frag. 16: 39

Pausanias
6.24.5: 89fn.14

Philo of Alexandria
On Drunkeness
171–75: 35
178–80: 84fn.6
181–83: 35
193–202: 51

Philostratus
491: 97

Photius
Bibliotheca
170a: 124

Plato
Alcibiades
1.119A–B: 43
Apology
19b–d: 69
23a–b: 67
28b–29a: 70
29b: 67, 70
31–32: 68
31c–d: 67
33–34: 68fn.23
40c–41a: 70
Cratylus
386a: 59
402a: 34fn.5
Crito
47–48: 68
50–54: 68
52: 68fn.23
54b–d: 70
Euthyphro
4b: 66
4e: 66, 68
6: 68
7e–8b: 67
10: 67
15b–c: 67
Meno
76c–e: 44
Parmenides
136a–c: 40
166c: 40
Phaedo
43b: 69
114d: 69, 70
115c–16: 70

Phaedrus
99d–100c7: 78
261d6–8: 43
Protagoras
171: 63fn.15
318a: 63
320c–f: 63
328c–d: 63
333e–34c: 58
Republic
1.329d: 69
2.377c–383c: 68
5.479: 78
7.515b–16d: 128fn.6
7.537–39: 78
Sophist
230b: 41
242d: 38fn.20
Theaetetus
166d–67c: 61–62
183e–84: 41fn.27
386a: 59
Timaeus
47c: 3

Plutarch
Life of Alexander, LII: 65–66
Life of Pericles, IV.3: 43
Moralia, "Adversus Colotum"
1108F: 53fn.4
1109A: 59
1110F: 53fn.4
1120C–E: 72
1120D–F: 72
1120E–F: 73
1121C: 73
1121D: 77
1121F: 98
1122B: 12, 109–10
1122D–E: 109
1123F: 109
1124A: 104
Moralia, "A Letter of Condolence
to Appolonius"
110: 108
Moralia, "Not Even a Pleasant Life
Is Possible on Epicurean Principles"
1089C: 108
Moralia, "On the Control of Anger"
461E: 108
Moralia, "On Tranquility of Mind"
470A–B: 108
474F–75A: 108

Sextus Empiricus
Adversus mathematicos
1.282: 95
6.53: 77
6.55: 77, 131
7.30: 93
7.48: 64, 72, 79
7.52: 33
7.53: 79
7.60–64: 58, 59–60
7.65–87: 51
7.87–88: 64, 72
7.90: 45
7.91–92: 46
7.115–16: 44
7.121: 44
7.122: 44
7.123: 45
7.125: 45
7.136: 54
7.137: 54
7.138–139: 52
7.140: 46, 55, 56
7.153–154: 103fn.19
7.158: 107, 109, 111fn.31
7.159–64: 35fn.10
7.159: 99fn.4, 103fn.19
7.161–64: 103
7.166–89: 119
7.166–68: 120
7.166: 113
7.169: 114
7.173: 120
7.176–79: 114, 120
7.184–89: 114, 115
7.190–200: 72, 139
7.194–98: 74
7.194–95: 77, 130
7.252: 103
7.291: 76
7.293–300: 77, 131
7.349: 36
7.352–66: 77, 130
7.358: 137
7.366: 137
7.385–87: 130
7.389: 61
7.390: 93
7.391: 137
7.402–22: 105, 106
7.402: 130
7.403–4: 76
7.427: 130

8.5: 72
8.151–53: 128
8.152–58: 136
8.154: 128
8.161–62: 128
8.163–70: 128
8.372–373: 133
8.348–50: 145
9.1–3: 131, 132fn.12
9.49: 15, 135
9.56: 58
9.140: 101fn.8
9.176: 102fn.17
9.182–90: 37
9.234–36: 128
9.336–67: 36
9.340: 128fn.7
10.6–36: 76fn.34
10.216: 36
11.1: 87
11.2: 69
11.18–19: 95, 137
11.20: 93, 96
11.110–67: 134
11.140: 96
11.155: 90, 133, 134
11.161: 14, 90, 134
11.164–66: 91
Outlines of Pyrrhonism
1.3: 112, 120
1.4: 137
1.8–14: 125
1.10: 133
1.13: 137
1.14–15: 137, 138
1.16: 137
1.17: 135, 137
1.19–24: 93, 137
1.19–22: 94, 140
1.19: 94, 137
1.20: 94, 137
1.23–24: 17, 135
1.25–30: 88, 133, 134
1.25: 90
1.28: 88
1.30: 107fn.26
1.33: 46fn.38
1.35: 107fn.26, 124, 137
1.38–39: 83
1.40–79: 35
1.62: 86
1.78: 130
1.87: 130, 137

1.90: 86
1.92: 44
1.101–3: 84
1.104: 130
1.113: 84, 130
1.114–17: 85fn.10
1.117: 130
1.118–23: 35
1.123: 130, 137
1.127: 137
1.128: 130
1.134: 130
1.135: 95, 137
1.140: 83, 130, 137
1.141–44: 33
1.144: 130
1.145–63: 51
1.163: 83, 130
1.164–77: 132
1.168: 127fn.3
1.177: 86
1.178–79: 132
1.187–209: 95
1.188: 78
1.191: 107fn.26, 138
1.193: 137, 138
1.194–95: 77fn.35
1.197: 138
1.198: 137, 138
1.199: 138
1.200: 137, 138
1.201: 138
1.202: 137, 138
1.203: 137, 138, 139
1.206–9: 138
1.207: 21
1.208: 137
1.210: 36
1.213–14: 52
1.213: 54, 94
1.215: 77fn.35, 130
1.216–19: 60
1.219: 58, 60
1.223: 137
1.224–25: 34
1.226: 120, 121
1.227–29: 114fn.36
1.230: 119, 121–122
1.231: 107fn.26
1.232–33: 99fn.3
1.232: 105, 107, 113
1.233: 111–12
1.234–35: 77fn.35

1.234: 113fn.34
1.235: 124
1.238–39: 135–36
2.10: 139fn.17
2.18–19: 34fn.4
2.20: 132
2.29–33: 77, 131
2.40: 127fn.3
2.48–69: 82
2.49: 130
2.50–60: 51
2.72–75: 35fn.10
2.74–75: 130
2.84: 131, 132fn.12
2.88–94: 137
2.98: 46fn.39, 55fn.7, 137
2.102: 136, 137
2.118–19: 128
2.144–204: 133
2.193–94: 86
2.195–97: 129, 138
2.204: 129
2.205–6: 86
2.211: 87fn.13
2.229: 86
2.241–44: 86–87
2.256–58: 58: 136
3.2: 15, 135
3.26–28: 128
3.28: 129
3.38–55: 76fn.34, 131, 133
3.63–150: 133
3.65–80: 41
3.119–35: 76fn.34
3.200–206: 126
3.218–34: 51
3.230–31: 126fn.2
3.236: 90, 133, 134
3.280–81: 86, 105fn.22

Simplicius
Aristotelis physica commentaria
22–24: 38fn.20
26: 44
160: 44

Stobaeus
2.7.2: 124

Suidas
Lexicon

Pyrrho 2.278: 71
Socrates 4.404: 71

Tertullian
De anima
9.5: 36
14.5: 36

Theophrastus
De sensu
7:45
9:44
27ff: 46
69: 52

Xenophanes
frag. 14–16: 33
frag. 18: 33
frag. 23–26: 33
frag. 34: 33
frag. 38: 33

Xenophon
Memorabilia
1.1.11–14: 66
1.1.11: 69
2.2: 70
2.8.4–10: 66
3.8.4–10: 66
3.13.4–6: 70
3.72: 70
4.2.12–23: 66
4.8: 69

Zeno
(The numbering in Lee is followed unless otherwise specificed.)
DK A.15: 43, 72
DK A.21: 42
frag. 1: 42
frag. 2: 42
frag. 5: 42
frag. 9: 41
frag. 11: 41
frag. 12: 41

General Index

Bibliographical entries are not indexed here.

Academic scepticism: main argument, 103–4; teaching practices, 106 n. 23, 118; Stoic influence, 110 n. 31, 116 n. 38; academic and Pyrrhonean scepticism, 111–12

Academy, 27–28, 97, 98 n. 1, 98–99. See Academic scepticism

Acusilaus, 33

Aenesidemus, 29, 83, 92, 96 n. 27, 97, 124, 125, 134; endorsement of Heraclitean doctrines, 32, 36–37

Agrippa, 96 n. 27

Alain, 11

Alcmaeon, 37

Aletheia, 19–22, 141. See Truth

Alexander of Macedon, 95 n. 25

Alexander the Great, 65, 81, 88

Alexinus of Elis, 70

Al-Ghazali, 28 n. 45, 35, 127 n. 5

Anaxagoras, 45–46, 47, 79, 80, 87, 101

Anaxarchus, 43, 65–66, 72, 76, 79, 80, 81, 92

Anaximenes, 47

Annas and Barnes, 86

Anonymous Iamblichi, 63

Antigonus of Carystus, 85

Antiochus of Laodicea, 96 n. 27, 97, 134

Antiochus the Academic, 119, 123, 124

Antipater, 108 n. 27

Antiphon, 51

Anti-realism, 5, 17–22, 26–27, 29–30, 65, 143, 146–52; in Arcesilaus, 109–10; in Carneades, 117–19; in early Pyrrhonism, 92–96; in later Pyrrhonism, 139–41; in Protagoras, 58–61. See Realism, Idealism

Antisthenes, 71

Antithesis, 31–32, 37–38, 50–51, 56, 100 passim. See Opposition

Aphasia, 9, 85, 90, 91

Appearances, 18, 55, 82, 92–97, 134–40

Appellas, 97, 134

Appelles, 88

Aquinas, 27

Arcesilaus, 12, 18, 29, 31, 66 n. 21, 77 n. 35, 98, 98 n. 1, 99, 100, 103, 104, 105, 105 n. 22; and equanimity, 107–8; and Pyrrho, 99 n. 3, 113; and Sextus, 112–13; anti-realism, 109–10; as a dogmatist, 113 n. 34; consistency, 11–113; natural belief, 109–11

Aristippus, 72, 74. See Cyrenaics

Aristocles, 76, 96

Ariston, 99 n. 3

Aristophanes, 76, 85

Aristotle, 4, 19, 27, 28, 29, 43, 48 n. 40, 53, 123, 139 passim; Aristotelean contraries, 31; on Protagoras, 61–64

Ascanius of Abdera, 87

Ataraxia, 87–89, 107, 122, 133, 134, 141. See Equanimity

Augustine, 10, 27, 116 n. 38

Bagot, Jean, 8

Bambrough, Renford, 26, 40 n. 25, 150 n. 10

Barnes, Jonathan, 17, 18, 34 n. 4, 37, 86, 86 n. 12, 127, 140

Bayle, 6, 17, 99–100

Beck, L. J., 101

Bergmann, Gustav, 8

Berkeley, 6, 20, 22, 23, 25, 27, 143, 147 n. 6
Burnyeat, M.F., 6, 17, 19, 22, 38, 75, 91, 102 n 15, 110, 140–42

Cause. *See* Pyrrhonism, Critique of cause/induction
Chrysippus, 99, 108
Cicero, 5, 15, 17, 35, 98, 100–104, 102 n. 14, 104, 105, 105 n. 23, 111, 113 passim; mitigated scepticism, 122–23; on plausibility, 115–19
Circularity. *See* Problem of the criterion
Circumstances. *See* Differences in circumstances
Clitomachus, 99, 108, 115, 116, 116 n. 38, 117
Cogito, 144 n. 2, 144–45
Colotes, 10, 12, 28
Commemorative signs, 128, 136
Consistency of scepticism, 9–12, 18; Arcesilaus' outlook, 111–13; Carneades' scepticism, 119–20; early Pyrrhonism, 94–96; later Pyrrhonism, 136–39. *See* Antirealism, Mitigated scepticism
Cornford, Francis, 28, 41 n. 26, 41 n. 29
Couissin, Pierre, 17, 197 n. 26, 110, 116 n. 38
Crates, 71, 98
Cratylus, 9
Criterion. *See* Problem of the criterion
Critias, 51
Cultural relativism. *See* 50–51, 83, 125–27, 127 n. 3
Curley, E. M., 102 n. 14
Cyrenaics, 24, 29, 72–77, 80, 96, 101, 139. *See* Aristippus

Daille, Jean, 8
Davidson, D., 26
Death, 69–70, 126
DeLacy, Philip, 53 n. 4
Demetrius the Laconian, 145
Democritus, 18, 28, 29, 52–57, 58, 72, 76, 79, 80, 81, 83, 88, 101, 108, 111 n. 31, 139; atomism, 31, 52–53; equanimity, 55–57; idealism, 53–55; on Protagoras, 61–64. *See* Metrodorus of Chios, Anaxarchus
Descartes, 4, 6, 7, 27, 75 n. 32, 101, 102, 102 n. 14, 144–45; academic version of his argument for scepticism, 101–2; as the father of modern philosophy, 6
Differences: in circumstances, 33, 54, 58,

72, 74, 83–84; in individuals, 59–60, 72, 73–74, 83; in senses, 44–45, 83; in species, 33, 35, 37, 53, 72, 83
Dillon, John M., 99 n. 5, 124 n. 1
Diocles of Cnidos, 113 n. 34
Diodorus Cronus, 71
Diogenes Laertius, 81–82 n. 1, 82, 84 n. 6, 85, 86, 89, 93, 95, 100, 108, 125, 134 passim
Diogenes of Sinope, 71
Dionysodorus, 60, 80
Dioscurides of Cyprus, 96 n. 27
Diotimus, 55
Dissoi Logoi, 49
Dogmatic claims/doubt, 10, 137–39. *See* Dogmatists, Undogmatic claims
Dogmatists, 86
Dorter, Ken, 128 n. 6
Dreams, 35, 59, 84, 101, 103

Elenchos argument, 66
Empedocles, 43–45, 79, 80
Epicharmus, 29, 37–38
Epictetus, 71, 76
Epicurus, 23, 28, 53 n. 4, 71, 89, 98 n. 2, 134, 139
Epoche, 18, 20, 21, 83, 107 n. 26, 111 n. 31, 119, 125, 140, 141
Equanimity, 55–57, 69–70. *See* Anaxarchus, *Ataraxia*, Indifference

Ferry, Paul, 8
Flintoff, Everard, 81–82 n. 1
Frankl, Victor, 13 n. 23
Frede, Michael, 17, 18, 19, 140
Freeman, Kathleen, 34, 37 n. 17, 41 n. 29

Galen, 11, 43, 71
Gallop, David, 39 n. 21, 40 n. 22, 40 n. 24
Gellner, Ernest, 151
Ghazali. *See* Al-Ghazali
God, 102, 102 n. 17, 135. *See* Religious scepticism
Goodman, Nelson, 22
Gorgias, 43, 51, 52, 75 n. 32, 79, 81 n. 1, 82, 83, 87, 129, 130, 139
Gouhier, Henri, 101 n. 12
Groarke, Leo, 28 n. 45, 40 n. 23, 70 n. 25, 102 n. 13
Guthrie, W. K. C., 35, 59 n. 12

Hallie, Philip, 3, 6, 11, 90, 140
Harrison, Jonathan, 149 n. 8
Hegel, 22

Hegesinus, 99
Heracleitus: Heraclitean opposites, 18, 19, 29, 31, 32, 34–37, 40, 47, 78, 83; Epicharmus' parodies on Heraclitean views, 38
Heraclides, 96 n. 27
Herodotus of Tarsus, 96 n. 27, 135
Hippias, 79 n. 36
Hippobotus: and Sotion, 96 n. 27
Hippolytus, 105
Hobbes, 16
Holbach, 15
Homer, 14, 82 n. 1, 83 n. 2, 89, 105
Hume, 4, 6, 7, 12, 13–14, 15, 17, 27, 56 n. 8, 109, 123, 127 n. 5; critique of cause, 6, 127–29, 128 n. 6; on the Pyrrhoneans, 14

Idealism: idealist truth, 6, 7, 22–25, 144–46; and early Pyrrhonism, 94; and later Pyrrhonism, 139; in the Cyrenaics, 72–77; in Democritus, 53–55; in Metrodorus of Chios, 64–65; in Monimus, 72
Illusion, 101, 103. *See* Dreams, Madness
Inconsistency of scepticism. *See* Consistency of scepticism
India: Indian influence on Pyrrhonism, 81–82 n. 1
Indicative signs, 128–29
Indifference, 71, 87–92, 121. *See* Equanimity
Individuals. *See* Differences in individuals
Induction. *See* Pyrrhonism, Critique of cause/induction
Infinite regress. *See* Problem of the criterion
Insanity, 54. *See* Madness
Internalism, 150
Isocrates, 43
Isostheneia, 125, 141, 104–7

Johnson, Oliver, 10, 11, 17, 86 n. 11, 86 n. 12
Johnson, Samuel, 8

Kant, 6, 13 n. 23, 20, 22, 23, 27, 140, 143
Kekes, John, 11
Kerferd, G. B., 28 n. 45, 43 n. 33, n. 34, 59 n. 12
Kierkegaard, 15
Kirk, G. S., 34 n. 5, n. 8
Kirk, Raven, and Schofield, 34 n. 5, 38 n. 20, 40 n. 22, 45–46

Lacydes, 99
Lee, H. D. P., 43

Le Loyer, Pierre, 8
Lennon, Thomas, 127 n. 5
Leucippus, 53 n. 4. *See* Democritus
Lewis, C. I., 11
Liar pradox, 101
Long, A. A., 124 n. 1
Lucian, 12, 13, 125
Lucretius, 10

Maccoll, Norman, 10, 11, 17, 28, 52, 91, 140
Madness, 35, 59. *See* Insanity
Malebranche, 127 n. 5
Mandeville, 16
Matson, Wallace, 6, 101
Medicine, 135–36
Megarians, 70–71, 87
Menodotus of Nicomedia, 96 n. 27, 135 n 13
Mental states. *See* Idealism
Metrodorus of Chios, 18, 29, 64–65, 76, 79, 80, 81, 92, 96, 101; idealism, 64–65
Metrodorus the Academic, 17, 122–23
Mill, 56 n. 8
Minton and Shipka, 9–10
Mitigated scepticism, 12–14, 17. *See* Antirealism
Molière, 12, 13

Norton, David, 18 n. 26
Numenius, 99, 99 n. 3, 100, 105, 113, 113 n. 34

Oenomaus, 144 n. 2
Oldfather, W. A., 76 n. 33
Opposition, 58, 72, 78, 79, 82, 82 n. 1, 125 passim. *See* Antithesis
Orwell, George, 152 n. 12
Other minds, 24, 73–74
Ou mallon, 52, 53 n. 4, 59, 78, 95, 105, 111 n. 31

Parmenides, 18, 19, 28, 29, 38–41, 47, 51, 78, 79, 81 n. 1, 87, 101, 129. *See* Megarians
Pascal, 15
Pathoi, 55, 130
Pausanias, 89 n. 14
Pithanon. *See* Plausibility
Plausibility, 113–23. *See* Probability
Plato, Platonism, 3, 4, 10, 19, 27, 18, 31, 32, 34 n. 34, 78, 79, 98, 101, 111 n. 33, 113 n. 34, 139; *Parmenides*, 40–41, 50, 78; on Protagoras, 61–64. *See* Academy
Plutarch, 11, 28, 43, 53, 77, 98, 104, 108, 109

Poincaré, Henri, 140
Polemo, 110 n. 31, 123
Popkin, Richard, 6, 8, 13, 28, 101
Practical criterion, 17, 18, 125, 134–36
Pragmatism, 64, 135–36
Praylus of the Troad, 91, 96 n. 27
Probability, 104–07. *See* Plausibility
Problem of the criterion, 7, 85 n. 10, 124,
   131–33
Protagoras, 18, 19, 29, 32, 43, 49, 50, 57–
   64, 79, 80, 81 n. 1, 82, 96, 111 n. 31;
   opposition, 58; anti-realist truth, 58–
   61; utility, 61–64
Ptolemy, 96 n. 27
Putnam, Hilary, 19, 20, 22, 26, 140, 149–
   50, 152
Pyrrho, 11, 18 n. 26, 29, 31, 43, 72, 81,
   83 n. 2, 85–96, 125, 133, 134, 135; and
   Arcesilaus, 99 n. 3, 120–22; and mitigated scepticism, 85–97; Indian influence
   on, 81–82 n. 1. *See* Pyrrhonism
Pyrrhonism, 21–22, 24 passim; early, 5,
   25, ch. 4; later, 5, 89, 92, 93, 94, 95,
   ch. 6; and academic scepticism, 111–12;
   and idealism, 94; consistency of early
   Pyrrhonism, 94–95; consistency of
   later Pyrrhonism, 136–39; critique of
   cause/ induction, 7, 127–29, 132–33;
   Pyrrhonean formulas, 125, 137–38. *See*
   Practical criterion
Pythagoras, Pythagorean doctrines, 19,
   31, 33, 47

Realism, 19. *See* Anti-realism
Relatives, 128
Relativity/mode of relativity, 83
Religious scepticism, 15–16
Rescher, Nicholas, 11, 86 n. 11, 86 n. 12
Robinson, John Mansley, 34 n. 5

Sight, 101
Signs, 128–29
Slote, Michael, 11
Smith, Norman Kemp, 6, 14
Socrates, 6, 28, 29, 66–70, 72, 79, 80, 85,
   87, 88, 91, 101; commitment to custom
   and convention, 67–69; equanimity,
   69–70; on death, 69–70; on Protagoras,
   61–62, 63 n. 15; mitigated scepticism,
   67–69
Solipsism, 6, 74 n. 26
Solmsen, Friedrich, 41 n. 29
Sophists, 49–52, 78, 79
Sorites, 100, 100 n. 9

Sotion, 96 n. 27
Species. *See* Differences in species
Stilpo, 71
Stoics, 10, 19, 71, 99, 100, 105–6, 106 n.
   23, 113, 122, 123, 124; Stoic and
   academic terminology, 110 n. 31. *See*
   Chrysippus, Zeno of Citium
Stokes, M. C., 40 n. 22
Stough, Charlotte, 10, 17, 21–22, 96 n. 26,
   116 n. 38
Striker, Gisela, 17, 18, 83 n. 5, 111 n. 32,
   115, 116–17 n. 38; on equal opposition,
   104–7
Suarez, 127 n. 5

Tarán, Leonardo, 40 n. 22, 41 n. 27
Tarrant, Harold, 99 n. 5, 124 n. 1
Telecles, 99
Thales, 47
Theiodas of Laodecia, 96 n. 27
Theophrastus, 123
Thoreau, Henry, 92 n. 18
Timon, 34, 37, 43, 86–89, 92, 94–98, 99 n.
   3, 125, 133, 134
Truth, 19–22, 26, 58–60. See *Aletheia*
Tsekourakis, Damianas, 109 n. 28

Undogmatic claims, 21. *See* Dogmatic claims
Unmitigated scepticism. *See* Mitigated .
   scepticism

Verdenius, W. J., 40 n. 25
Vlastos, Gregory, 43 n. 34
Von Fritz, K., 41 n. 29

West, M. L., 40 n. 25, 41 n. 26
Wilbur and Allen, 34 n. 5
Williams, Bernard, 4, 6, 22
Winch, Peter, 26, 150 n. 10
Wittgenstein, Ludwig, 20, 26, 140, 147–
   50

Xeniades, 75 n. 32, 79, 81 n. 1, 82, 129,
   130
Xenocrates, 123
Xenophanes, 32–34, 35, 38, 47

Zeller, Eduard, 17, 66, 91, 99 n. 3, 140
Zeno (of Citium), 71, 110 n. 31
Zeno (of Elea), 41–43, 45 n. 36, 47, 71, 79,
   87
Zeuxippus, 96 n. 27
Zeuxis (of the angular foot), 96 n. 27, 97,
   125, 134